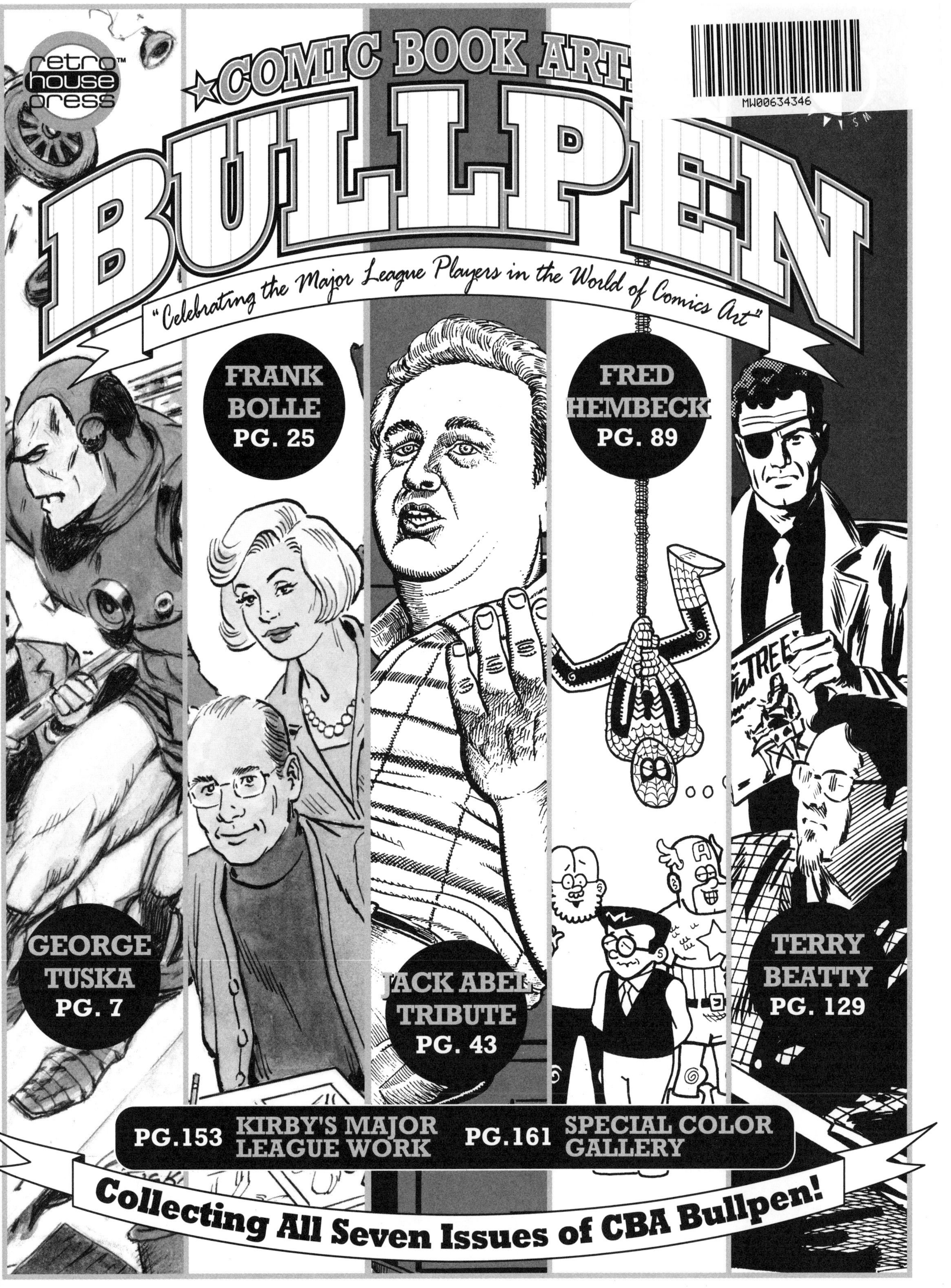

retro house press™
★COMIC BOOK ARTIST
BULLPEN
"Celebrating the Major League Players in the World of Comics Art"
FRANK BOLLE PG. 25
FRED HEMBECK PG. 89
GEORGE TUSKA PG. 7
JACK ABEL TRIBUTE PG. 43
TERRY BEATTY PG. 129
PG.153 KIRBY'S MAJOR LEAGUE WORK
PG.161 SPECIAL COLOR GALLERY
Collecting All Seven Issues of CBA Bullpen!

COMIC BOOK ARTIST
BULLPEN
The Complete Collection

Jon B. Cooke
Edits, Design, Production, and Original Publisher

Rick Parker
Guest Associate Editor, *CBA Bullpen* # 3/4

John Morrow
Collection Publisher

Proofread by Rob Smentek

Along with additional material, this volume is a compilation of
Comic Book Artist Bullpen #1-6 published by RetroHouse Press. *CBA Bullpen* #7 appears for the first time.

"The Tuska Technique" ©2021 John D. Coates.

"Beatty At The Drawing Board" ©2021 Jason Strangis.

Special Thanks to Michael Netzer.

Cover Art by
Jack Kirby
Inks by Mike Thibodeaux • Colors by Tom Ziuko
Art © the estate of Jack Kirby

Published by

TwoMorrows Publishing
10407 Bedfordtown Rd., Raleigh NC 27614

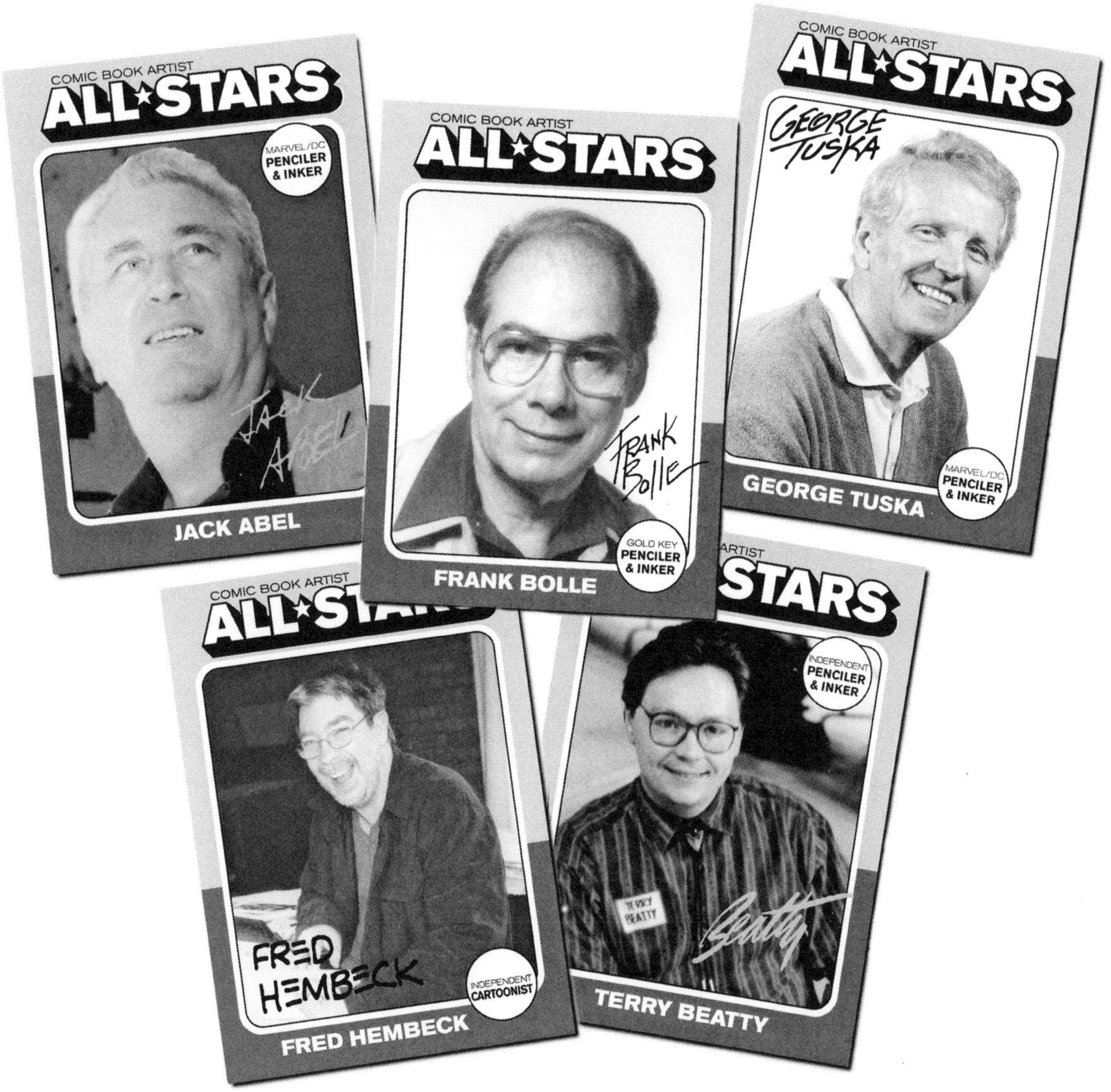
COMIC BOOK ARTIST
ALL★STARS
MARVEL/DC PENCILER & INKER
JACK ABEL
COMIC BOOK ARTIST
ALL★STARS
FRANK BOLLE
GOLD KEY PENCILER & INKER
FRANK BOLLE
COMIC BOOK ARTIST
ALL★STARS
GEORGE TUSKA
MARVEL/DC PENCILER & INKER
GEORGE TUSKA
COMIC BOOK ARTIST
ALL★STARS
FRED HEMBECK
INDEPENDENT CARTOONIST
FRED HEMBECK
STARS
INDEPENDENT PENCILER & INKER
TERRY BEATTY
TERRY BEATTY

What in heaven's name was I thinking…?

By 2003, I'd been in the "magazines-about-comics" game for seven or so years and it was then I came up with the "brilliant" idea to self-publish a spin-off of my relatively successful *Comic Book Artist*. Melding the notion of a sports dugout with a certain publisher's production department, I developed the title *Comic Book Artist Bullpen*, with the notion I'd start a little side-gig with my own fanzine while, at the same time, produce my regular periodical for then-publisher Top Shelf. Post-9/11, advertising (my profession during much of the 1990s) had suffered a critical slowdown and, father to three young boys, I had to find a way to keep the money coming in. Maybe a bi-monthly, 20-page, Xeroxed, self-cover 'zine boasting an interview with a comics professional and designed by me would help fill the house coffers.

I did have a good number of faithful *CBA* readers and access to subscribers' addresses, so I reached out with a mail announcement and the response was okay, enough to build on, thought I. But my business plan (if you can call it that) was fundamentally flawed from the get-go and, however enthusiastic I was and however confident that I could meet my ambitions, I had difficulty facing the fact that I am no businessman. So *CBA Bullpen* didn't work out in the long run, much to my regret. Best as I can recall, it started in late 2003 and, by the end of 2004, the game was over. But, man, the experience did have its moments!

On the negative side, besides the fact that my nifty li'l mag would not continue, I couldn't afford to print up the fifth* issue, a comprehensive and entertaining chat with Terry Beatty, though it was entirely finished. That was a curveball, to say the least.

But what was published was pretty cool, especially the "Jack Abel Remembered" tribute in #3/4, which includes comic-style remembrances from an array of industry pros, from legends such as Joe Kubert, Walter Simonson, and Marie Severin, down to the tireless Marvel bullpen assistants who worked side-by-side with Jack before he passed away in 1996 while working at his desk. It's a remarkable historical artifact, never mind a heartfelt, sometimes hilarious, send-off to a 45-year comics veteran, and it is one that my now-publisher, John Morrow, and I have wanted to get into print for a number of years now. And we couldn't be more delighted to share it with a wider audience.

I hope you enjoy the following as much I enjoyed putting it all together. I doubt I'll ever stop doing publications and, you never know, I might just return to the 'zine scene in the autumn of my years. My very first foray was in 1973 or so, when I caught the bug; why quit now?

Jon B. Cooke

---

* The last issue of *Comic Book Artist Bullpen* was numbered #7, but it was the fifth edition released as the Jack Abel tribute (#3/4) and the Fred Hembeck interview (#5/6) were each double-issues with combined numbering.

The Story Behind the Cover

In 1984, Jack Kirby was enlisted to produce illustrations for General Mills' breakfast cereal packaging featuring a gang of athletic "Honeycomb Kids," which were used as 3-D poster giveaways. That three-dimensional effect is evident in the repro above (so—no—it's *not* printed off-register!). There were two additional posters—one with girls roller-skating, the other with boys racing in a BMX biking competition, and a never used fourth illo, and all were inked by Mike Thibodeaux.

Dedicated
to the Home Team

The Cooke Boys
Benjamin, Joshua, and Daniel

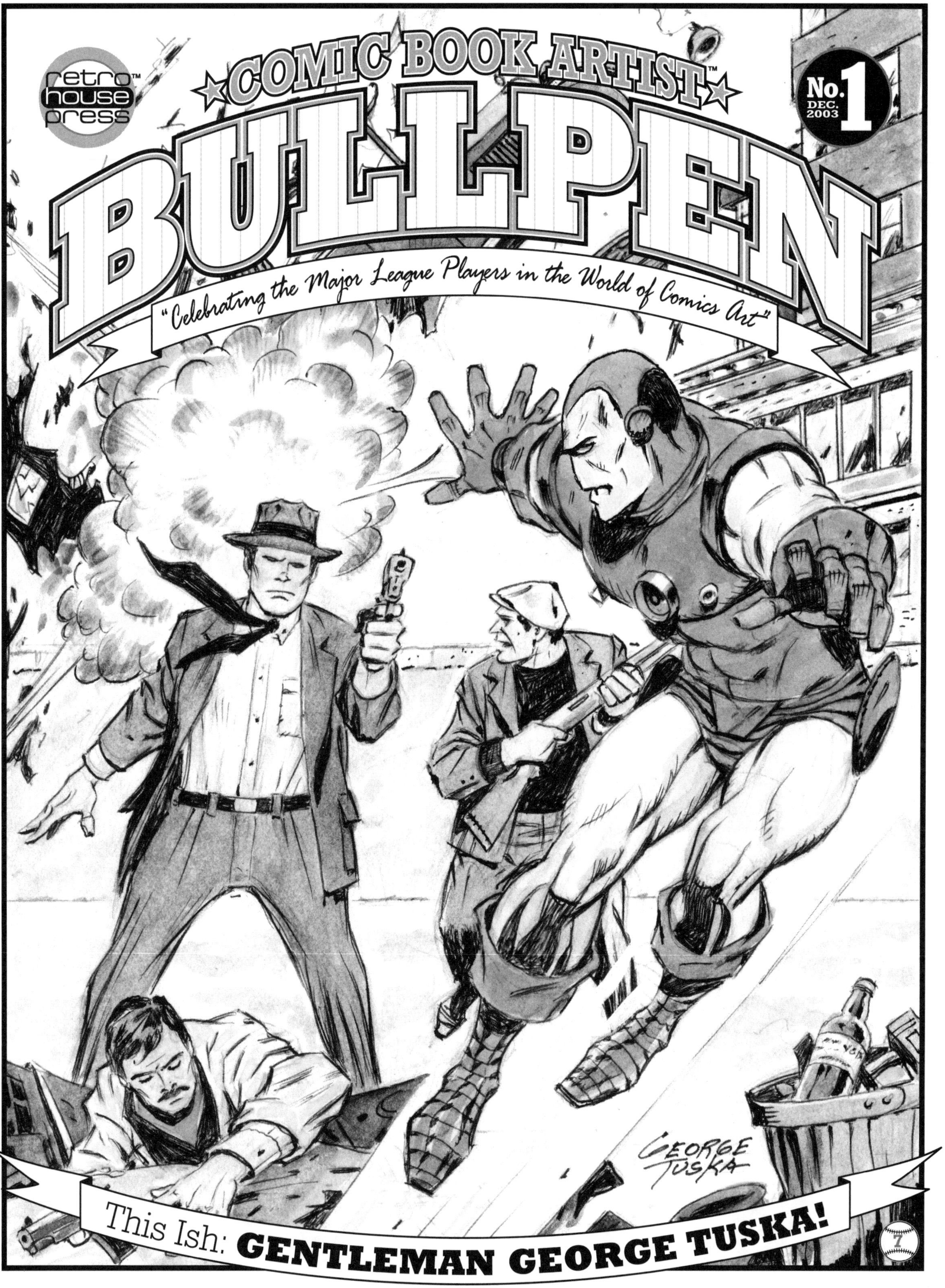
retro house press
COMIC BOOK ARTIST
BULLPEN
No. 1 DEC. 2003
"Celebrating the Major League Players in the World of Comics Art"
GEORGE TUSKA
This Ish: GENTLEMAN GEORGE TUSKA!

The Tuska
Interviewed & Transcribed

"Gorgeous" George Tuska — as Stan "The Man" Lee affectionately dubbed the handsome artist—has a career in American comic books spanning over 60 years, from his start with the legendary Will Eisner, in 1939, through the "Marvel Age" into the 1980s. Though perhaps most known for his extensive work on Iron Man, his initial claim to fame came as a very highly-regarded artist on the Charles Biro crime comics of the '40s, when he first was considered an "artist's artist." CBA Bullpen is proud to present George as our debut feature.

John D. Coates: *Before we begin, allow me to thank you for this opportunity to discuss your long and illustrious carrier.*

George Tuska: My pleasure, John.

John: *Before drawing professionally, did you draw for any local periodical, newspaper or local school publication?*

George: I only drew for personal enjoyment. It was only after I left home for New York when I began to get paid for drawing professionally. This was around 1936. I began art school at the National Academy of Design.

John: *While in art school, did you work professionally?*

George: I was employed by a cosmetics company and designed jewelry. Aside from that, I first began drawing professionally with comic books.

John: *In attending art school, was your original intent to draw comic books or did comics simply provide a means of employment until an advertisement agency or newspaper strip position was available?*

George: I always knew I wanted to draw though, at the time, I hadn't decided how to make a living at it. Originally, I was simply looking for work and comics kept me busy. [*laughter*] Once I began, I became deeply involved and enjoyed it immensely. It was a great outlet for, not only my art, but it allowed me to create, as well.

Top: *Photo of George Tuska, courtesy of Mike Gartland.*
Right: *Panel detail from George Tuska's pencil job in* What If? *#5. Jerry Ordway shared this piece, reproduced from photocopies of the original pencil art. Jerry told us, from the late '70s to the mid-'80s, then Marvel editor-in-chief Jim Shooter would give fledgling inkers reams of these copies to practice their inking. TM & ©2021 Marvel Characters, Inc.*

Technique
by John D. Coates

Special Thanks To:
Robert Pollak, Jerry Ordway, Pat Lang, Jerry K. Boyd, Axel Kahlstorff, John Berk, Frank Motler, Bill Howard, Bob Conway, Matthew Hull, John Canfield, Troy Pierce, Mark Foy, and Eric Decarlo.
For Supplying Images for This Interview

John: *Once you graduated, how did you begin looking for work in the art field?*

George: Being young, I didn't have an agent. Also, with the Depression, all work was tough to come by. Around 1938, I felt confident enough to draw professionally, so I began using an artist employment agency. These agencies would keep your portfolio on file. Different publishers would use the agencies to acquire young and cheap artists for various projects. If you were lucky, the publisher would eventually hire you full-time. Either way, it was great exposure for the artists to be seen by publishers.

John: *Was it here that you became involved in comic books?*

George: Yes. While at one of these agencies, the Eisner & Iger Studio had seen my portfolio and asked I send on some samples. I guess they liked my work because they hired me.

John: *Was it at Eisner & Iger Studio that you decided to draw comic books for a career?*

George: Yes. I found that I loved the creative atmosphere in the studio and in the industry.

John: *Let's talk about the old studio system for a moment: Though you worked for the Eisner & Iger studio, your work appeared under numerous comic book publishers such as Brookwood/Speed, Fox, Fiction House, Quality, and Fawcett, to name a few. Could you briefly explain the studio system?*

George: In those days, publishers would farm out their work to a studio like Eisner & Iger. The publisher would either specify what type of strip they wanted the studio to create or would leave the idea up to the studio. Most of the time, the publishers would ask the studio to replicate a strip similar to whatever character-type was already popular on the newsstand. The studio would then create, write, pencil, ink and letter the strip in-house, ready to be printed. The studio would then supply the finished book to whatever printer the publisher had predesignated. Under this system, a publisher could have their competitors' books being produced beside one another, by the same creators!

John: *Looking back, do you see any advantages to the old system?*

George: Not really. I prefer freelancing, though you sometimes miss the camaraderie of other artists. But, being young, I liked being around other young artists, I found freelancing allows more freedom to work at your own pace. The privacy is also nice. With the studio system, you stayed in the office from nine o'clock in the morning to whenever the work was complete that day. You would sit at your table in a room surrounded by other artists and you had to draw, regardless of your creative mood, motivation, etc. That could be stressful. Also, I would get easily distracted. It was sometimes hard to concentrate on your work with other people in the room, talking, and looking over your shoulder. All this would only add to

Left: *George Tuska fan R. Robert Pollak shared this color commission piece by the artist, showing just how dynamic George's work is today. Art ©2021 the estate of George Tuska. Iron Man TM & ©2021 Marvel Characters, Inc.*

Portions of this interview originally published in *Comic Book Marketplace #31*, January 1996. Edited by Gary Carter.

Above: *"Spike Marlin,"* Speed Comics #1 [Oct 1939]. Harvey Comics. George Tuska's very first published work! **Inset right:** *"Zanzibar,"* from Mystery Men Comics #1 [Aug. 1939]. Fox Publications. **Below:** *"Cosmic Carson,"* from Science Comics #1 [Feb. 1940]. Fox Publications. TM & ©2021 the respective copyright holders.

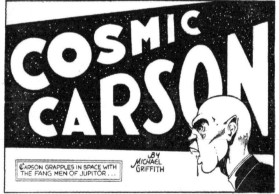

the stress if a tight deadline was looming.

John: *At Eisner & Iger, what was the first character you remember working on?*

George: I believe that would have been "Spike Marlin." The strip was mostly adventures at sea-type stories, fighting modern-day pirates, criminals, etc. Great fun. After that job, they gave me others, as well. I remember I created "Cosmic Carson" and "Zanzibar the Magician." Both standard adventure fare and very fun to draw.

John: *From an artistic perspective, how did the studio operate?*

George: Speaking for my-self, Will Eisner and I would outline the plot. From that, I would complete the story, pencil, and inks. I would then hand off the finished pages to be lettered, and so on.

John: *Would Eisner go over your art to give it a "house" art style?*

George: In some panels, yes. He would suggest I change this or that. Mostly we would discuss layouts, but he rarely changed the art. Will would always make sure you clearly understood what he wanted prior to starting to draw. He had confidence in the people he hired. Very supportive.

John: *What type of story do you prefer to draw?*

George: Adventure, crime, action, and science-fiction. I tend to draw the types of stories that interested me as a child. Lots of action!

John: *What type of script do you prefer the writer provide: Synopsis or detailed panel-by-panel description?*

George: Synopsis. I can then dictate the flow of the story and layout. When work-ing from the strict panel-by-panel script, it's too confining and boring to draw. Limits the imagination and creativity of the drawing.

John: *Do you prefer to as-sist the writer with the script?*

George: Sometimes, if the plot and story are good, I usually stay fairly close to the script. Regardless, I draw what I like as long as it follows the plot.

John: *Back to the Eisner & Iger Studio: Who were some of the other artists in the studio?*

George: Some of the greats: Lou Fine, Bob Powell, Charlie Sultan, Nick Cardy, and John Celardo come to

mind. With the studio environment and close quarters, we became friends at once. It's also the nature of the work and the fact that we were all young and hungry!

Incidentally, Nick Cardy and I have become reacquainted in recent years. We run into each other as guests at the various comic conventions. He's still got it and draws as beautifully as ever. Of course, he's also one of the nicest people you'll meet. A real gentleman. We joke about how far we've come since we began working in obscurity in 1939 to make ends meet, producing a new thing called a "comic-book," and now, over 60 years later, we're guests-of-honor at conventions for doing it! [*laughter*]

John: *Any interesting anecdotes regarding these gentleman?*

George: I remember Bob Powell was always a very fancy dresser, always up on the latest fashion. Of them all, Lou Fine was the artist I admired the most and whom I thought was the most talented. He did beautiful work with a Japanese brush and inks. Very dedicated.

John: *How long did you stay at Eisner & Iger?*

George: Until 1941, when I was drafted. I was stationed in

Columbia, South Carolina, at Fort Jackson.

John: *You're kidding! I grew up in Columbia! Of course, my memories are probably happier than yours!*

George: You could say that! [*laughter*]

John: *What exactly were your duties?*

George: I worked in the headquarters drawing plans for artillery equipment to be used in Army manuals. The drawings were used to teach troops how to use the equipment, etc. Very technical work but not very challenging or creative. Anyway, I received a medical discharge in 1943, when I lost hearing in my left ear in a training accident.

John: *Did you go directly back into drawing comic books?*

George: Yes. I did work for most of the main publishers: Fiction House, Fawcett, Street & Smith, Harry "A." Chesler, St. John, and a few others. With most of the men who had drawn comic books in the war, artists were scarce. I simply called up the publishers and was hired.

John: *Where the working conditions different from what you had remembered?*

George: It was strange because, as I said, most of the artists I knew had gone to war. Like most of the home-front duties, many publishers had hired woman to draw the comics. Though they were very talented, I missed the camaraderie from the prewar studio days.

John: *Was it difficult to adjust as a civilian after the Army?*

George: Oh, yes! Though I had experienced discipline in the Army, I had fallen out of the habit of drawing comic books. That's a completely different type of discipline. Fortunately, it came back to me fairly quickly. I think it helped that I then began to freelance at home versus working in a studio.

John: *During the mid-1940s through the early '50s, you seem to have had an affinity for working on crime stories. The first work that comes to mind is* Crime Does Not Pay, *published by Lev Gleason. In Ron Goulart's 1986 book,* The Great History of Comic Books, *he writes that you have been referred to as, "the premier crime comic artist." Also, you were mentioned in the book by Mike Benson,* Crime Comics: The Illustrated History. *Mike writes, "Tuska was one of Biro's favorites to illustrate his stories during the late '40s, and it was [Tuska's] version of 'Mr. Crime' which remains the most memorable." [Mr. Crime was the host of* Crime Does Not Pay, *a prototype of EC Comics' Crypt Keeper and company, a character who introduced stories.] Did you request for them to give you crime stories?*

George: Not really. Charles Biro simply handed me the scripts. Most of my stories in that book were written by Bob Bernstein, a pretty prolific writer. I guess they liked my work because I kept getting scripts! [*laughter*]

John: *Did you think the stories too violent?*

George: The stories were presented as fictional and in good fun. I always felt that the kids could tell the difference.

John: *How did you first meet Charles Biro?*

George: While submitting samples, I met Charles and we became friends. He later became my boss on *Crime Does Not Pay.* Charles is probably best known for his gruesome crime covers.

In many ways, he was the first to really do crime-themed comics, or at least to where they were popular. We kept in touch through the years, until his death in 1982. He had a heart-attack while driving. He was a gifted man.

John: *During this period, do you remember working with any other artists of note?*

George: Not "with," because I was freelancing. However, I did become close with Jack Kirby and Bob Powell. Jack was a true talent. I remember his work was always a little on the edge for its time. Not like an Eisner with graphic design, but Jack would put so much energy and imagination into each page. Personally, Jack was a well-liked, respected and big-hearted.

Bob Powell was a wonderful artist. Very technical. Bob and I became closer when we both worked with Joe Simon on *Sick* magazine, in the early 1960s.

John: *Let's talk about your Atlas Comics work. This would have been around 1949 or 1950. Any particular reason you worked so closely with that publisher?*

George: Not really. At the time, Martin Goodman was the publisher. I had been looking for more work and showed him some samples. He was looking for experienced artists and hired me. Martin was a shrewd businessman, but could be difficult. All in all, I enjoyed working with him. Also, it's about this time—

late 1940s/early 1950s—when I met Stan Lee.

John: *How could Martin be "difficult"?*

George: He was the publisher and boss, and I was the artist and employee. The nature of an artist is to always try and produce the best work possible, while the publisher has to get the books out the door on time and pay the bills. Sometimes the artist is unrealistic, sometimes it's the publisher. Just your typical art vs. business concerns.

John: *What was Stan Lee like in those days?*

George: Stan was like he is today, only younger! [*laughter*] Always enthusiastic and full of story ideas. If I remember correctly, he wrote most of the stories I drew for Atlas. Of course, I didn't know it then, but Stan would remain an integral part of my comics' career later.

John: *In the early '50s, the comic book market was downsizing. Did you stay in the industry?*

George: No. Around 1952 or 1953, the comic book market was no longer lucrative for publishers. Many just closed shop. With no employment in comics, I was fortunate to find work with the Associated Press

Newspaper Syndicate, drawing a then-popular strip, *Scorchy Smith*. John Terry had originated the strip in the 1930s. Anyway, *Scorchy* was pretty much your standard adventure strip. The hero was dashing and sort of a troubleshooter. He fought criminals, smugglers, hunted treasure, etc. Oh yeah, he also always got the girl! [*laughter*] There I wrote, penciled, and inked both the Sundays and the dailies.

John: *I believe Frank Robbins drew the strip prior to your arrival. Did you meet with him or John Terry to discuss the art or story direction of the characters?*

George: Never spoke to John, but I did meet Frank. We discussed the strip in general terms, but with me writing and drawing the strip, it quickly became my own.

John: *Very impressive! I'm curious, at your peak, how many finished pages (story, pencils and inks, ready to be lettered), could you complete in a day?*

George: With comics, about two to three pages a day. When drawing the newspaper strip, I would produce a little more.

John: *How many hours did you work in your average day?*

George: Too many! [*laughter*]

John: *With comic books, what was your creative process?*

George: For a 28-page comic story, I would first divide the plot synopsis into seven-page quarters. As each quarter was completed, I would return that quarter to the publisher for approval. I could then make any changes in the office. The pages would then be passed to the letterer, etc. I would then go back to my studio at home and complete the next quarter's worth of pages, and so on.

John: *And with your newspaper strip work?*

George: Totally different process. When drawing a newspaper strip, you're limited to how you lay-out the story. Limited in the sense that you only have three or four panels to work with. This can make it easier to lay out the page, or frustrate you. Remember, these strips were daily and needed to provide the reader with enough story to move along the plot. That can be difficult in the limited panels, day in and day out. Anyway, I would take the script, complete the artwork, and turn in a few weeks' worth of dailies at one time. This kept me ahead of the deadline, but was very hard work.

John: *In the early 1950s, while you were doing the Scorchy Smith strip, the comic book industry was under siege and subject to Congressional Hearings. Dr. Frederic Wertham had accused comic books of causing juvenile delinquency. What do you remember about that time?*

George: It was a very unfortunate situation. The entire comic book industry suffered. As everyone knows, a lot of very good artists were put out of work and hurt professionally.

John: *Though you were out of the comic book field at this time, what was your opinion of the work produced by publishers like EC Comics?*

George: I thought it was a little gory for the times, but so was some of my crime comics' work. This was the nature of the business. Gory, yes, but all in good fun. Certainly not to the point of a Congressional hearing.

John: *Why do you think this happened?*

George: During the 1950s, comic books were just for children so I think parents thought them too violent for their kids.

Above column, top: *Tuska splash panel from* Journey Into Mystery #11 *[Aug. '53].* **Middle:** *Spaceman #4 [May '54] splash by Tuska.* **Bottom:** *Another Tuska splash panel, this one from* Menace #5 *[July '53].* **Column at right, top:** *That's right, padnah! Another Tuska splash panel, this one from* Black Rider #19 *[Nov. '53].* **Middle:** *Tuska splash panel,* Jungle Action #2 *[Dec. '54].* **Bottom:** *Guess who drew this splash panel from… hey, we can't find the credit reference, but we know, like all the rest on this Tuska page, it was published by Atlas Comics. ©2021 Marvel Characters, Inc.*

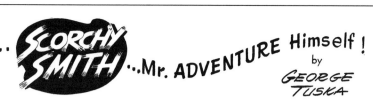

...SCORCHY SMITH ...Mr. ADVENTURE Himself!
by GEORGE TUSKA

SCORCHY SMITH pioneered the air age for comics page readers.

Scorchy Smith in wartime carried out authentic combat missions, at the adventure strip level.

Scorchy Smith afterwards rode the crest of the interplanetary adventure cycle.

Now, Scorchy Smith is making new adventure history. Where and how? We can't rightly say, pardner, because by the time you get this he's very likely made a new landing.

We're dead sure of just one thing—that the brilliant young artist, George Tuska, will keep flowing from his board the best drawn, liveliest, fastest moving, most genuine adventure strip available anyplace, from anybody, at any price. You can see for yourself. But watch out for the Scorchy Smith habit. It's catching!

This is George Tuska, the chap whose clean, technical art style and knack for adventurous yarns have placed SCORCHY SMITH in the very front of the derring-do parade.

Standing 6 feet 1 inch and weighing 195 pounds, Tuska looks more like a professional football player than an artist. He certainly does not look his 37 years.

A native of Hartford, Conn., and a World War II army veteran, he lives with his wife and two little girls at Hicksville on Long Island. He learned adventure strip art the hard way—by actually producing it for more than 12 years. His hobby? Serious art in oils and water colors!

Here are just a few graphic examples of SCORCHY SMITH in action...

Above: The newspaper syndicate that handled Scorchy Smith, *AP Newsfeatures,* sent out this promotional broadsheet, complete with Tuska biography, to prospective clients throughout the country. Courtesy of the artist. ©2021 the respective copyright holder.

Centerspread: George Tuska proudly displays two framed Iron Man *covers—the original art for #5 and 8, owned by collector Troy Pierce—at the 2002 MegaCon comics convention, held in Orlando, Florida. Iron Man TM & ©2021 Marvel Characters, Inc.

Also, comic books were an easy, beatable target. The industry was not considered legitimate and the publishers were not unified. Most publishers simply gave up, instead of fighting. Luckily, most of the artists I knew personally, turned to advertising or other venues, and continued to work. It was a scary time if you had a family to support.

John: *Was there ever concern among the newspaper syndicate artists that this hearing on comic books could spill over into newspaper strips?*

George: Not at all. As an illustrated story, newspaper strips were always considered more reputable, and for all ages. Again, comic books, at that time, were created, written, drawn, and marketed to children. That's the difference, that perception. Also, who would want to take on a newspaper syndicate? This was prior to television when newspapers were the primary source of news, and much more influential

than today. As mentioned earlier, comic books were an easy and beatable target.

John: *Considering the newspaper syndicate who published Scorchy Smith, did they have a position on these hearings? Did they feel threatened in any way?*

George: No, but they did have certain rules about violence. For example, I could not show hands around someone's neck, strangling. No facial expressions of agony or overt suffering. Most of the violence was implied and off-panel. When I had to show it in the strip, it was done in such a way as not to be excessive. Pretty challenging when you're working on an adventure strip! [*laughter*]

John: *My research found that, in the late 1950s, while still on Scorchy Smith, you somehow found time to step back into the world of comic books and also draw for such publications as Archie Comics'* Adventures of the Fly *and* The Double Life of Private Strong *[The Shield], Crestwood Publications'* Black Magic, *Hasting's* Eerie Tales, *Pastime's* Weird Mysteries, *and Harvey's* Alarming Adventures. *When did you find the time?*

George: I did all that? [*laughter*] Well, while on *Scorchy,* I would get calls from comic book publishers asking me to help out. Most were only four- to six-page stories. The extra money was nice!

John: *In 1959, you left the* Scorchy Smith *strip and began to do the* Buck Rogers *dailies and Sunday page strip. How did this come about?*

George: I had been on *Scorchy* for about five years. Maury Brickman called and offered me the *Buck Rogers* strip. Maury was an editor for the publisher. He and Robert Dille, who worked for the National Syndicate out of Chicago, told me that Murphy Anderson was leaving the strip and they

needed an artist. Being the more popular strip, I accepted.

John: *Considering the* Buck Rogers *strip involved an established character, as opposed to* Scorchy Smith, *were you restricted artistically as to how you could handle the character? As I understand it, the Edgar Rice Burroughs estate closely monitors any interpretations of the Tarzan character.*

George: No. The syndicate never had any issues with my interpretation. Howard Liss wrote the strips. He'd submit them to the syndicate prior to my receiving them, so I only saw the final, approved script.

John: *What was the artistic process while doing* Buck Rogers? *Was it similar to your* Scorchy Smith *or comic book schedule?*

George: For the most part. Howard wrote the strips, I worked from home, and I both penciled and inked it. No assistants. Someone at the syndicate would letter the pages. Unlike with *Scorchy*, where I was a one-person shop, on *Buck*, I had little or no input on the scripts. This was an adjustment. For five years, I was doing it all. Nothing against Howard's scripts, but when I also wrote the story, I felt my illustrations were more complete.

John: *In speaking with your wife, Dorothy, she indicated that, while doing* Buck Rogers, *you received a invitation from Johnny Carson to appear on* The Tonight Show?

George: Oh, yes. This was during the 1960s when the country was caught up in the Space Race. Mr. Carson had liked my *Buck Rogers* and also thought it would be topical to have me on his show. I received a letter of invitation to appear. Unfortunately, I could not take the time away from the strip, so I had to decline. Very flattering, though.

John: *National Syndicate canceled* Buck Rogers *in 1965. Did you immediately come back to the comic book field?*

George: Yes. Re-enter Stan Lee in my life! Once it was discon-

tinued, I began to look for work again. With Stan now running Marvel Comics, about a month before *Buck* was cancelled, I called Stan to get work. He welcomed me with open arms! I worked for Stan through the late 1970s and for Marvel, on-and-off, until about 1987. Over 20 years.

John: *Though touched on earlier, any comments on Stan Lee?*

George: Stan was a great inspiration and fun to work with. During creative meetings where plots were discussed, Stan would actually demonstrate the story as he proposed it! [*laughter*] Not only that, but he would act out the different characters to illustrate their personalities. It made for a fun, creative atmosphere. I want to also add that Stan was also a good businessman, as well. Sometimes I think that part of Stan is lost in his public persona.

John: *While freelancing for Marvel*

Above: *For collector R. Robert Pollak's unpublished Buck Rogers portfolio, George Tuska some very handsome pencil and full-color pieces, including this tabloid-sized pencil art in the 1980s. Courtesy of Mr. Pollak. Art ©2021 the estate of George Tuska. Buck Rogers ©2021 Buck Rogers Company.*

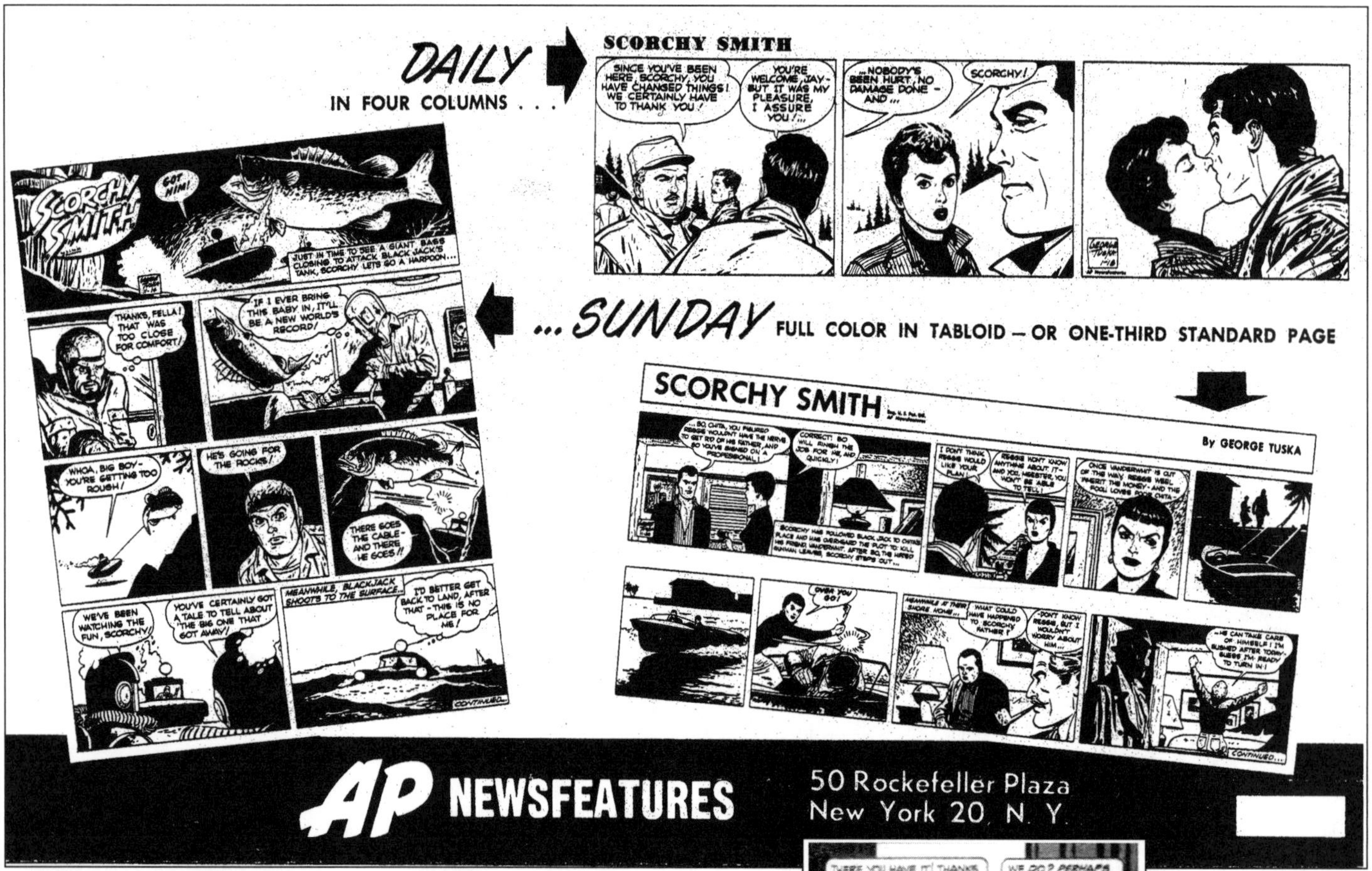
DAILY
IN FOUR COLUMNS . . .
SCORCHY SMITH
SINCE YOU'VE BEEN HERE, SCORCHY, YOU HAVE CHANGED THINGS! WE CERTAINLY HAVE TO THANK YOU!
YOU'RE WELCOME, JAY-BUT IT WAS MY PLEASURE, I ASSURE YOU!...
...NOBODY'S BEEN HURT, NO DAMAGE DONE - AND...
SCORCHY!
SCORCHY SMITH
GOT HIM!
JUST IN TIME TO SEE A GIANT BASS CLOSING TO ATTACK BLACK JACK'S TANK, SCORCHY LETS GO A HARPOON...
THANKS, FELLA! THAT WAS TOO CLOSE FOR COMFORT!
IF I EVER BRING THIS BABY IN, IT'LL BE A NEW WORLD'S RECORD!
WHOA, BIG BOY-YOU'RE GETTING TOO ROUGH!
HE'S GOING FOR THE ROCKS!
THERE GOES THE CABLE-AND THERE HE GOES!!
WE'VE BEEN WATCHING THE FUN, SCORCHY!
YOU'VE CERTAINLY GOT A TALE TO TELL ABOUT 'THE BIG ONE THAT GOT AWAY!
MEANWHILE, BLACKJACK SHOOTS TO THE SURFACE...
I'D BETTER GET BACK TO LAND, AFTER THAT - THIS IS NO PLACE FOR ME!
CONTINUED...
...SUNDAY FULL COLOR IN TABLOID — OR ONE-THIRD STANDARD PAGE
SCORCHY SMITH
By GEORGE TUSKA
CORRECT! BO WILL FINISH THE JOB FOR ME, AND QUICKLY!
I DON'T THINK REGGIE WOULD LIKE YOUR PLAN!
OVER YOU GO!
WHAT COULD HAVE HAPPENED TO SCORCHY FATHER?
-DON'T KNOW REGGIE, BUT I WOULDN'T WORRY ABOUT HIM...
CONTINUED...
AP NEWSFEATURES
50 Rockefeller Plaza
New York 20, N. Y.

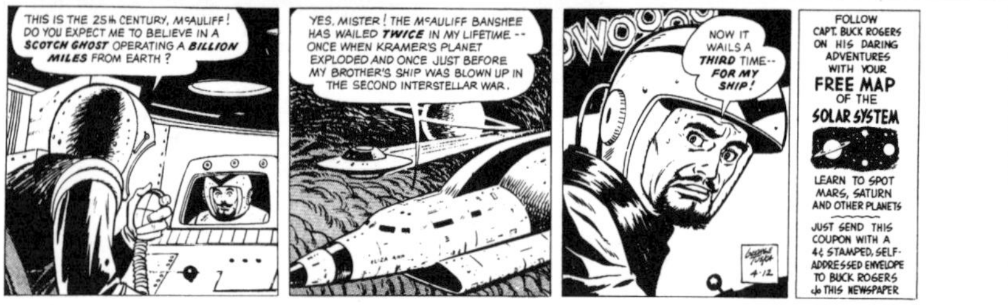
THIS IS THE 25th CENTURY, McAULIFF! DO YOU EXPECT ME TO BELIEVE IN A SCOTCH GHOST OPERATING A BILLION MILES FROM EARTH?
YES, MISTER! THE McAULIFF BANSHEE HAS WAILED TWICE IN MY LIFETIME.-- ONCE WHEN KRAMER'S PLANET EXPLODED AND ONCE JUST BEFORE MY BROTHER'S SHIP WAS BLOWN UP IN THE SECOND INTERSTELLAR WAR.
NOW IT WAILS A THIRD TIME-- FOR MY SHIP!
FOLLOW CAPT. BUCK ROGERS ON HIS DARING ADVENTURES WITH YOUR FREE MAP OF THE SOLAR SYSTEM
LEARN TO SPOT MARS, SATURN AND OTHER PLANETS
JUST SEND THIS COUPON WITH A 4¢ STAMPED, SELF-ADDRESSED ENVELOPE TO BUCK ROGERS c/o THIS NEWSPAPER

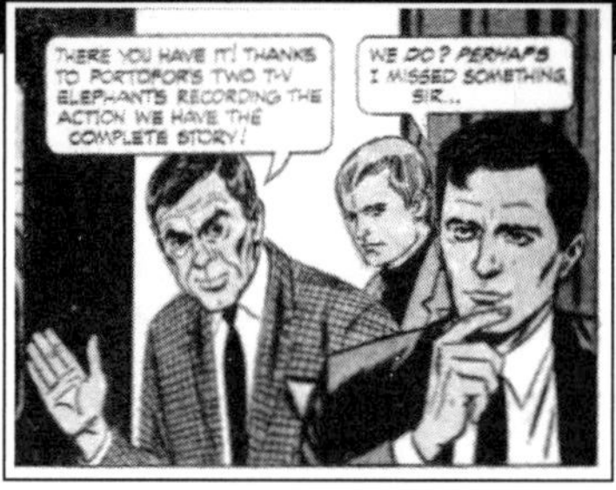
THERE YOU HAVE IT! THANKS TO PORTOFOR'S TWO TV ELEPHANTS RECORDING THE ACTION WE HAVE THE COMPLETE STORY!
WE DO? PERHAPS I MISSED SOMETHING, SIR...

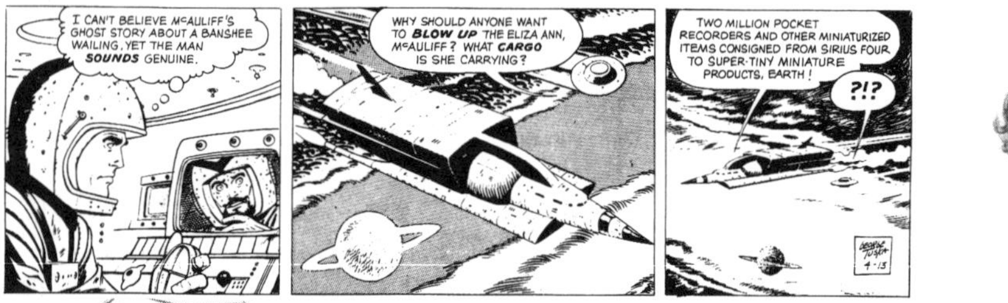
I CAN'T BELIEVE McAULIFF'S GHOST STORY ABOUT A BANSHEE WAILING, YET THE MAN SOUNDS GENUINE.
WHY SHOULD ANYONE WANT TO BLOW UP THE ELIZA ANN, McAULIFF? WHAT CARGO IS SHE CARRYING?
TWO MILLION POCKET RECORDERS AND OTHER MINIATURIZED ITEMS CONSIGNED FROM SIRIUS FOUR TO SUPER-TINY MINIATURE PRODUCTS, BARTH!
?!?

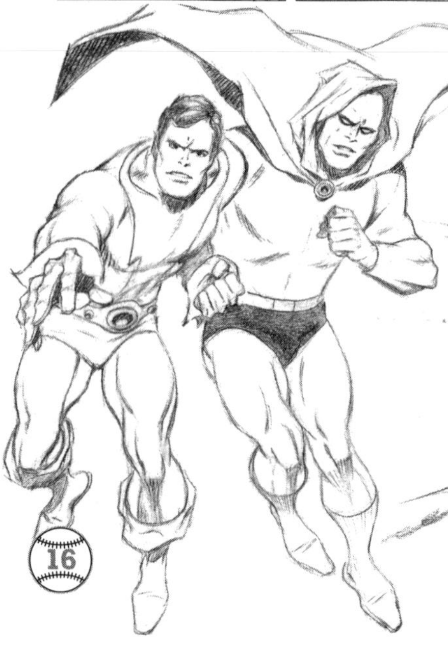

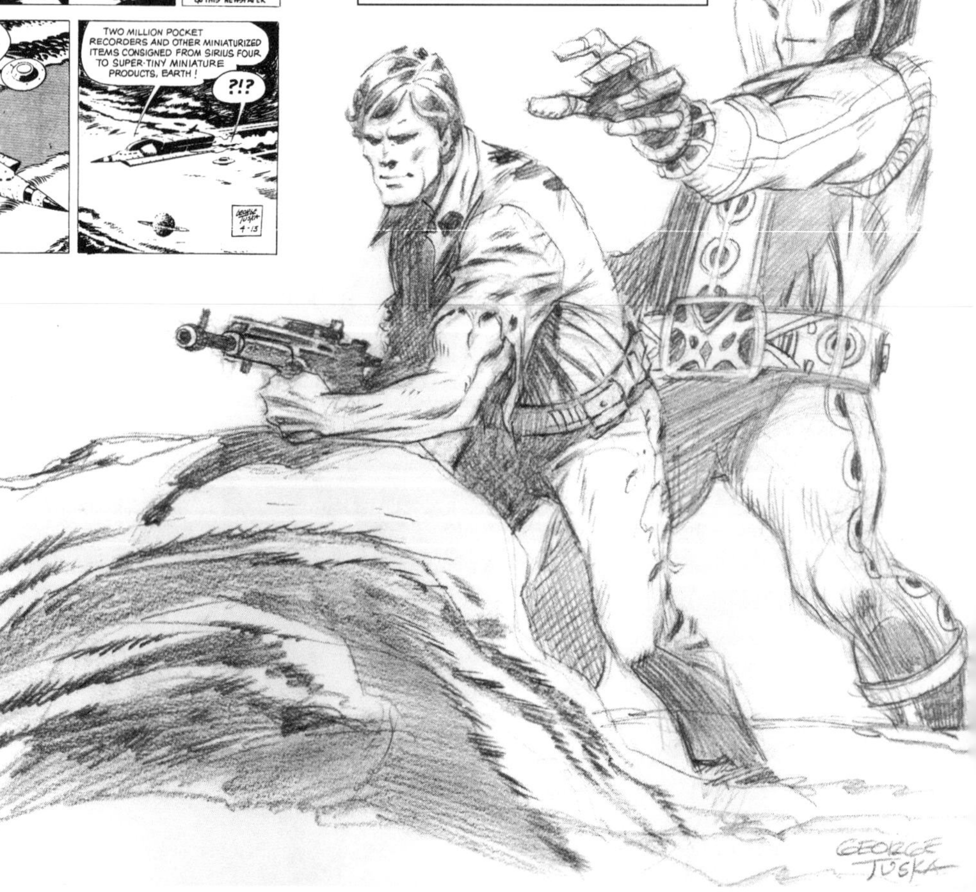
GEORGE TUSKA

Previous page: *(Clockwise from top) Other side to the AP Newsfeatures broadsheet promoting Scorchy Smith. ©2021 the respective copyright holder. Panel from The Man from U.N.C.L.E. #3 [Nov. '65]. Gold Key. ©2021 the respective copyright holder. 1980s Scorchy Smith commission piece by George. Courtesy of R. Robert Pollak. Art ©2021 the estate of George Tuska. ©2021 the respective copyright holder. T.H.U.N.D.E.R. Agents commission piece, courtesy of Jerry K. Boyd. Art ©2021 the estate of George Tuska. Characters ©2021 Thunder Agency. '50s Buck Rogers daily strip drawn by George Tuska. ©2021 the respective copyright holder.*

This page: *(Clockwise from above) Buck Rogers commission piece courtesy owned by R. Robert Pollak. Art ©2021 the estate of George Tuska. Buck Rogers ©2021 Buck Rogers Co. Splash panel from The Double Life of Private Strong #2 (Aug. '59). ©2021 Archie Publications. Tuska T.H.U.N.D.E.R. Agents piece courtesy of Jerry K. Boyd. Art ©2021 the estate of George Tuska. Characters ©2021 Thunder Agency. Spyman #1 cover by Tuska (Sept.'66). ©2021 the respective copyright holder.*

CAPTAIN AMERICA, LIVING LEGEND of WORLD WAR II

"the FINAL SLEEP"

TWO OF THE *SLEEPERS* HAVE ALREADY *AWAKENED!!* BUT I MUST SOUND THE *WARNING* ABOUT THE *THIRD!*

BLAZING STORY: **STAN LEE**
BURNING LAYOUTS: **JACK KIRBY**
BLISTERING ARTWORK: **GEORGE TUSKA**
BURNT-OUT LETTERING: **ARTIE SIMEK**

AFTER A DARING LEAP TO EARTH FROM THE BACK OF THE 2ND DEADLY *SLEEPER CAPTAIN AMERICA* RACES TO THE NEAREST *NATO* INSTALLATION TO OFFER HIS SKILL, STRENGTH, AND *LIFE*, IF NEED BE, TO COMBAT THE *RED SKULL'S* INHUMAN CREATIONS!

LOOK!! SOMEONE CRASHED THRU SECURITY!

HALT! HALT AND BE RECOGNIZED!

NATO ARMY CORPS INF. DIVISIONAL HEA...

IT'S CAPTAIN AMERICA!

I DON'T CARE IF HE'S SOUPY SALES...

--WE'VE GOTTA *STOP* HIM!

Above: *Beautiful splash page sporting Jack Kirby's layouts with finishes by George Tuska.* Tales of Suspense #74 [Feb. '66]. **Below left:** *Tuska's cover art for* Hero for Hire #1 [June '72] with some John Romita, Sr. alterations. **Inset right:** *Tuska cover art to* The X-Men #39 [Dec. '67] and The Avengers #48 [Jan. '68]. TM & ©2021 Marvel Characters, Inc.

MARVEL COMICS GROUP

LUKE CAGE, HERO for HIRE

1 JUNE 20¢

SENSATIONAL ORIGIN ISSUE!

America, Daredevil, Iron Man, *and* The Avengers, *to name a few. Any favorites?*

George: Probably Captain America. He is a very dynamic and physical character. Lots of action and very heroic.

John: *Though your work continued to appear across Marvel's line of titles, the work you're most associated with is* Iron Man. *With one or two exceptions, you drew every issue of the title from 1968–78. Do you have an affinity for the character?*

George: When I first began drawing *Iron Man,* it immediately appealed to me. Where the Iron Man persona was invincible, the Tony Stark character was very fragile. I liked the contrast. It was interesting that the invincible persona—Iron Man—was held together by the fragile character—Tony Stark. The Stark character was also fun to draw. Very Stylish.

John: *During this period at Marvel, you began to ink more as opposed to penciling. Did you tire of penciling?*

George: Nothing that dramatic. The main heroes were already scheduled with their regular art teams. Unlike today, in the mid-1960s, Marvel didn't publish that many monthly titles. While waiting for an opening, I inked for a while. Given a choice, I would rather pencil and have another artist ink my work. I feel more involved with what goes on the page if I do the pencils.

John: *That's odd. Many pencilers I've spoken to would rather ink their own work.*

George: Well, if time permits, so would I. But, by having someone else ink my pencils, I could draw more pages. Besides, I would never allow an artist to ink my work if I did not like the finished product.

John: *Around this same time, in the mid- to late 1960s, your work appeared in Harvey's* Thrill-O-Rama *and* Spyman *comic books. How did that come about?*

George: Through [editor] Joe Simon. I had known of Joe since the early days, but had never known him personally. He liked my art and offered me work. I think I only drew a couple issues and maybe a cover or two. Joe also was publishing a *MAD*-type magazine, called *Sick*… satire and the like. We worked together for years on those and became very close personally. It helped that we lived fairly close to one another, as well.

John: *Aside from Marvel, Gold Key, and Harvey, your work also appeared in Wally Wood's Tower Comics. How did that come about?*

George: I just dropped in one day and was offered work! [*laughter*] I was still mainly working for Marvel, but many times I would finish that assignment early. While waiting for the next Marvel script, I would

Comics, did you write any scripts?

George: No. I worked from plot synopsis. Although I did provide input into the writing by indicating dialogue in the margins for some of the characters. I believe this was practiced by quite a few of the artists at the time. The nature of drawing from a synopsis makes it a natural progression to provide input. Stan wrote most of the stories, which was why they read so well. He has a flair for writing.

John: *Did Stan ever give you a moniker? For example; Jack "King" Kirby, "Jazzy" John Romita?*

George: Oh, yes! It was embarrassing! I was "Gorgeous" George Tuska. Really, it was all in good fun and just Stan's way.

John: *Starting in the mid-1960s at Marvel, your pencils appeared in a wide range of titles, from* Tales to Suspense, Uncanny X-men, Ghost Rider, Incredible Hulk, Captain

drop by other publishers and try and pick up additional work.

John: *What was working with Wally Wood like?*

George: I didn't work in the office, but we met occasionally. Always very pleasant.

John: *This brings us up to the late 1960s and early '70s, when you began to free-lance for DC Comics, as well as Marvel. Like Marvel, your work also appeared across DC's line of titles. I remember your back-up stories starring the Legion of Super-Heroes [in* Superboy*]. Other work that comes to mind is* Teen Titans, *with Nick Cardy inking.*

George: I really didn't connect with those characters. It had nothing to do with Nick's inking. I loved what he did over my pencils. Who wouldn't? His inking seemed to add to my pencils, without losing my style or the drawings original intent.

John: *How did you get into DC Comics?*

George: I had known Carmine Infantino since the early days and submitted samples. Carmine was the publisher at the time. Anyway, he gave me the *Teen Titans* book. Evidently, Nick was no longer available to both pencil and ink the book.

John: *You continued freelancing for both Marvel, DC Comics, and various other publishers throughout the 1970s. In '78, you again left the comic book field for a newspaper daily and Sunday syndicated strip. This time it was the new* Superman *strip. How did that come about?*

George: With the success of the Christopher Reeves *Superman* movie, DC was developing a new Superman-based newspaper strip. At the time, Vince Colletta was the art director for DC. We had met in the early 1960s at Marvel. Vince called to offer me the new strip. He was the principle inker on the strip, as well.

John: *After 15-plus years hiatus from drawing newspaper strips, had it changed any?*

George: A little. I think the biggest difference was that the scripts on the *Superman* strip lacked quality. I could never get anyone at DC interested in getting better scripts. After over five years of drawing it, I finally left the strip in 1983.

John: *Did you make your concerns known to the writers or editors?*

George: I went to one editor, but nothing came of it.

Eventually, Joe Orlando took over as strip editor and the scripts began to become much better. Unfortunately, by that time, I had lost interest in the strip and went back to drawing monthly comics for DC like *Masters of the Universe, Firestorm, Green Lantern,* and *Justice League.*

John: *Around this time, in the mid-1980s, your work in the comic book field became less frequent. Any particular reason?*

George: I was tired. After over 15 years back in the business—not including the 1940s and 1950s—I decided to take it easy.

John: *What did you do during your hiatus?*

George: I like to paint and on occasion have done posters for DC and Marvel, and cover re-creations for fans.

John: *In 1987, your last comic book work was the* Masters of the Universe *movie adaptation for Marvel. Any chance of a return to*

Inset left: *Tuska cover art for* Sub-Mariner #41 *[Sept. '71] &* Iron Man #5 *[Sept. '68].* **Right:** *Gorgeous George Tuska color commission job done for R. Robert Pollak, starring the character most associated with the artist. Art ©2021 the estate of George Tuska.* **Above right:** *Courtesy of collector Troy Pierce, the original cover art to* Iron Man #8 *[Dec. '68]. All characters TM & ©2021 Marvel Characters, Inc.*

the field of comic books?

George: Today, it's a new field with new tastes, but thanks for being kind. I'd be open to it, but I'm happy just doing commissions and cover re-creations for fans, as well.

John: *Any general Impressions of the industry today?*

George: A mixture: Some of the art is sub-par. Some artists can't even draw the most simple human figure. I see some artists trying to cover up their inability to draw the human form by drawing all sorts of patterns, heavy shading. Exaggerating the human form is fine with comics, but you must be grounded. If you never learned to draw the human form correctly, how can you know what to exaggerate from?

Jack Kirby is a perfect example of how to do it right. I can't understand why some artists don't care about their craft. On the other hand, some artists today really do take the art form to new heights, into places I never dreamed of when I started back in 1939. Overall, the art today is more lively and colorful than in that era. Very imaginative layouts, powerful visually, and explosive. But I do think there is an overall lack of understanding of how to sequentially tell a story. Maybe that's just what the editors want.

John: *Well, if the artists of today are reaching new heights, it's on the foundation built by artists such as yourself.*

George: Thank you.

John: *Another trend in comics over the past ten years is to blur the lines between the hero and the villain.*

George: To show some

characters in this light is realistic. To have all the characters act this way is boring and unimaginative. I would think that there is no better time than today to feature a truly heroic character.

John: *But can't the same excuse be used with your 1940s crime comics work?*

George: Not at all. The difference is that we always portrayed violence as wrong, not a solution. Though we would show the violent act, the bad guy would always face some form of consequence. Today, many characters seem to be shown to be "bad guys," and the violence is shown as something to aspire.

John: *Again, I can't thank you enough for this opportunity. I feel fortunate I was able to conduct this interview, but more so, the fans have been fortunate for having been able to enjoy your wonderful work and the entertainment you've provided through the medium.*

George: Thank you. I can truly say I never thought it would come to this. Through interviews such as this, and when I attend conventions, it's very touching to learn that fans enjoyed my work as much as I loved doing it. I'm very lucky to be remembered this fondly.

Interview ©2021 John D. Coates & the estate of George Tuska.

Tuska Testimonials

As told to John Coates & Peter Depree

Will Eisner

George was quite a fine man. I still remember him very fondly. He was a very nice fellow and we got along very well. He was a quiet, big fellow, a big handsome man who worked at Eisner & Iger. As a matter of fact, I refer to him in my book, *The Dreamer,* in one sequence where he punched out Bob Powell, who made some remarks that angered Tuska! Tuska was rather shy and I think there was a girl in the office he was sweet on, and Powell made a remark about that one day. This was in the shop, while we were all sitting around, and Tuska got up, very slowly and kind of sadly, and slugged Powell. [*laughter*] Then sat down and apologized later. Said he was sorry he got angry, but he lost his temper. He did not come with me when I did *The Spirit.* He remained behind. Tuska had a very, very clean style, and a very, very pleasant style. His characters had a moralistic look to them. They were classy comics [with] a very clean, sharp, strong line. His characters always looked very nice, very clean, and good-looking.

Stan Lee

In then old days, many artists were fast and a few were good. George excelled at both. I can't speak highly enough of him or his work. George was probably the most complete artist I ever worked with. And that includes everybody! George was not only a great artist, but he understood the reproduction aspect of the printed page. His lines were always just thin or thick enough… his blacks and shading were just right… so that nothing was lost in the printing. That's talent!

    I tried to get George on [the] *Spider-Man* [comic book] for years, but he was always too busy. But George did pinch hit on the *Spider-Man* newspaper strip more than once. He was always at the ready and I knew that if I were behind a deadline, I could depend on George, regardless of what else he was working on!

Carmine Infantino

When I was just getting started in the business, I studied George's attitude and professionalism. I realized that if I were going to be successful in this industry, he was someone who I would need to emulate. His artwork has the same integrity he has: Clear and honest.

John Romita, Sr.

Even as a child reading comics in the 1940s, I knew and admired George's work. Looking at George's panels was like watching a silent movie, frame by frame… he's *that* good a storyteller! George's work defines the visual medium in the proper light. During the 1950s, while at Atlas Comics, whenever I was in the

office and saw George's work, I would grab up as much as possible. For years, I wanted him on *Spider-Man,* but he was too busy. George is as good a figure- and character-man as anyone in the business… and he stacks with the best.

Joe Simon

I worked with George a long, long time. We were very good friends. Tuska was penciling the *Buck Rogers* comic strip when started working with me [1959], but that was winding down. He had such a wonderful ink style; I'm surprised they would have someone else ink that strip. We kept him busy for about 15 years on *Sick.* It required an illustrative style, so he didn't have to modify his technique. He helped us on *Young Romance* and *Young Love,* as well. He also worked with me on *The Adventures of the Fly* and The Shield in *The Double Life of Private Strong,* in the late '50s, for Archie Comics. He did a lot of work for us at Harvey, too, including Spyman and Bee-Man. He was happy and we were happy. It was a very friendly relationship; it wasn't like he was working for me or I for him. I was so happy to get artists like George because there was never a boss/employee relationship ever with any of my artists.

    I remember George liked to paint. He would paint oil on canvas board. If he didn't like his paintings, he would burn them up! Every spring, he would take them out in his back-yard and burn the ones he thought were bad! The neighbors were probably scared to death of him! It was like "The Rites of Spring": George Tuska burning his paintings!

    I like to think George has a very good memories of us. I know I do of him.

Above: *Portrait of the artist. Courtesy of Mike Gartland.* **Below:** *As a longtime hobby, George Tuska would dabble in watercolor and oil painting. Here's a superb example of the latter. ©2021 the estate of George Tuska.*

Portions of this text originally published in *Comic Book Marketplace #31,* January 1996. Edited by Gary Carter.

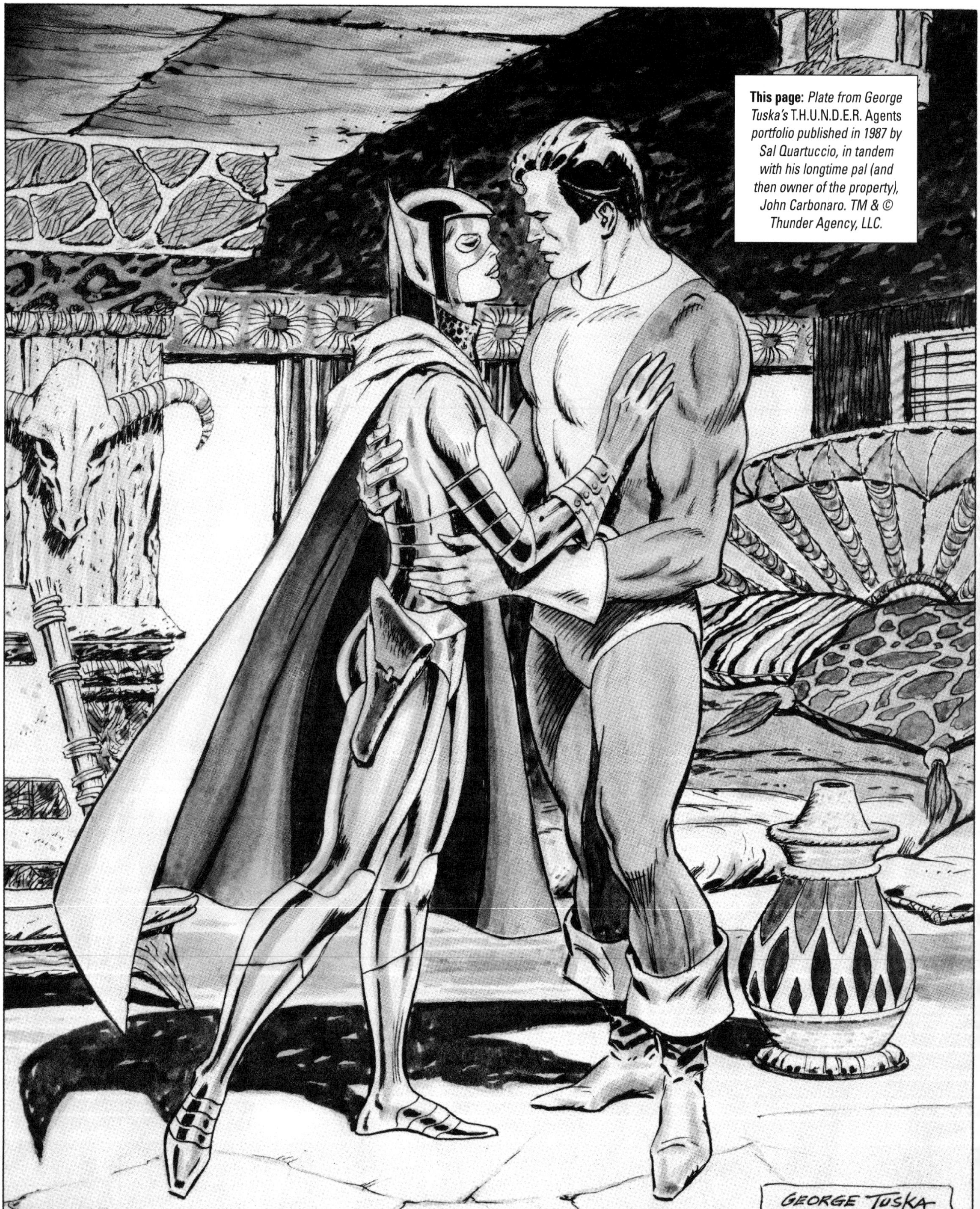
GEORGE TUSKA
1986

This page: *Plate from George Tuska's* T.H.U.N.D.E.R. Agents *portfolio published in 1987 by Sal Quartuccio, in tandem with his longtime pal (and then owner of the property), John Carbonaro. TM & © Thunder Agency, LLC.*

Below: *Rare example of George Tuska's ink-wash work, a panel from his singular contribution to the Warren horror magazines, "A Vested Interest," Creepy #8 [Apr. '66]. ©2021 Warren Publications.*

...WEREWOLF!

Tuska Portfolio

Above and inset: *In recent years, the artist has been devoting more of his energies to painting. Here are two examples of his new-found love. Courtesy of and ©2021 the estate of George Tuska.*

23

George Tuska: CBA All-Star!

COMIC BOOK ARTIST
ALL★STARS

George Tuska

MARVEL/DC
PENCILER & INKER

GEORGE TUSKA

001

GEORGE TUSKA
PENCILER • INKER • WRITER

BORN: 2/26/16 BIRTHPLACE: HARTFORD, CT
SCHOOL: NATIONAL ACADEMY OF DESIGN
1st PUBBED: "Spike Merlin," 1939 (Tem/Holyoke)

G.T. STARTED DRAWING AT 8, ENCOURAGED BY HIS MOTHER & INSPIRED BY SAT. EVENING POST MAGAZINE ILLUSTRATORS!

MEMORABLE WORK:

IRON MAN
MARVEL COMICS

PROFESSIONAL COMIC BOOK/STRIP ART HIGHLIGHTS

YEARS	PUBLISHER	FEATURES/GENRES
1939-40	VICTOR FOX	Includes some writing. Zanzibar, Cosmic Carson, etc.
1940-46	FICTION HOUSE	Innumerable strips which include some writing. Wilton of the West, Greasemonkey Griffin, Werewolf Hunter, Kayo Kirby, Kaanga, Planet Payson, Cosmo Corrigan, Shark Brodie, and others
1940-46	FAWCETT	Captain Marvel, Golden Arrow, El Carim, Nuoka, Doctor Voodoo
1946-55	LEV GLEASON	Crime comics: Crimebuster, true hero series, Crime Does Not Pay
1947-53	PINES	Black Terror, Buckaneers, Doc Strange, Phantom Detective, Looie Lazybones, s-f, horror, romance
1950s	CRESTWOOD	Romance, horror
1950s	ATLAS/MARVEL	Western, horror, s-f, crime, romance, war
1954-59	AP NEWSFEATURES	Scorchy Smith (newspaper strip)
1959-67	NAT'L NEWS SYND.	Buck Rogers (newspaper strip: dailies until '65, Sundays until '67)
1959	ARCHIE	The Fly, The Shield
1964-'80s	MARVEL	Iron Man, Captain America, The Avengers, Daredevil, The Champions, Ghost Rider, The Hulk, Sub-Mariner, Shanna, Doctor Strange, Doctor Doom, X-Men, Ka-Zar, Luke Cage, Black Goliath, Tigra, Godzilla, Dracula, Planet of the Apes, The Thing, and many more strips
1966-68	TOWER	T.H.U.N.D.E.R. Agents, Raven, Weed
1967	HARVEY	Spyman
1970-80s	DC COMICS	The Legion of Super-Heroes, Teen Titans, Challengers of the Unknown, mystery, Superman, Superboy, Batman, Firestorm, Green Lantern, Justice League of America, Masters of the Universe, & much more
1978-83	DC COMICS/CTNYNS	World's Greatest Super-Heroes (newspaper strip, dailies & Sundays)

Iron Man ©2003 Marvel Characters, Inc.

Collect 'em All!

Trading card data compiled with reference to Who's Who of American Comic Books, *1st edition.*

COMIC BOOK ARTIST™ BULLPEN was published between 2003–04 by RetroHouse Press, C/o Jon B. Cooke, P.O. Box 601, West Kingston, R.I. 02892 USA. Jon B. Cooke, editor. Vol. 1, #1, Dec. 2003. All characters © their respective copyright holders. All material © their creators unless otherwise noted. ©2021 Jon B. Cooke. Cover acknowledgement: Cover acknowledgement: Iron Man TM & ©2021 Marvel Characters, Inc. Art ©2021 the estate of George Tuska.

Bullpen Extra!

Above: *Buck Rogers poster by George Tuska, commissioned by (and courtesy of) R. Robert Pollak for his mid-'80s unpublished portfolio. Buck Rogers ©2021 the Buck Rogers Company.*

★ COMIC BOOK ARTIST ★

BULLPEN

"Celebrating the Major League Players in the World of Comics Art"

retro house press

No. 2 JAN. 2004

This Ish: **THE ARTISTRY OF FRANK BOLLE!**

25

FRANK BOLLE
ARTIST OF SOLAR

Interview by Jon B. Cooke

Transcribed by Steven Tice

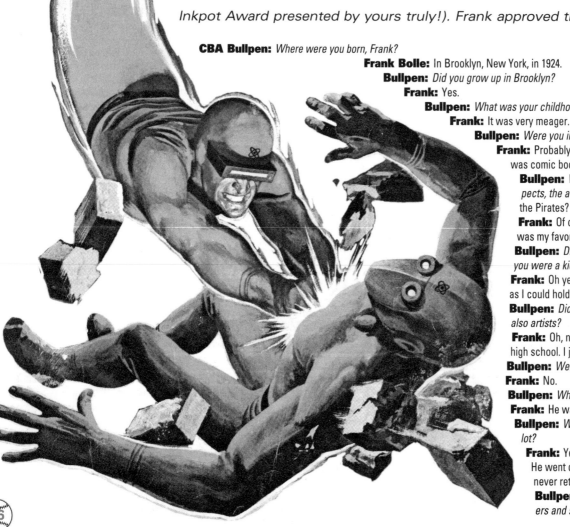

A humble and good-natured man, Frank W. Bolle counts himself as a seasoned comic book artist who has also had a significant career drawing a multitude of newspaper comic strips, children's books, and magazine illustration. The editor had the opportunity to interview the artist via telephone on June 20, 2003, in preparation for moderating a Bolle panel at last year's International Comic-Con: San Diego (where the artist received the coveted Inkpot Award presented by yours truly!). Frank approved the final transcript.

CBA Bullpen: *Where were you born, Frank?*

Frank Bolle: In Brooklyn, New York, in 1924.

Bullpen: *Did you grow up in Brooklyn?*

Frank: Yes.

Bullpen: *What was your childhood like?*

Frank: It was very meager.

Bullpen: *Were you into comic strips as a kid?*

Frank: Probably my only recognition of art was comic books coming out at that time.

Bullpen: *Were you into the usual suspects, the adventure strips like* Terry and the Pirates?

Frank: Of course. *Terry and the Pirates* was my favorite strip.

Bullpen: *Did you start drawing when you were a kid?*

Frank: Oh yes. I started drawing as soon as I could hold a pencil.

Bullpen: *Did you have friends who were also artists?*

Frank: Oh, no, not until I got to junior high school. I just did it all on my own.

Bullpen: *Were your parents creative?*

Frank: No.

Bullpen: *What did your father do?*

Frank: He was a Merchant seaman.

Bullpen: *Was he away from home a lot?*

Frank: Yes. I didn't really know him. He went out to sea one day and never returned.

Bullpen: *Did you have any brothers and sisters?*

Frank: No, I was an only child.

Bullpen: *When did you see drawing as a career possibility?*

Frank: I had no real examples of which way to go until I got to junior high school. We had, besides recess and other classes, one period a week which was an art class. I guess I was always drawing in the art class, and the teacher said I should go to the High School of Music and Art, which, of course, I'd never even heard of before. So she filled out an application for me when I was ready to graduate from junior high. So I went to the High School of Music and Art. I had no idea where it was. It was an hour away from where I lived, and I had to have someone show me how to get there. [*chuckles*] I had to take an entrance exam and I was accepted, and that's when the whole world opened up to me.

Bullpen: *The high school was in Manhattan?*

Frank: Yes. I had to walk a mile to get to the subway, and then it took forever to get to 135th Street. That's way uptown, and that's coming from Brooklyn, so it was quite a trip. A lot of times, especially when the time changed, it was dark in the morning, and I'd get home when it was dark at night. It was a long day, because besides the regular curriculum, we had an extra hour of either art or music, depending if you were a music or an art student.

Bullpen: *This was obviously fortuitous to happen to a poor kid from Brooklyn, right?*

Frank: Oh, yes. I saw things there I never saw before. In Brooklyn, I had no outlet of knowing there were other jobs besides the daily work my neighbors did. In fact, my mother thought I should become a baker, so I would always have bread in the house. [*laughter*]

Bullpen: *Where are your parents from originally? What's their ethnicity?*

Frank: Central Europe, Austria.

Bullpen: *Did you have classmates of any note when you were in high school?*

Frank: Oh, yes. My best friend, who I've known since 1939, is Leonard Starr, the comic strip artist who recently drew *Little Orphan Annie*.

Bullpen: *Leonard Starr? Whoa! There's an illustrious friend!*

Frank: Yes! I still see him every week. [*laughs*] We just celebrated our 65th anniversary of friendship!

Bullpen: *Wow! He's obviously renowned for doing the syndicated strip,* On Stage with Mary Perkins. *He's a great artist!*

Frank: Right!

Bullpen: *You were about 12 years old when American comic books pretty much started?*

Frank: Pretty much, yeah.

Bullpen: *Did you notice comics when they started to come out? Did you have an interest in them at all?*

Frank: Yes! I didn't have the money to buy them. I could go to the movies for a dime, where they gave away some free comic books. That's when I first got the idea of drawing comic books. I used to draw pictures, make up my own stores and then I'd show them to my classmates. I'd do them over the weekend, so when I went to school on Monday, I would have the sketchbook with me with panels drawn in it and finished stories. I would write my own mysteries and science-fiction stories. That's when I got started in comics, by doing them on my own.

Bullpen: *Were they dramatic strips?*

Frank: Yes, usually.

Bullpen: *What was New York like when you were growing up? Were you in the thick of the great Depression?*

Frank: Yes, but it was pretty nice. Sometimes we would go into Manhattan. Subways were only a nickel, and it only took 20 minutes to get there, maybe a half-hour. We could walk into

Inset left: *Portrait of the artist, Frank Bolle. Courtesy of FWB.*

Opposite page: *Frank Bolle didn't do the final painting on this issue of* Doctor Solar, *but it is likely he composed the layout. ©2021 Penguin Random House, LLC.*

Below: *Frank Bolle illustration of Luis de Torres and company for the children's magazine* World Over. *Courtesy of the artist.*

Inset right: *Splash page by Frank Bolle from* Robin Hood *#52 [Nov. 1955].* ©1955 Sussex Publishing. **Below:** Robin Hood *#4 [May 1956], cover by FWB.*

Below: *Cover detail by Frank Bolle from an issue of Sussex Publishing's* Robin Hood. ©1955 Sussex Publishing Co.

Central Park any time of the day and feel perfectly safe. You never—ever—thought, no matter how late you came home from a movie or somewhere, or were a teenager on a date, that you had anything to worry about. The city was so friendly and nice in those days.

Bullpen: *Did Brooklyn pretty much live up to its reputation as it was portrayed in the movies as being quite a tough place to grow up?*

Frank: No. Only some neighborhoods were rough. Most of the places I was in were very nice. We always had nice neighbors and kids got along great. Though there *were* some neighborhoods where kids were always getting into trouble…

Bullpen: *There weren't the kid gangs, like the Dead End Kids or anything like that?*

Frank: No. There were some, but they were not as bad as the Dead End Kids.

Bullpen: *What neighborhood did you grow up in?*

Frank: Williamsburg.

Bullpen: *When you went to the school, what was the emphasis you took? Illustration?*

Frank: It was more general than that. It didn't really emphasize any particular kind of art, it just gave you a fundamental view of the whole field in general. We saw slides of Michelangelo, work like that, architecture, some paintings, some of the old Renaissance paintings. But no one emphasized anything in particular.

Bullpen: *So what was the curriculum?*

Frank: Well, we would have a regular day with English, math, science, and gym, classes like that. Then there was that extra hour where you had a painting or a craft class. In the craft class, you made things, would use clay or something like that, and construct three-dimensional things. It was pretty general. A lot of graduates would later become psychiatrists and doctors, and some never painted again. They just had a liking or a feel for art, had some talent, but would

go onto other professions. Some of girls just got married and let their husbands make a living. [*laughs*] Some did animation on TV, some were in the Hollywood cartoon business, and others did become painters

In the beginning, I had no idea I could make a living in *any* field. I thought I might become an art teacher, because that was what I liked the most. Then one of my teachers said,"You're too good. You shouldn't teach; you should just do it!" So I couldn't quite appreciate the compliment. [*laughs*] But I was always outstanding in my class. It was only until later on when I thought, "Maybe I'll get into comics." But, before I could start a career, I turned 18, so I was drafted and went off to war.

Bullpen: *Did your mother fathom what your interests were? Was there support there?*

Frank: Well, no, there was no encouragement. There was support in the sense, "Just enjoy what you're doing, but you've gotta become a baker." But there was no encouragement. No one in my neighborhood really understood that you could have a career in art. They weren't people who went to museums, bought art books, and things like that. So I was in kind of limbo there. I had no idea.

In the service, when I was stationed out of town — in Chicago, for instance, where I went to museums and started to get an appreciation of culture — I got to see there were other things in life, beyond the working class existence in Brooklyn, you see? So I began to realize I didn't have to be a baker, that I could be an artist.

Bullpen: *You mentioned a number of people who graduated the school did not go on to pursue, perhaps, careers in the arts, but became professionals in medicine or law. Did you think that there still was an advantage to going to that school anyway for them? Do you think it may have imbibed them with a certain attitude about life that could have been helpful, regardless of their final vocation?*

Frank: Well, sure! The musically inclined became musicians in one way or another. They knew it was a good school, so I guess they went there. One of my art student friends became an interior decorator. Another became an art director in television. So, it wasn't always in the art field, but something that was related, like interior decorating, furniture design, and things like that. Some became artists in some form or another, but it depended on how much they wanted to do it. In a lot of ways, it was hard work. One of the girls I knew in high school, she was a terrific painter. She had such a good feeling for painting. She admitted she was lazy, she wasn't going to work that hard. She just got married several times, four or five times. [laughter] I still know her. I don't see her a lot, but she calls me every once in a while. In fact, I went to her last wedding, which was the fifth, about two years ago. [laughter] She was sort of a high school girlfriend, but not *my* girlfriend.

Bullpen: *[Laughs] "Thank* you!" How did you meet Leonard?*

Frank: Well, we were in the same class. I met him in an English or math, and he had a sketchbook and he would be doodling as I was doodling. I thought he was pretty good and he thought I was pretty good. Then we found out we were in the same art class, and we became the two best in the class. We were always buddies together, would talk about the movies we liked, and things like that. We rode the train together. He lived in downtown Manhattan and I was in Brooklyn. A lot of times, I would meet him on the train coming with a couple of other fellows who caught the same train, and the four of us would go off to school and leave at the same time. Then we'd have lunch together in the lunchroom. So we hit it off right away. We have the same sense of humor, love funny stuff, tell jokes, and we got along great. To this day, we still get along great.

Bullpen: *Is Starr his birth name?*

Frank: No. His parents were Russian. His last name was originally Staradub. Then, when he graduated, when he was going to go into business, changed his name to "Starr" for short.

Bullpen: *But threw in an extra "R" for fun? [laughs]*

Frank: Yes. So it was a hard name for people to pronounce.

Bullpen: *Where were you on December 7, 1941?*

Frank: It was Sunday morning. I was home

drawing and I had the radio on. That's when I heard about Pearl Harbor.

Bullpen: *Was it a moment when you realized everything would changed?*

Frank: No, I was just baffled at what was going on, because I knew the Japanese ambassadors were here talking about trade and peace, stuff like that, which had been reported on the radio. Then, suddenly, this surprise attack. I had no idea where Pearl Harbor was. But a short time later, I sure found out and we knew there was a problem, there was something serious going on.

Bullpen: *In what year were you drafted?*

Frank: In 1943.

Bullpen: *Did you see the war as inevitable?*

Frank: Oh, yes, I expected it. In fact, I graduated in '42, and then went to Pratt Institute. I figured I would stay there as long as I could until they called me up. I was there for six months. I went in September and, by March, I was drafted. By March 15, I was already in the service. I was 18 years old and was just baffled by the whole thing. I'd never left Brooklyn except to go to school, and I was a kid who never had money. I was a very poor kid who was suddenly traveling on a train, going to Virginia, camping up there for a couple weeks, where I got a physical, and all that stuff. Then, next thing, I was shipped off to the Virginia Army Air Base, and basic training. My eyes must have been wide open, because I was taking everything in. I was like Alice first visiting Wonderland. I had been very secluded in

Above: Frank Bolle work depicting the Blonde Phantom and Tim Holt as Red Mask. Art courtesy of and ©'04 Frank Bolle. Characters ©2021 the respective copyright holders.

Inset left: The bodacious Blonde Phantom as drawn by Frank Bolle.
Below: Frank's cover detail of Red Mask from Tim Holt #27 [Jan. 1952].

10¢

EXTRA DIMENSION BY FRANK BOLLE

GUNFIRE ROLLS OUT ACROSS A LITTLE VALLEY—

ALL THIS TRAINING SURE HAS PAID OFF!

WHY DO THE WORST OUTLAWS OF THE WEST GATHER AT A LITTLE RANCH SOUTH OF BULLET? WHO IS THE MAN WHO TRAINS THEM TO KILL AND ROB.? WHERE IS REDMASK? WHAT WILL HAPPEN WHEN THE MASKED RIDER OF THE RIO GRANDE COMES FACE TO FACE WITH THE KILLERS WHOSE GOAL IS—

"TARGET: REDMASK!"

Brooklyn, so I never knew much of the outside world, and suddenly here I am! So it was *quite* an experience.

Bullpen: *Were you afraid?*

Frank: No, I don't think I was ever afraid. I was very athletic. Basic training was a breeze for me. I'd won every race I was ever in in high school—or in *any* school—and, in fact,

when I lived in Brooklyn, there wasn't a fence in the neighborhood I didn't jump over. I climbed *every* fence. I was one of those kids who would run downstairs and then, the last 20 steps, I would leap down. Being athletic was like being Errol Flynn. I had wings on my feet! So going from basic training, the physical stuff was nothing. In fact, I would always wind up helping someone carry his rifle after marching 20 miles.

But I did have some funny experiences because I had no experience with woodsy stuff. I'd never been in the woods. Bivouac was a strange thing to me, living in a little tent on the ground. [*laughter*] It was a whole new experience for me!

Bullpen: *Were you popular in school?*

Frank: Oh, yes, I always had friends. I was always liked. I was very easygoing, pleasant, always kidding around—pleasantly, not maliciously. Even to this day, people say, "Are you *always* this cheerful?" When I went to the doctor a few weeks ago, I'd injured my knee, and he says, "Well, it just could be a little arthritis." I said, "'*Arthritis*'? I'm too *cheerful* to have arthritis!" [*laughter*]

Bullpen: *You gotta be cranky, huh? [laughs] Misdiagnosis!*

Frank: Yeah! It proved to be nothing, I'd just strained my knee.

Bullpen: *Did you go to the movies as often as you could?*

Frank: At least once a week. It was 15¢ at that time. That was when I had an allowance. I earned money by delivering ice. That's when people had ice boxes, y'know? I was making some money delivering ice. I'd carry a 50-pound chunk of ice for a couple of blocks to someone's house. We went to the movies at least once a week.

Bullpen: *When you and Leonard were graduating, the war notwithstanding, what were your plans? What did you hope to do?*

Frank: We were both figuring on going to Syracuse. Then, when the war broke out, we thought, "We'd better to stay near home." That's why we went to Pratt Institute, because it was only a subway-ride away, and that was right in Brooklyn. Anyway, Pratt was an art school, engineering school, architectural school. I lasted six months. I almost finished the first year, but not quite. Then I was off to war.

Bullpen: *Why stick close to home?*

Frank: Well, because I knew if I went off into the service, I would be gone for several years. So I figured, if I've got six months to stay around, I may as well stay at home.

Bullpen: *How were you able to go? Did you get scholarships? Did you work and save money?*

Frank: Well, Pratt wasn't that expensive, but my stepfather was willing to pay. I think it was like $300 a term or something like that. It wasn't a lot. It was a lot in *those* days, but it wasn't a lot when you think of it now.

Bullpen: *When did your mother remarry?*

Frank: At just about that time. I was very glad she wouldn't be home alone.

Bullpen: *So, obviously, your stepfather was supportive of you?*

Frank: Yes.

Bullpen: *You went through basic training. Where did you go from there?*

Frank: Well, for awhile, since I was an artist, they put me in a small camouflage unit. For six months or so, I went around giving talks and lectures and demonstrating how things can be hidden and disguised or put up false images for planes, observers to be misled, things like that. It was interesting. I went to a lot of different bases and demonstrated these things. But eventually I wound up with an Air Force ordinance and engineering outfit, and that's when I went overseas. I was in the Pacific. I would have liked to have gone to Europe, because that always sounded nice, but I finally wound up in the Pacific.

FRANK BOLLE'S EXTRA DIMENSION!

Frank added as a postscript to his interview transcript: "Maybe I should mention that in the 1950s, when 3-D movies suddenly became popular, and even some books were printed in 3-D (but you had to wear special eyeglasses), I went to [ME editor] Ray Krank and [ME publisher] Vincent Sullivan while I was drawing *Tim Holt*, and said I could draw my own "3-D effect" illustrations of Holt, and you didn't even need to wear the special glasses. By using perspective and having people and objects come in and out of the panel, it could have a sort-of 3-D look. They loved the idea, and I did it 'til the fad faded [#39-41, Dec. '53-Apr. '54]. Some people still come up to me and say they still remember that pseudo-3-D effect."

Bullpen: *When you were stateside doing the camouflage talks, how long did that last for?*

Frank: It lasted maybe about eight months.

Bullpen: *By the time you were shipped overseas, had D-Day already taken place? That was June of '44.*

Frank: No, I was still stateside at one of the air bases, but I left soon after that.

Bullpen: *What did you want to do as a job? Was getting a syndicated strip the focus?*

Frank: In the beginning, it was. When I first started to do comics, I was so busy doing that so I didn't really think of comic strips until later. I thought getting a syndicated strip would have been nice. That would be a nice final goal to make.

Bullpen: *In the sense of getting the recognition?*

Frank: Yes, but also enjoying something I could do well.

Bullpen: *But you must have recognized how much work would be involved in doing a daily strip, right?*

Frank: Oh, yeah! Sure.

Bullpen: *So how long were you in the service?*

Frank: Three years. I got out in 1946.

Bullpen: *So did you see action in the Pacific?*

Frank: Some, yes. Just some. In fact, I was there, ready to go into Japan. We were all on Okinawa by that time, and we were ready to invade Japan when they dropped the "Big Bombs."

Bullpen: *Was there anything particularly horrific which had an impact on you?*

Frank: It was kind of scary. There's a very helpless feeling when bombs go off and you have absolutely no control. It's really a helpless feeling. Things are blowing up and all you can do is duck.

Bullpen: *Was hearing about the tenacity of the Japanese a constant anxiety on you? That you were in for a hellacious fight?*

Frank: Yes.

Bullpen: *What was the feeling when Nagasaki and Hiroshima were bombed?*

Frank: In a way it was a relief, but we didn't quite understand what it was. We didn't have radios with us or anything like that. Someone heard a report somewhere and came running into our outfit and saying they just dropped "an automatic bomb" on Japan.

Bullpen: *"Automatic bomb"?*

Frank: He heard it, but he didn't quite understand what he heard. So everyone said, "What the hell is an 'automatic bomb'?" And we didn't learn for weeks, because we didn't have any communications where we were. That was up-to-the-minute. So it wasn't until later we found out it was an "atomic" bomb, which we had never even heard of. Then it turned out that Japan surrendered, so we were relieved. But we were still there in our tank, deep in mud, living in tents. Then we had the worst typhoon they'd ever had in 20 years or so, which just blew everything away. From what I heard, some of the ships blown onto shore are still there. [*Jon laughs*] Someone I met told me they had recently been to Okinawa, and…

Bullpen: *The boats are still there, on the beach?*

Frank: —they saw some big ships on the beaches! I said, "Oh, yes! I remember those ships!" Y'know, a ship is *so* huge, when you're standing next to it on a beach! You'll see a ship out in the water, how big it is, but you don't see the hull. [*Jon laughs*] It goes down under the waterline another 50 feet! And here this ship, this giant tanker or cargo ship, is on the beach, and you're standing there, and it's like you're standing in front of the pyramids! It was amazing. Everything we had blew away! I went to the mess tent to get some food, and by the time I stepped out, the wind and the rain blew all the food out of my mess kit!

Bullpen: *[Laughs] That was one typhoon!*

Frank: Yes, it was! Tents were blown away, guys were running around getting ropes and pulling their tents back and trying to put stakes in the ground and retie them to trees. Oh, it was one mess. So, it was one thing after another.

Bullpen: *Did you have any chance to take in any of the native culture?*

Frank: No. When I was in Okinawa, we didn't have any kind of leave The capital, Naha, was a little village. Nothing was taller than one or two stories high. I'm sure now it's got skyscrapers and I wouldn't remember it at all. But it was very primitive. Very

little villages, here and there. It was an island you wouldn't think much of.

Bullpen: *Did you ship back directly from Okinawa to the States or did you join the occupation of Japan?*

Frank: No. One of the guys and myself were driving to headquarters, because we had to go get some inoculations, and he was driving and we were on a mountainous road. We made a turn, suddenly there was no road there, so we went off the cliff. The vehicle was smashed and we were lying across some rocks. I was unconscious, but woke up to hear somebody moaning. It was like being awakened out of a sleep because I hear someone in pain. It turned out that *I* was the one doing the moaning. My leg was torn apart and I had a broken jaw.

Bullpen: Whoa! *How far of a drop was it?*

Frank: Well, enough to smash up a jeep. Luckily, maybe an hour or so later, another vehicle came along with some guys from my own outfit. They saw us, climbed down, picked us up, and took us to the hospital.

Above: *Example of early Frank Bolle work in* Tim Holt.

Left: *The cowpoke himself, Tim Holt, from the 1941 RKO Western,* Thundering Hoofs. ©2021 *the respective copyright holders.*

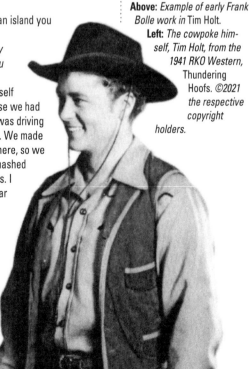

It was a M.A.S.H. [Mobile Army Surgical Hospital] outfit, just in a tent, and they had no X-ray machine or anything, so they just set my jaw and gave me some antibiotics for my leg which was torn open.

Bullpen: *You had a compound fracture in your leg?*

Frank: No, my leg wasn't broken; it was torn from ripping against rock after rock.

Bullpen: *A laceration on your leg.*

Frank: Yeah, so they just bandaged it and reset my jaw. To this day, my jaw has never been the same. It's a little off.

Above: Frank Bolle contributed mightily to the magazine, Boys' Life, for a number of years, even going so far as to work in fellow National Cartoonists Society member Dik "Hagar" Browne's style for the Pee-Wee Harris strip. Courtesy of the artist. ©2021 the respective copyright holder.

Bullpen: *How was the guy you were riding with?*

Frank: I think he had a broken leg and a fractured arm. I didn't see him after that, because he went elsewhere and I went to another hospital because I couldn't eat food, so they had to put me in a place where there were other patients who also couldn't eat. I had to be on a liquid diet. They were giving me penicillin for my leg. It was the first time they must have been using penicillin, because it was the worst thing. The shots were *so* painful, and they were giving me penicillin shots every couple of hours, night and day. Not only did it hurt, but—and I know penicillin now is a lot different—but I tell ya, it was so painful when it was injected, I could *taste* it!

Bullpen: *Eeooww!*

Frank: [*Chuckles*] I can remember to this day what it tasted like… and it wasn't pleasant.

Bullpen: *Did you consider yourself lucky?*

Frank: I guess so, since I came out of it all right, but I didn't like being all banged up.

Bullpen: *How long were you in recuperation?*

Frank: About three months.

Bullpen: *You were 20 or 21?*

Frank: Yeah, I was about 20, 21, something like that.

Bullpen: *You never saw the guy you were with again?*

Frank: No. They flew me back to the States, mostly because they didn't have milk and other nutritious liquid food, and whatever they had to give me as something to…

Bullpen: *Oh, for calcium to build up your jaw bone?*

Frank: Yes. So after I was in the hospital there for about a month, I flew back to the States, and was at the military hospital in Utica, New York. I was there for two more months, and by March, I went back to Fort Dix and was discharged. That was '46.

Bullpen: *So you flew from Okinawa to the West Coast?*

Frank: Yes, to Hawaii. I stopped in Hawaii, then to San Francisco, then I was in a hospital in San Rafael for a few days, from there to Denver, then to somewhere else, then to Utica, New York.

Bullpen: *What was it like to fly over the Pacific? You were in a prop plane, right?*

Frank: Yes.

Bullpen: *Was it loud?*

Frank: Oh yeah! My teeth were wired, and my little tiny rubber bands were hooked to each other, and they said, "If you get nauseous, you've got to cut those rubber bands, because you'll swallow your own vomit."

Bullpen: *And suffocate?*

Frank: So I sat by a window on this plane that had no interior decorating, where you sat on a bucket…

Bullpen: *Was it insulated at all?*

Frank: It was a DC-3 something… More like a cargo plane. A bunch of guys who also were medical people were with me. Anyway, I just keep reading this magazine, every single word, so I wouldn't think about where I was, so I wouldn't get nauseous if we hit some rough air or anything like that. Landing on some of those islands, it looked like you were landing on an aircraft carrier. You'd look down, "We're gonna land on *that?*" It looked so small.

Bullpen: *Now, what was Leonard's experience during the war?*

Frank: Oh, he had a great experience! He had had rheumatic fever as a kid and he was 4-F, so he didn't go in! He just drew comics. He was my buddy who I wrote letters to, to tell him what I was doing.

Bullpen: *So you came back to the States and became a civilian. Did you return to Brooklyn?*

Frank: Oh yes. I had no place else to go. I went back and lived in my little room in Brooklyn, where my mother was still living.

Bullpen: *How did the comic book market look? It busted by the end of '46 and into '47, right?*

Frank: No, they were still doing great. In fact, as soon as I came back, I went to work with Leonard. I penciled stories and he inked them, and we also wrote stories together.

Bullpen: *For DC Comics?*

Frank: No, we started off by doing some stuff for *Crown Comics*. Then we did some stuff for DC and some of the other magazines. I don't know if I can remember. It was so long ago.

Bullpen: *Do you remember what you did for* Crown? *Superheroes, crime…?*

Frank: They were super-hero stories. I can't remember the name of the strip, but we started off doing stuff I was so anxious to get going on. This was 60 years ago, so I don't remember.

I just remember doing a *lot*.

Bullpen: *Have you had a chance in later years to look back at that work at all?*

Frank: No, because I don't have any of the comic books or any of the originals, because the publishers didn't return them in those days.

Bullpen: *How do you imagine your talents were at the time?*

Frank: They were pretty good. I have some things, but only of stuff I did after Leonard got married and moved out onto the island [Long Island]. We had had a studio together and then I just went on my own, because he had his accounts out there and my accounts were still in the city.

I worked for Magazine Enterprises. Someone told me M.E. was looking for an artist. So I went there, they liked what I had done, and they gave me a seven-page spy story to illustrate. When I brought that back, they said, "Can you do Westerns?" I said, "Sure! I love Westerns." So they gave me a script for *Tim Holt,* who was a movie star cowboy at that time. I did the first story, they liked it, and from then on—I don't know how many issues—I did *Tim Holt, Red Mask,* and then *Best of the West.* So I was working for them for about 10 years. I would go into their offices every week. I would pencil a story, bring it in, they would give me another script, I would pencil that, bring that in, pick up the last one that was lettered, then ink it and bring that in. So it was a regular routine of going in every week and either picking up or dropping off pencils, or dropping off finished inks.

Bullpen: *Who were you dealing with over there?*

Frank: Ray Krank was the editor. Vincent Sullivan was also there. He had his hand in the Superman thing with *Action Comics* #1.

Bullpen: *That's right! He was their first editor.*

Frank: Right. Then he started his own line of comics with M.E. I did stuff for them for years. I did romances, but mostly

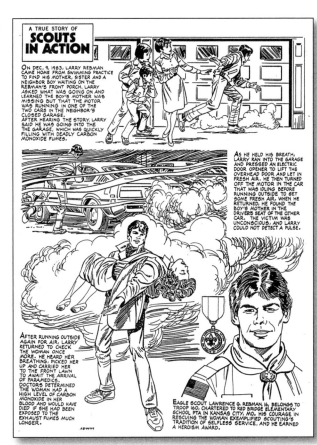

Westerns, and some other adventure strips.

Bullpen: *Prior to that, had you gone around to the different publishers and tried to get work?*

Frank: Yeah, I did some work for DC and Marvel, a few things. But with them you either penciled or you inked or you colored. I penciled some stories, a *Superman* story maybe, or inked it. I just didn't feel quite satisfied. Whereas, with Magazine Enterprises, I could do *everything.* I could pencil it *and* ink it, and I'd feel I did a complete job. That's why I always stuck with companies who let me do the whole thing.

Bullpen: *You just didn't like the whole assembly line process?*

Frank: Yes, it wasn't as satisfying. If I had to ink, I would be spending more time correcting the other artist's pencils. I guess I just wanted to be a real artist.

Bullpen: *As close as you could be in a commercial field?*

Frank: Right. Then I went around with my stuff and I illustrated books, I did magazine illustrations.

Bullpen: *What books did you illustrate?*

Frank: I illustrated a *lot.* I illustrated a soccer book, a scuba-diving book, a boxing book… I illustrated a whole series of

Inset left: Frank Bolle illustrated the Boys' Life feature, Scouts in Action for a stretch. Courtesy of the artist. ©2021 the respective copyright holder.

Below: Frank also drew the Bible Stories feature for the Boy Scout magazine. Courtesy of the artist. ©2021 the respective copyright holder.

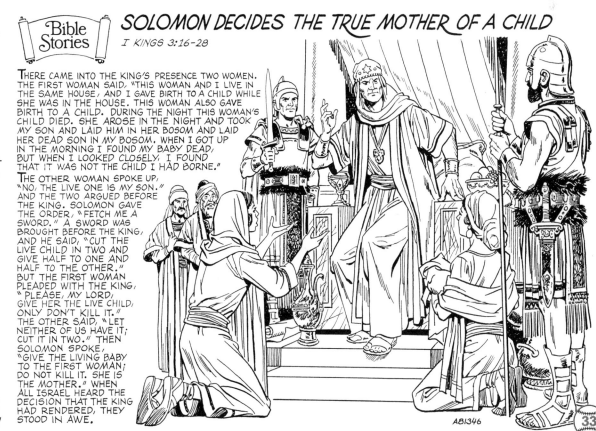

ONLY A TREMENDOUS *DOWNPOUR* CAN PUT OUT THIS FIRE BEFORE IT STRIKES THE LAB BUILDINGS!

Above: *Nifty panel drawn by Frank Bolle from* Doctor Solar, Man of the Atom #8 *[July 1964].*

Below: *Detail from same. Doctor Solar TM and ©2021 Penguin Random House LLC.*

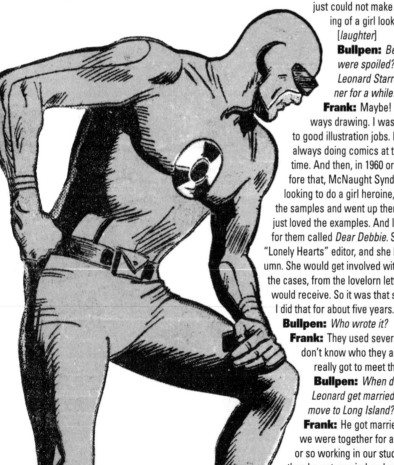

Sherlock Holmes books and adventure novels…

Bullpen: *How did you get those jobs?*

Frank: I just took some of my samples around and showed them to the editors.

Bullpen: *Did you always look to the illustration field as something to aspire to?*

Frank: Yes, illustration was one of the things I liked to do. I saw some good illustrations in magazines I liked, and I always drew attractive women. I was always surprised that some guys just could not make a drawing of a girl look pretty. [*laughter*]

Bullpen: *Because you were spoiled? Having Leonard Starr for a partner for a while!* [*laughs*]

Frank: Maybe! So I was always drawing. I was attracted to good illustration jobs. But I was always doing comics at the same time. And then, in 1960 or a little before that, McNaught Syndicate was looking to do a girl heroine, so I took the samples and went up there, and they just loved the examples. And I did a strip for them called *Dear Debbie*. She was a "Lonely Hearts" editor, and she had a column. She would get involved with some of the cases, from the lovelorn letters she would receive. So it was that sort of thing. I did that for about five years.

Bullpen: *Who wrote it?*

Frank: They used several writers, I don't know who they are. I never really got to meet the writers.

Bullpen: *When did Leonard get married and move to Long Island?*

Frank: He got married in 1947, we were together for about a year or so working in our studio, and then he got married and moved out to Huntington. I just went back to working in my apartment in Brooklyn. But I still saw him pretty often. He was working on several different comic books, but I didn't get to see all of them. He worked on that stuff and I worked on my stuff and we just

got together whenever we could.

Bullpen: *So, in the late '40s, you're working for Vince Sullivan doing romances, Westerns, and material like that. Did you work on any crime material?*

Frank: Yeah, every once in a while there would be a detective story or something like that. Every once in a while, someone else would call me from DC or Timely [Marvel] when they needed something and I would do a romance story for them.

Bullpen: *Who did you know over at DC?*

Frank: If I heard the name, I would probably remember.

Bullpen: *There was Shelly Mayer, there was Mort Weisinger.*

Frank: Shelly sounds familiar. I don't remember. I did a few romance stories for them, but then I would get involved in something else. I illustrated some children's stories and some children's records. They had records with pictures not on the cover, but on the record itself, and I did a whole series of those. So I was always doing something.

Bullpen: *Magazine Enterprises was pretty much a mid-level company within the field, right?*

Frank: Yes.

Bullpen: *So had you worked in the assembly-line process, could your page rates have been higher? Was there a trade-off?*

Frank: There probably was, yes. But I enjoyed what I did, and it wasn't hard work doing it. [*laughs*]

Bullpen: *Let's say you had a seven-page story. How long would it take to do?*

Frank: Oh, I was fast. I could pencil it in two days.

Bullpen: *Did you do any writing?*

Frank: Sometimes, but not a lot. I wrote and illustrated some children's stories I did on my own, because they were just different, just imaginary things I like to do. Every once in a while, I would write a Western for *Tim Holt*, take it to the editor, and if he liked it, would let me illustrate it. A little different than the other stories. I worked for good writers, I just enjoyed doing it.

Bullpen: *By the early '50s, when Frederic Wertham's* Seduction of the Innocent *and the Senate Subcommittee on Juvenile Delinquency came along, how did that affect you?*

Frank: I remember it, but it didn't really affect me because I didn't do anything in the material I worked on that would be controversial in any way. You know, I didn't draw naked women or anything bad happening. It was never gory or anything like that, so it didn't really bother me.

Bullpen: *But did you see that comic books in general were being threatened, or did you feel safe where you were?*

Frank: I felt safe. I don't think anyone did anything bad, I didn't understand what they were complaining about. I don't think it affected me that much.

Bullpen: *Now, the children's books you did, were any of them for Western Publishing?*

Frank: Yes, they were for the Golden Books. I did some with Doubleday and for Lion Press. Some of the big publishing outfits in town.

Bullpen: *You freelanced for a length of time with Western, right? On their line of comics, Gold Key?*

Frank: Oh, yes! A *long* time. Ten, 15 years. I did *Doctor Solar*, *Boris Karloff* horror stories, *Grimm's Tales*, *Twilight Zone*, and a bunch of others. There, too, I'd come in and deliver one thing and pick up another already-lettered job, ink it, and then bring that back, pencils. I'd go in every week with something, so it was continuous. There was never a break. I was always doing something. They just loved my stuff. I got along great with the editors, they always enjoyed having me come over, and we'd chat for a while.

Bullpen: *Who were the editors?*

Frank: I had several. There was Wally Green, Paul Kuhn, Denise Van Lear, and a couple of others who came and went. Some people were only there for a short time. And Matt Murphy. They were a great bunch, and I worked for them for a long time. They just loved my drawings. In fact, one of the editors once told me—because the writing was very good—he said some of the stories were a little far-fetched, but he always gave them to me because I always made them look believable.

Bullpen: *All of the material you did for Gold Key was pretty much straight stuff? You didn't do any kind of cartoony material at all?*

Frank: No.

Bullpen: *Did you have other friends in the field, besides Leonard?*

Frank: Yes. One of my close friends was John Prentice. Tex Blaisdell, who did mostly backgrounds for all the different guys. Howard Post, who did real cartoony stuff. A lot of my friends were cartoonists.

Bullpen: *Now, during the '50s at DC, Prentice and Leonard Starr and Reuben Moria were pretty much the house style. Did you contribute to DC during that time when they were publishing* Mr. District Attorney, Big Town *and* Gang Busters?

Frank: Yes, I did a few stories, but not that I can remember any of them that stood out.

Bullpen: *Did you see yourself as belonging to this kind of school? It's more related maybe to Alex Raymond than to Milton Caniff. John Prentice seems to epitomized this DC look of the day. He had this look. Did you feel that you belonged to that?*

Frank: No, I never really felt that I belonged to any particular school, although I did work with John for about 30 years. While I was doing all my own work, John was very slow at what he did. He never got out of first gear. He was very precise and very slow, so at the end of every month he was always a week late. So, for 30 years, I always helped him out that one week. [*laughter*]

Bullpen: *Was it always a given that you were going to be called in to help that week, or was John always in a panic?*

Frank: Well, when it started out, he would call and ask me if I could help him with another week. Sometimes I just did the pencils and he would ink, sometimes I would do the whole week's worth of strips. So yeah, for 30 years I did that extra week of worth almost every month. [*chuckles*]

Bullpen: *This was on [the syndicated strip]* Rip Kirby?

Frank: On *Rip Kirby*, yes.

Bullpen: *You ghosted a lot of* Rip Kirby?

Frank: Oh yes.

Bullpen: *Did you know Stan Drake?*

Frank: Oh sure! I even helped Stan sometimes with [the syndicated strip] *Juliet Jones.*

Bullpen: *Wasn't he another guy who was always behind?*

Frank: Well, a lot of times he would be playing golf…

Bullpen: *Right.* [*laughter*]

Frank: I didn't do a *lot* for Stan, but for John I did something every month. Then, when Stan did *Blondie*, he couldn't do *Juliet Jones*, because it just took too long to do the *Blondie* dailies and Sundays. So I took over the *The Heart of Juliet Jones* for the next 10 years or so, until it ended.

Bullpen: *You got full credit for that?*

Frank: Yes.

Bullpen: *Did you like doing romance?*

Frank: Oh, I loved it! It was great! I enjoyed it very much. I always enjoyed drawing good-looking girls and having a nice, soap-opera-type story. While I was doing that, I was also drawing *Winnie Winkle*. I started *Winnie*, I think, in 1976, something like that. I did that until 1996. I did that *while* I was doing *The Heart of Juliet Jones. And* helping John out on *Rip Kirby!*

FRANK BOLLE

BORN IN N.Y., JUNE 23, 1924. I STARTED BY DRAWING ON ANY SCRAP OF PAPER I COULD FIND. I WENT TO THE HIGH SCHOOL OF MUSIC AND ART. FROM 1943 TO 1946 I SERVED WITH THE ARMY AIR FORCE AND CONCLUDED MY MILITARY CAREER ON OKINAWA BY THE SEA. ON MY RETURN I FREE LANCED WHILE I WAS STUDYING AT PRATT INSTITUTE. I STARTED ILLUSTRATING COMIC BOOKS, CHILDREN'S BOOKS AND ADVENTURE MAGAZINES. FOR SEVERAL YEARS I WROTE AND ILLUTRATED "CHILDREN'S TALES" A SYNDICATED SUNDAY PAGE. NOW I'M WORKING FOR "BOY'S LIFE, DOING THEIR CARTOON FEATURES. ALSO DOING SUNDAYS AND DAILIES OF "ENCYCLOPEDIA BROWN" BOY DETECTIVE! I ALWAYS TRY TO FIND TIME FOR SOME OIL PAINTING BUT I DO MANAGE TO GET SOME WATER COLORS FINISHED. I STILL ENJOY MY WORK AND EACH DAY I LOOK FORWARD TO GETTING TO WORK IN MY STUDIO. FOR RELAXATION I HELP MY WIFE, LORI, AROUND THE BARN WHERE SHE KEEPS HER 4 HORSES, WHICH SHE TRAINS AND SHOWS. THE WHOLE FAMILY USED TO RIDE, BUT DAUGHTER, LAURA, IS GROWN UP AND IS IN ADVERTISING. SON, FRANK, LOOKS LIKE HE'S GOING TO BE A CARTOONIST.

Above: Frank Bolle's autobiographical essay as seen in the 1980 National Cartoonists Society Album.

Below: After the passing of Alex Kotsky, Frank Bolle took over penciling chores on the syndicated newspaper comic strip, Apartment 3-G. These two dailies (sporting inks by Lisa Trusiani) are from May 2 and 3, 2001, respectively. Courtesy of the artist. ©2001 North America Syndicate, Inc.

[laughter]

Bullpen: *Did you have assistants?*

Frank: No. I do everything myself.

Bullpen: *That's a lot of work!*

Frank: Yes.

Bullpen: *Any writers you remember that you work with? Or did you write, yourself?*

Frank: No, the scripts always came right from the syndicate. I think Fred Fredericks wrote *Rip Kirby*. Some of the writers I would only meet casually as they were leaving the office and I was coming in to deliver something at the publisher, so I never really got to know the writers, so I can't really give you much information on them. But they were usually good, like Paul S. Newman, Gardner Fox, some of the others. If I met them, I only met them casually as they were leaving, or coming in as I was leaving. But I got their scripts, which was okay with me. So I was always busy doing one thing or another.

Bullpen: *What was your family situation?*

Frank: I got married when I was 25. I was married for seven years, then we got divorced. I had two children, but I don't see them very often. They were influenced too much by their mother, who was not as nice as I was. It's okay. I did my best. I took care of them when they were kids. But now they're grown people.

Bullpen: *Are you married again?*

Frank: Yeah, I got married again and I've been happy now for 46 years.

Bullpen: *I've heard a lot about Stan Drake. He did not have the easiest of lives and perhaps he put himself in some situations that weren't good for himself. I recall hearing stories of him having a bucket of ice under his drawing tablet so, at four o'clock in the morning, he would stick his foot into the ice to make sure that he would stay awake. [laughter] It was a grueling routine, apparently. Whether or not he was playing golf during the daytime—maybe Stan wasn't economizing his time well—it was still tough to get the work out. But you look at the fact he was an extraordinary artist who just did wonderful material, and he ended up aping Chic Young.*

Frank: Yes.

Bullpen: *Do you think that these artists are as appreciated as they should be?*

Frank: I don't know. The people who knew him appreciated what he did. They could see what great work he was able to accomplish. Choosing *Blondie* was his own choice, and I don't know why he did that. I guess he did it for the money.

Bullpen: *But do you hope these creators who you knew and admired are remembered?*

Frank: I really don't know. His friends remember him. Stan was a funny kind of person. He drank a lot. Outside of golf, sitting at a bar was the only physical activity he did. In all the years I knew him, he never invited me to his place. He never invited anyone I knew to his place. A lot of times when people invited him to their house, he didn't show up.

Bullpen: *I've got an index of comic book art that came out in 1996, and the listing for you is just way too short. There's just no way this is anywhere near complete. Obviously, it's focused on super-heroes. It says that for a period of time in the early '70s, you worked for Marvel?*

Frank: Yes.

Bullpen: *What prompted you to go over?*

Frank: I illustrated some of their mens magazines like *True, Odyssey,* and *Male.* I did some full-page illustrations for them, whether Hawaiian people or cowboys or soldiers. But I did a few of those and then one of the other editors liked what I do, so I remember she wanted me to do some comics. So I did some romance stuff. I just don't remember what I was doing for them.

Bullpen: *I first encountered your name between 1973 and '74, when you inked a good amount of work for Marvel that included* The Avengers, Werewolf by Night, *a Sub-Mariner story,* The Defenders. *It was as if you showed up for six months, then you were gone, disappeared. But you did do an awful lot of work in those six months, then you vanished. Was it just pretty much to tide you over during a particular fallow period?*

Frank: Not really, because I was always doing other stuff. But I think I got involved with the syndicate then, doing both comic books and working for a syndicate. I did stuff for Universal Syndicate: *Encyclopedia Brown.* I did a series of novels I illustrated in comics called *Bestseller's Showcase,* dailies and Sundays of some of the best-selling books at that time, like *Raising the Titanic,* and a few other sto-

ries. One of the writers they used would break it down so it could be in dailies and Sundays. Each adaptation would last about eight weeks, condensed like *Reader's Digest*. I received a really good response with that, because I had to make up my own char-

Inset left: *For about four or five years, Frank Bolle drew the exploits of boy detective Encyclopedia Brown for the Universal Syndicate. These dailies are from May 9 and 10, 1980, respectively. Courtesy of the artist. ©2021 Universal Press Syndicate.*

acters from what I read in the script, and I was busy with that. So if I stopped doing comic books for DC or whoever, it was because I got really involved with a really tight, weekly deadline, where I was doing weekly dailies and Sundays, and also probably doing some book illustrations at the same time.

In the early 1970s, Stan Lee or one of his features editors called me and I did some work over at Marvel Comics. I always got along well with editors.

Bullpen: *[Laughs] Man, you didn't stop to breathe, did you?*
Frank: No.
Bullpen: *Were you able to take any vacations?*
Frank: Yes. One of my artist friends said I was one of the fastest " drawers" in the West. [laughter] Do you know of Gil Fox?

Bullpen: *Sure!*
Frank: Well, he's the one who goes around telling everyone, he says, "Frank is the fastest artist in the world." He saw me draw a portrait of someone who wanted me to draw their kids, and he was standing there and said, "You got a likeness. And you did it in two minutes! Instead of sketching, you wrote it! And you got a likeness and it's well done… No wonder you do so much stuff! You *are* the fastest draw in the West!"

Bullpen: *Was it somewhat addictive to work at this pace? The way you most enjoy working is just to have this enormous workload?*
Frank: No. In fact, I never knew I was doing it like that. To me, it just came naturally. Just like jumping over all the fences in Brooklyn.

Bullpen: *[Laughs] Where there's a headline for this interview. [laughter] Did you have a particular thing you most enjoyed? Did you enjoy the strips or the comics stories? Or did you like it all?*

Below: *From 1976 to '96, Frank Bolle drew the* Winnie Winkle *syndicated newspaper comic strip. This Sunday page example appears courtesy of the artist. ©2021 the respective copyright holder.*

The STEEL-SMASHING RETURN of **MAGNUS ROBOT FIGHTER** 4000 A.D.

WRITTEN BY: ROGER McKENZIE
ART BY: FRANK BOLLE

Above: *Curiously, Dan Spiegle was chosen as artist on* Doctor Solar *for the late '70s revival, while Frank drew the Magnus back-up strip.*
Below: *Detail from* Boris Karloff *story. Courtesy of the artist. Magnus ©2021 Penguin Random House LLC.*

Frank: I liked it all. I went to Pratt on the G.I. Bill, and I worked in watercolor, learned about landscapes, I did some watercolor landscapes. Up until then, whenever I looked at landscapes, they were only backgrounds for my figures. I never even thought of landscapes as anything special. Then I started doing watercolors. So whenever I'm not doing comics, I'm painting landscapes, watercolors or oil paintings. I never showed them until recently. I joined a local club where I met artists who are teachers and are professional painters. When they had an exhibition, I didn't dare show my paintings because these people paint every day, and I only do a painting once or twice a year, because I'm busy with my commercial art. So I didn't want to show my work that I painted for myself. The thing is, for the past five years or so, they've talked me into showing it, and every time I've shown one of my paintings at the show, I've won something.

Bullpen: *Good for you!*

Frank: I've won first prize, second prize, best in show, I've won three gold medals in a row at three different shows. They think that I'm terrific, even these people who paint every day. So my whole background of drawing has helped so much, my drawings and my compositions may be strong. They have a definite look about them. People would look at a whole bunch of paintings and say, "Is that one of yours?" I'd say, "Yes." They'd say, "Yeah, that's what I thought." My work has a certain personality… Maybe they're masculine… They have a certain look about them where the composition is well-balanced because I draw so much.

Bullpen: *Do you sell them?*

Frank: Yes, I do.

Bullpen: *Did you ever look at doing your own thing, creating and owning your own property, whether it's a syndicated strip or comic book? Something that could pay you over a period of time. You know what I mean? Having your own property.*

Frank: No, I never really thought of it. I did some writing when I wrote my own children's stories which I had published. But it's a whole different gear sitting down and writing than it is drawing. Right now, I wouldn't have the patience to sit down and write anything. I just accepted that people who were professional writers were good enough to work with. If I had an idea for something, I don't remember it now. I probably did, but I was just always busy doing something else.

Bullpen: *How was your income throughout your career pretty good?*

Frank: It was always good, yes.

Bullpen: *You were able to do what you wanted and to sock away for the future?*

Frank: Yes. To a certain extent, sure.

Bullpen: *Did you receive much recognition from fans?*

Frank: Oh, yes, I would get letters. I had shopping bags full of letters I just could

never get around to answering. I'd answer some, but, as I said, there were shopping bags full of letters.

Bullpen: *Was this when you were doing the strip?*

Frank: Always. Some when I was doing the strips, some when I was just doing comics. One guy wrote and said he used to sneak up into his attic and read his father's collection of *Tim Holt*s and other Westerns. He wrote, "That's how I got started to read, and now I'm a fabulous reader." Because his father collected the old comic books. So he wrote and thanked me for doing it. So, yeah, I still get all kinds of strange letters from some people who remember things I did years ago.

Bullpen: *Now, was there any particular emphasis with some of these fans on the* Doctor Solar *stuff and the super-hero material you've done?*

Frank: Yeah, a lot of people liked *Doctor Solar*. I did that title for quite a few years. I don't know how many issues I did.

Bullpen: *Did Paul S. Newman write those?*

Frank: He probably wrote most of the scripts, yes.

Bullpen: *What did you think of the character?*

Frank: Oh, I thought he was good, because he was more normal than a muscle-bound super-hero. Even though he went about in a costume and he was well-built, he wasn't bulging.

Bullpen: *What* was *with that green thing?*

Frank: That was the color of his skin. I don't remember why. They did that all the time.

Bullpen: *I believe they did that from the start. As a kid, I always thought it was mis-colored because it was never referred to in the issues I read. [laughs] Somebody sent me some layouts for cover layouts that were followed by a painter — George Wilson, maybe — whoever painted the covers, which really definitely seem to be done by you.*

Frank: I did some… I drew some in black-&-white. They had someone on staff who colored the covers.

Bullpen: *You've just always stayed at it? You didn't have a period of time when you were looking for work?*

Frank: No, it just seemed one thing led into the next. I just accepted whatever came along and always enjoyed what I was doing.

Bullpen: *Did you join the National Cartoonist Society?*

Frank: Yeah, back in the '60s sometime.

Bullpen: *Do you go to the Westport meetings?*

Frank: Yeah. The local chapter. If you're from New York, Connecticut, Massachusetts, and New Jersey, we meet here in Westport. A couple of years ago, I went to Boca Raton, when they had the annual awards dinner. The year before that, they had it at the Twin Towers, in Manhattan. So I go to a lot of the dinners here when they meet in Westport, three or four times a year. I go and see some of the cartoonists.

Bullpen: *What was the comic book material that you were doing in the '70s and '80s?*

Frank: In the '70s, I was still doing stuff for Western Publishing: *Boris Karloff* and *Twilight Zone*. Also in that time, I was working for *Boys' Life* magazine.

Bullpen: *Johnstone and Cushing had the comic book account in the '60s. Did [onetime J&C production manager] Al Stenzel have the account after he left Johnstone and Cushing?*

Frank: For a while he did, yes.

Bullpen: *So were you with Stenzel?*

Frank: No, I was on my own. Someone had told me the magazine was looking for someone to illustrate, so I went down to their offices, in New Jersey at the time, and I showed them some samples. And from that point on, I did the *Bible Story*, which I liked, because it was altogether different costumes. I did *Pee-Wee Harris, The Tracy Twins, Scouts in Action*. And then I did the science-fiction stories they had.

Bullpen: *Did you mock Dik Browne's style for* Pee-Wee Harris *and* The Tracy Twins?

38

Frank: Yes, I could do that. I can do *anything*. [*laughter*]

Bullpen: *And how long did you freelance for* Boys Life?

Frank: I did that for about 20 years, from 1977 to 1996. At the same time, I was drawing *Winnie Winkle* dailies and Sundays.

Bullpen: *Do you have any idea who wrote the material?*

Frank: No, they had their own writers. They had other freelance writers. I wrote a couple. When I'd get a good idea for *Pee-Wee Harris*, a funny little cartoon type of story. I did several, maybe altogether five in all the years. I did a few *Tracy Twins*. But the other stories were scripts that they bought. You know, those science-fiction things, I can't remember all the titles. But yeah, I did those for all those years, while I was doing *Winnie Winkle*. See, that was just a monthly thing. W*innie Winkle* was every week. So was *Juliet Jones.*

Bullpen: *Now, when you were doing the* Boys' Life *material, did you do the same process? Did you send pencils to them, then they sent them back to you, and then you inked? Was it lettered in-between?*

Frank: Nope. I sent them finished art.

Bullpen: *Who did the lettering?*

Frank: I did.

Bullpen: *Really? Had you always done your own lettering?*

Frank: Not in the beginning. When I lived in the city, I always brought a job in and they would have it lettered, and that's the way it was done. But when I moved to Connecticut, I couldn't find a letterer. I hired one guy and he was always late. Then I said, "I should have already sent this in." He said, "Well, my grandmother got sick, I had to drive over, and when I pulled out of the driveway, I ran over my dog, and had to take my dog to the doctor…" [*Jon laughs*] But the thing is, he gave me that *same* excuse *every* time!

Bullpen: [*laughs*] *"How many dogs have you got, mister?"*

Frank: And how many *grandmothers*? [*laughter*] So I realized, "I'd better learn to letter." So I did my own. Then when Leonard couldn't find someone to letter *Annie*, he would ask, "Could you letter *Annie* for me?" So for 10 years, the last 10 years of

Inset left: 1970s advertising art by Frank Bolle. Courtesy of the artist. ©2021 the respective copyright holder. **Below:** *Frank also contributed to Jim Warren's black-&-white horror magazines. These two pages are from his work—coincidentally also written by Doug Moench, who would collaborate eight years later with Frank on the* Alice in Wonderland *adaptation for Marvel Classics Comics (see next page)—which appeared in* Vampirella *#7 [Sept. 1970]. Courtesy of the artist. ©2021 Warren Publishing, Inc.*

Alice's Adventures in Wonderland

by Lewis Carroll

Alice, a childish story take,
And with a gentle hand
Lay it where childhood's
dreams are twined.
In memory's mystic band,
Like pilgrim's withered wreath of flowers
Plucked in a far off land.

ADAPTED BY DOUG MOENCH

ILLUSTRATED BY FRANK BOLLE

at Saint Paul's Church, near Columbus Circle.

Bullpen: *A little hot down there wasn't it?*

Frank: They had a huge basement. You needed to come up for air a couple of times. The guy that produces it, Joe Petrilak, talked me into it. He even came up here, picked me up, and took me down there.

Bullpen: *What was your experience? Did you enjoy it?*

Frank: Yeah, it was okay. I sold some things and met some people. Then I saw some dealers who had my originals I never got back and they were selling them. Some were selling *Tim Holt* pages, which I never even got back, because in those days, they either threw them away (because they didn't print them here in New York, but in Racine or someplace way out West). So I'm walking around this convention and there I see a whole big stack of *Tim Holt*s some guy sitting there is selling.

Bullpen: *Did you have any words with him?*

Frank: No. [*chuckles*] No, I just looked at them and said, "Hi." He said, [*uncertain voice:*] "Hi, Frank." He saw my name tag. He must have known that I was the guy that illustrated them. [*laughs*]

Bullpen: *How did you feel about that?*

Frank: Well, I was disappointed they were never returned to me. What could I do? I'm not going to get upset about it.

Bullpen: *Are you going to be doing that in San Diego? Are you going to be selling original art*

Frank: I'm bringing some of the things that I did. Unfortunately, I don't have any *Doctor Solar*. None of those were returned to me. Those were thrown away or someone else got them in Racine, Wisconsin, where they were printed. So I'm bringing some of my *Twilight Zone*s and *Boris Karloff* pages, some *Winnie Winkle* strips and some other things I've done.

Bullpen: *Did you get the original art back from the* Boys' Life *work?*

Frank: Some of it, yes, but not all.

Bullpen: *Overall, when you look back on your career, what was your favorite thing that you did?*

Frank: I think *Winnie Winkle* was nice to do, because I could see it in my daily newspaper and colored on Sunday. A lot of things I've done, like *Juliet Jones*, I hardly ever saw because it was always in some other paper, out of town, somewhere else.

Bullpen: *What was the premise of* Winnie Winkle?

Frank: It was a soap opera. She was in the fashion business, but had a family, a husband, two children, and a mother and father. *Winnie Winkle* goes back to the 1920s. I was the third artist to do the strip, but I updated it. It was more cartoony when I took it on, but they didn't like that look anymore because it was out of date, and they wanted something more modern and fashionable. So I made Winnie look like a beautiful illustration, good-looking with a handsome husband and a mother and father who were really homey-type people. The parents would create funny situations. Like, the father would borrow the car and smash it by not opening the garage door and driving right in. [*laughter*] Stuff like that. So, it was a family strip, though she would also get involved with models and people in the fashion industry or show business. So it was that kind of soap opera thing, which was nice, because I could illustrate interesting characters and draw nice looking people.

Bullpen: *At its height when you were on it, what was the number of papers* Winnie *was in?*

Frank: Oh, it was quite a lot, but mostly on this side of the Mississippi, because a lot of the mail I would get always seemed to be from Chicago, Pennsylvania, Florida, or Kentucky, places which made it seem the sales people didn't go over to the West Coast for some reason (when they really should have).

Leonard's *Annie*, I did the lettering.

Bullpen: *[laughs] Frank, seriously, when did you sleep?*

Frank: I slept like a baby!

Bullpen: *[laughs] You were able to find time to sleep?*

Frank: Yeah! I had time to do that. I also walked a couple of miles every day, and I mucked around in the barn. We had several horses in our barn. My wife taught riding and I also like to ride.

Bullpen: *Comics fans, a great number of them anyway, are prejudiced in favor of the super-hero material, and I think it helps to enlighten them to look at your career. You can have a long, productive career, like Frank Springer and a number of other guys, who worked in and out of the comics field. There were other outlets, like Boys' Life. There were options.*

Frank: Right.

Bullpen: *Have you been invited to comic conventions prior to this year's San Diego Comic-Con?*

Frank: Well, some of the comic conventions we've had in New York. I went to one in Madison Square Garden and then several

Bullpen: *Were you disappointed when it was canceled?*

Frank: Yes, very much so.

Bullpen: *What did you do when you got that news?*

Frank: Well, I started painting some more, doing portraits. I did a painting of my dog, and my wife showed it to our veterinarian, and he said, "Gee, could you do a portrait of *my* dog?" So I said, "Sure." I did that, and some other people wanted me to paint their dogs, because the vet hung up copies in his waiting room. Then I got calls for months from people who wanted to get a painting of their horse or dog as an anniversary or birthday present. My prices were reasonable, a couple of hundred dollars or three hundred, depending on the size of the portrait. So I was doing that in my spare time, because I was only doing *Juliet Jones* and *Boys' Life*. So I was doing these paintings, and the more I did, the more people kept wanting me to do one for them. Then one of the people who went to the vet for their dog, who was a real dog lover, she saw my paintings. She produced dog products, so she called me up and asked would I be interested in doing work for them. So, I must have done several hundred dogs by now. These are watercolor paintings. I do them commercially, too, for a dog company that has frames for photographs, but the frame itself has pictures of that particular breed on it. So if I paint a Labrador retriever, I'll have a head and four more dogs still sitting or lying down in full figure. Paintings and watercolors. I've done plenty. They have a catalog full of my dogs. That's what I did when *Winnie Winkle* ended.

Then, a year later, *Boys' Life* made a complete change and they dropped me from everything. They put out a real crummy-looking magazine with real goofy, ugly-looking stuff. Pee-Wee Harris, who was a cute little Boy Scout, now has a head like a football and looks like a dwarf. He's got these little legs about two inches long, and got this big football head. Is that the new trend: ugly comics?

Bullpen: *It's probably a holdover from the Nickelodeon cartoons, the animated shows a lot of kids watch. Tom Eaton is the cartoonist on all that* Boys' Life *comic strip stuff now.*

Frank: So I stopped working for *Boys' Life*, which had been a nice big account I had. So I continue doing these dogs and portraits. Then I did caricatures of people who wanted to use them as gifts. Someone was retiring from an airline company, who apparently had everything, but they wanted to give him something that he didn't have. So I did a caricature of him—a nice one, not ugly. I made it look like the person, but in a humorous way, without offending the subject. He and everyone liked it so much, all the officers in that company wanted one! So I had to do nine more. [*laughter*]

So, I was always doing something. Then, in 2000 or '01, they ended *The Heart of Juliet Jones*, but they called me right back and

asked, "Can you do [syndicated newspaper strip] *Apartment 3-G*?" It's about three girls. Have you ever seen it?

Bullpen: *Sure! This was after artist Alex Kotzky had passed away?*

Frank: Right. So I'm doing *Apartment 3-G* now.

Bullpen: *[Laughs] Wow, you just don't quit! [laughter] So there's no talk of retirement, I take?*

Frank: No, no. Some of my friends have retired. Leonard Starr retired and he hasn't drawn anything. He quit *Little Orphan Annie* three years ago and hasn't drawn a single line since. I don't know how he can do that! But he watches a lot of TV.

The minute I stop drawing, I do a painting. I also do other stuff: I get out every day. Yesterday, I had lunch with a friend of mine who was in the same outfit when we were in the service. I met him when I was 18 years old, in 1943. He was the first buddy I made in the service. We were together for about a year-and-a-half before we split up. But I still see him now. We talk about old times and some of the characters we knew, and we had a nice time.

Bullpen: *Are you looking forward to the San Diego Comic-Con?*

Frank: In a way. I don't know what to expect. I don't know what I'm getting myself into.

Bullpen: *Prepare to be overwhelmed. [laughter]*

Frank: Yeah, I'm sure I will be!

***

Collection Editor's Note: *Frank Bolle died on May 12, 2020, at the age of 95. He is survived by his wife, Lori Bolle, and children, Laura and Frank. Even as old as 91, Frank was still drawing syndicated newspaper comic strips!*

FRANK BOLLE

Above: *Slightly modified splash page detail from* Werewolf By Night *#6 [June 1973], penciled by Mike Ploog and inked by Frank Boole (who worked for a brief period at Marvel as an inker).* **Below:** *For a few issues of* The Defenders *during scripter Steve Englehart's Avengers/Defenders war, Frank Bolle inked Sal Buscema's pencils. Panel detail from #10 [Nov. '73]. TM & ©2021 Marvel Characters, Inc.*

Frank Bolle: CBA All-Star!

COMIC BOOK ARTIST
ALL★STARS

FRANK BOLLE

GOLD KEY
PENCILER
& INKER

FRANK BOLLE

Collect 'em All!

Trading card data compiled with information supplied by Frank Bolle.

COMIC BOOK ARTIST™ BULLPEN was published between 2003–04 by RetroHouse Press, C/o Jon B. Cooke, P.O. Box 601, West Kingston, R.I. 02892 USA. Jon B. Cooke, Editor. Vol. 1, #2, Jan. 2004. All characters © their respective copyright holders. All material © their creators unless otherwise noted. ©2021 Jon B. Cooke. Cover acknowledgement: All characters ©2021 their respective copyright holders. Art ©2021 the estate of Frank Bolle.

Bullpen Extra: Bolle's Paintings

Courtesy of and ©2021 the estate of Frank Bolle.

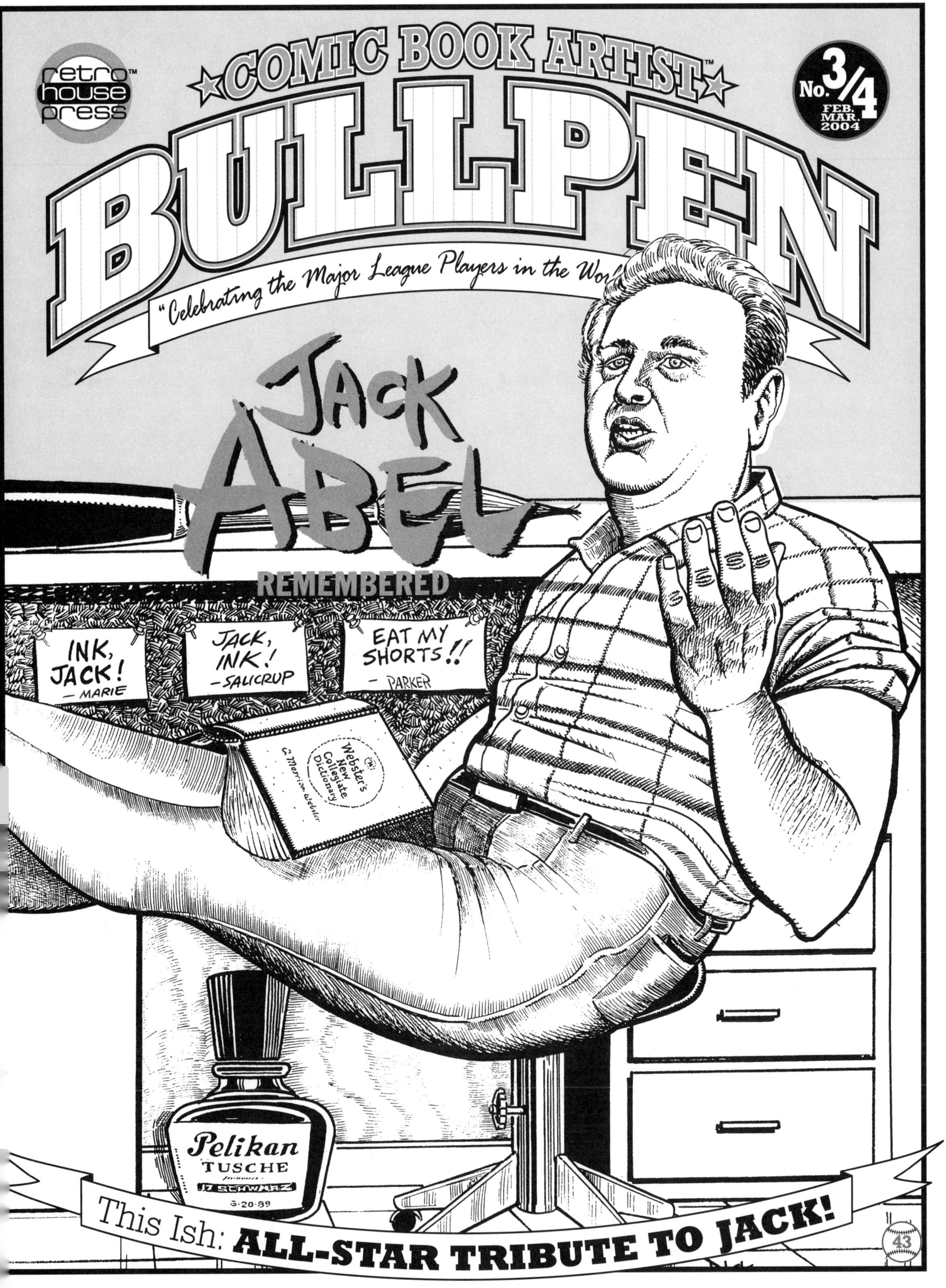

retro house press
COMIC BOOK ARTIST
BULLPEN
"Celebrating the Major League Players in the Wor
No. 3/4
FEB. MAR. 2004
JACK ABEL
REMEMBERED
INK, JACK! —MARIE
JACK, INK! —SALICRUP
EAT MY SHORTS!! —PARKER
Webster's New Collegiate Dictionary
G. Merriam Webster
Pelikan
TUSCHE
17 SCHWARZ
G-20-89
This Ish: ALL-STAR TRIBUTE TO JACK!

Dear Jan,

I want to thank you so much for the beautiful books you published as a tribute to my husband Jack Abel.

I also want to thank all the guys that contributed to the books. And a special thanks to Rick Parker for not giving up on this dedication to Jack!

Jack was a great guy and respected by many.

My children and I miss him very much and recall his great sense of humor very often. You certainly would have liked and enjoyed his humor too.

If there is anything I can possibly do to be of any help in anyway please let me know.

With sincerest appreciation for all you have done, I remain.

Sincerely yours
Adele Abel

4-6-04

44

★COMIC BOOK ARTIST★
BULLPEN
BULL SESSION

It's fitting that Jack Abel should be honored in the pages of a magazine called *Comic Book Artist Bullpen*. Not only was the fabled artist a lifelong fan of America's Greatest Sport and its winning-est professional team, the New York Yankees, he also was a mainstay in a number of honest-to-goodness comic book artist bullpens, from Wallace Wood's Connecticut studio, where Jack shared space with Woody, Syd Shores, and numerous Wood assistants, to Neal Adams and Dick Giordano's Continuity Associates studio, where dozens of young artists would get their start in the funny-book business and be first introduced to the charming and affable Abel, to the Mightiest Bullpen of Them All: Marvel Comics, where Jack spent a big part of his career, as inker, art corrector, and proofreader, and where he perhaps became more beloved than ever, judging by the accolades former Marvel staffers bequeath to Jack in these pages. And, as you'll read in Jack Morelli's wonderful essay on the beloved artist's athletic prowess herein, Jack was no slouch behind the plate, as well. So we hope the crusty curmudgeon is looking down approvingly at this publication from way-on high.

I never got to meet Jack, who died in 1996 at his desk in the Marvel Comics Bullpen, but I sure wish I had, judging from the love and affection felt for the silver-maned artist that's so apparent in virtually every page in this tribute to the man. Apparently, Jack made a positive impression on just about every type of soul involved in this business, whether talented legend/peer or punk rocker production assistant. Plain and simple, the guy was a very special human being.

I only knew of Jack by his work in the comics themselves, whether as a mainstay on the Bob Kanigher-edited DC Comics' war books of the 1960s—the exploits of Gunner, Sarge, and Pooch in *Our Fighting Forces* being his most memorable stint—or as the ubiquitous journey man inker on many, many DC and Marvel Comics over a 20+ year stretch, and, over the years, it wouldn't be a surprise to find his work in Charlton, Gold Key, and Tower comics, among other publishers. Jack was, indeed, ready, willing, and able.

But I had no idea what kind of man Jack Abel was when I first received a package from my pal Sal Amendola a few years ago, one labeled by Sal with a note to me that said, "You'd probably be interested in this." Inside was a Xeroxed set of pages of some 40- to 48-page comic book titled "Jack Abel Remembered," featuring strips by an amazing array of talents, including Joe Kubert, Walter

Simonson, Sergio Aragonés, Kyle Baker, Joe Sinnott, Dick Ayers, Alan Weiss… I mean, a *stellar* group, to say the least. Well, I don't need to wax on this too much—you have the production in your mitts right now, so you be the judge—but suffice to say this unpublished tribute book was a superb and worthy effort.

Needless to tell ya, I pounced on the phone and called Sal about this hitherto unknown Abel tribute to find out just what the hell the status was on its publication. Sal shared that cartoonist Rick Parker had been behind the project, serving as editor and compiler, but that it had failed to find a publisher. Naturally, I contacted Rick and asked if maybe I could feature the tribute as some *Comic Book Artist* special of some kind. Rick kindly gave permission and the initial plan was to feature this as the second *Comic Book Artist Special Edition*. But, alas, *CBA SE #2* was not to be—long, boring story—and the book was shelved until *CBA Bullpen* came along.

Many folks contributed to Rick's initial tribute, some who have since moved since last Mr. Parker has seen them, so if anyone knows of a contributor who has not received comp issues of this special issue, be sure to drop us a line with contact info so we can zip some copies their way.

Special thanks are due to a number of people for their efforts on behalf of this issue. First, kudos to Sal Amendola for first cluing Yours Truly in on this great work. Second, to Rick Parker, for going above and beyond the call of duty—gathering the material, making scans, answering inane questions, being a mensch—to see his dream finally see the light of day. Third, to Jack Abel's lovely bride, Adele, and his son and daughter, Gary and Randi, for permission and participation in this celebration. Lastly, allow us to extend our deepest appreciation to the writers, artists, letterers, and friends of Jack Abel who gave so much of their talents in this wonderful show of appreciation for one man who made a difference in their respective lives. Such public displays of affection are clearly what makes life worth living and I am so proud and happy to help these lovely testimonials see the light of day, so now everyone can see what impact adorable Jack Abel made in some peoples' lives. Jack, I hardly knew ye, but here's hoping you enjoy this loving presentation. We love ya, you magnificent bastard!—**The editor.**

Above inset: Rick Parker wanted us to use the above—a cartoon of Jack Abel by R.P.—as back cover, but we couldn't mess with our current format. Rick also hesitated to use his cover art—fearing it would appear self-serving—but we had to insist. So don't blame the artist, folks! We think Rick did a great cover ourselves!

abel's egg cream routine

a foreword by jack's son, gary michael abel

Above: *The Big Man himself, Jack Abel, in a picture courtesy of Alan Kupperberg.*

My father, Jack Abel, passed away on March 6, 1996, at the age of 68. It was truly a sad day for everybody who knew and loved him. But, because he was beloved by so many in the comic book industry, many talented people have come forth to put together a lasting memorial to the man who Marvel Comics has dubbed "The World's Toughest Proofreader."

But comic books were not the only things Jack Abel was all about. A wonderful husband, father, father-in-law, brother and (most recently) a loving grandfather. My dad was a die-hard sports fan, and he had a keen sense of humor, and was seemingly an endless supplier of useless information.

To those of us who loved him and miss him, what a wonderful remembrance this book will be. My family and I want to thank all of the people who gave of their time to make this publication possible.

As an extra bonus, I would like to relate one of my favorite memories of my father. As any proper parent should do, my father taught me right from wrong, good from bad, and how to root for the New York Yankees. One other thing he instructed me about was the appreciation of a good egg cream, that deliciously unique beverage, originated in the greater New York City area. Just recently, my girlfriend, Lerian Mora, and I were taking an evening stroll along the local waterfront and we stumbled upon a little hole-in-the-wall place that calls itself Coney Island West. You see, we live in Marina Del Ray, a small California beach community, just outside of Los Angeles. Needless to say, egg creams in these parts are very hard to find, but Coney Island West not only makes that East Coast confection, but they make 'em very well. Naturally, this discovery prompted me to think about my father as I took my first sip of a Coney Island West egg cream.

When I was about four years old, my father used to take me to a candy store in Queens for an egg cream. To a little kid, the tall glass with all that white foam was just too much to handle alone. So it became a ritual for my father to take the first sip, after which I would finish the job. Well, one time, my father sat me down at the counter of our favorite candy store and ordered up one tall, cold egg cream. The woman working the fountain obliged and I immediately looked for my father to take that first sip. But he was nowhere in sight. So I did what any small boy would do and I just sat there staring at my drink, not saying a word. Finally, the lady asks what's the matter and I reply, "I need my father to start it off." She then went to hunt him down, finding my dad browsing the comic book rack off in the corner, and he came over and took that required first sip, then turning the rest over to me. For the next five minutes, all was good in this little boy's world as I gulped down that egg cream my dad had started off for me.

So, while you read this book, wherever you live, and if it's possible, find yourself a good egg cream, take a first sip, think of my dad, and give a hearty toast in memory of Jack Abel.

— **Gary Abel**

Inset below: *As a gift, Jack Abel drew this for his friend Rick Parker.*

TO MY PAL, RICK—
JACK ABEL

Art ©2021 the estate of Jack Abel. Characters TM & ©2021 Marvel Characters, Inc.

Below: *Rick Parker pencils the legendary Big Apple liquid confection: the egg cream. Note the message to the inker.*

JACK--
PLEASE INK!
Rick
2004

©2021 Rick Parker.

JACK ABEL ...A "BRIEF" INTRODUCTION!

WORDS BY RICK PARKER
ART BY MARIE SEVERIN

OH... HELLO! I REALLY DIDN'T EXPECT TO BE HERE... BUT YOU SEE, LAST YEAR... WELL,... I PASSED AWAY... SO A BUNCH O' MY BUDDIES PUT THEIR REGULAR WORK ASIDE AND GOT TOGETHER THIS COMIC BOOK AS SOME SORT OF TRIBUTE, I GUESS...

IT'S REALLY NOT JUST ABOUT ME...IT'S ABOUT ALL COMIC ARTISTS... AND IT'S ABOUT THE MEDIUM OF COMICS, TOO! IN MOST CASES, THESE NICE FOLKS WROTE AND DREW THE STORIES THEMSELVES, ALTHOUGH THAT'S NOT HOW COMICS ARE USUALLY DONE ...USUALLY ONE SPECIALIZES -- PENCILER, INKER, LETTERER...

SO ANYWAY... WHAT WAS I SAYING... OH YEAH, SO I'M HAPPY TO BE BACK WITH YOU AGAIN--ALBEIT THIS TIME AS A COMIC CHARACTER R...

≶ ahem ≷

YOU SEE, BIG JOHN VERPOORTEN LUMBERED INTO MY ROOM HERE A WHILE AGO AND SAID, "JACK, TAKE A MINUTE TO INTRODUCE THESE "STORIES" THEY DID ABOUT YOU... FREE-OF-CHARGE, I MIGHT ADD." AND I SAID... WELL, NEVER MIND WHAT I SAID! WALLY WOOD TOLD ME THEY EVEN GOT MARIE SEVERIN TO HELP OUT!

THAT'S HER NOW!

JUST VISITING, JACK!

COMIC BOOK HEAVEN

C&I SCH

JABEL

I REMEMBER · OLD DOUBLE-Y

WELL, I COULDN'T FIGURE OUT WHAT TO SAY, SO BIG JOHN SAID, "JUST INTRODUCE THE STORIES! IT'S EASY!"

JACK ABEL

SO... HERE I AM... AND WITHOUT FURTHER ADO, I'D LIKE TO INTRODUCE THE STORIES, THE FIRST OF WHICH APPEARS ON THE NEXT PAGE.

SO, THANKS A LOT, MEN... OH!! YOU, TOO, LISA!!!

47

JACK ABEL... AS I REMEMBER HIM...

I REMEMBER JACK AS: DARK-HAIRED, FUNNY, LACONIC AND VERY PLEASANT COMPANY. WE DIDN'T "HANG OUT" AND OUR RELATIONSHIP EXTENDED TO THE TIMES WE MET AT THE OFFICE (D.C.). WE WERE BOTH HIRED PENCIL-AND-INK GUYS WORKING FOR BOB KANIGHER (OUR ESTEEMED EDITOR).

JACK WAS AN EX-NAVY GUY, BUT HIS NAVAL HISTORY WAS RARELY A SUBJECT IN OUR DISCUSSIONS. MORE OF OUR TALKS INVOLVED; "GOTTA GET SOME *SLEEP!* AFTER 48 HOURS, IT'S LIKE I'M WALKIN' ON *MARSHMALLOWS!!!*" THAT, AND "GOTTA STICK AROUND UNTIL BOB FINISHES WRITIN' THE LAST PAGE OF MY SCRIPT. LET'S EAT." THESE COMMENTS COULD'VE COME FROM EITHER OF US.

CIRCA: 1960

ON MY RARE VISITS TO *MARVEL* (YEARS LATER), IT WAS GREAT TO SEE JACK'S BULK BENDING OVER HIS BOARD. KINDA MADE THE WORLD RIGHT. AN OPPORTUNITY TO SHOOT THE BREEZE... ABOUT OLD TIMES AND NEW TIMES.

IT WAS JACK'S SHOULDER I TAPPED WHEN I NEEDED HELP ON *"THE GREEN BERET"* (A BELATED AND NOW DORMANT STRIP). HE WAS THERE. FOR ME... AND FOR MANY, MANY OTHERS. A GOOD GUY WHO WILL BE REMEMBERED.

A STAR is BORN...

A FEW CENTURIES AGO, A BUNCH OF US GRACEFULLY AGING PROS WERE THE YOUNG TURKS OF COMICS.

HEY! THIS IS A CONTINUITY AD, CIRCA 1973.

WE LIVED IN THE BIG APPLE AND WE ALL HUNG OUT AT CONTINUITY, NEAL ADAMS' AND DICK GIORDANO'S STUDIO ON E. 48th STREET. THE GOOD OLD DAYS.

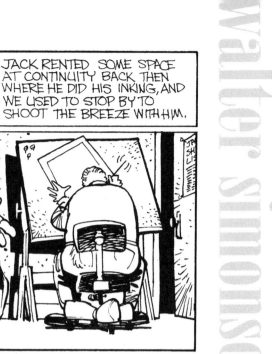

JACK RENTED SOME SPACE AT CONTINUITY BACK THEN WHERE HE DID HIS INKING, AND WE USED TO STOP BY TO SHOOT THE BREEZE WITH HIM.

THERE WERE A LOT OF US AROUND.

APPROVED BY THE COSMIC CODE AUTHORITY

ME / CHAYKIN / MILGROM / STARLIN / HAMA / RALPH REESE / RUBINSTEIN / TERRY AUSTIN / BOB W

"...AND THIS IS JUST OFF THE TOP OF MY HEAD. I'M LOUSY AT CARICATURES SO YOU'LL JUST HAVE TO READ THE LABELS AND TAKE MY WORD FOR IT, BUT CONTINUITY WAS A GREAT PLACE TO HANG WHEN WE WERE YOUNG.

— E. ENGLEHART

COPYRIGHT © 1996

AND TRYING TO MAKE JACK LAUGH WAS ONE OF OUR FAVORITE SPORTS. SO WAS LISTENING TO HIS CURMUDGEONLY TALES ABOUT FELLOW (OLDER) PROFESSIONALS.

BACK WHEN I DREW BATTLESTAR GALACTICA FOR AWHILE, I SHOWED JACK SOME OF THE PAGES I WAS INKING.

HE TOLD ME MY STAR-FIELDS WERE SUB-PAR, TOO REGULAR, AND HE SHOWED ME HIS AP-PROACH TO DOTTING THE BLACK SKY WITH PRO-WHITE.

INSTEAD OF THIS...

"...THIS!"

THE RESULTING VISUAL REALLY SUGGESTED A STRUCTURED UNIVERSE, AND OF COURSE, WAS AN OUTGROWTH OF JACK'S METHODICAL APPROACH TO HIS CRAFT.

ACTION FIG.

I WAS DELIGHTED WITH THE RESULTS AND EVERY TIME I DREW A STAR-FIELD, I THOUGHT OF JACK AND HIS TIP.

THAT'S STILL TRUE, EXCEPT THAT NOW, AFTER I DRAW THE FIELD, I PUT IN AN EXTRA STAR.

THAT'S JACK'S STAR.

BLESS YOU BUDDY, GODSPEED.

©2021 Walter Simonson.

walter simonson

"JACK ABEL AND THE HAIRY ARM SYNDROME" by "his Pal" Rick Parker '04

"ABOUT 20 YEARS BACK, I HAD A JOB DOING LETTERING CORRECTIONS IN THE MARVEL BULLPEN.

"IT WAS MY GOOD FORTUNE TO HAVE HAD THE DRAWING TABLE RIGHT BEHIND JACK ABEL.

"ONE DAY AN EDITOR WHO HAD SHOWN SOME INTEREST IN MY ARTWORK HAPPENED BY.

SAY... HOW'D YOU LIKE TO DO A COVER FOR ME?

"THIS BEING MY FIRST PROFESSIONAL ART ASSIGNMENT, I WAS NATURALLY ANXIOUS TO IMPRESS.

SOAR! ZIP! I'M GONNA BE RICH!! NOT FOR LONG!!

"I WAS HOPING THAT ONCE THE WORLD SAW WHAT A "GREAT JOB" I WOULD DO ON THAT COVER, I WOULD BE BESIEGED WITH OFFERS OF HIGH-PAYING ILLUSTRATION WORK.* *WHAT A DREAMER!!

"I WAS PROVIDED WITH A PRELIMINARY SKETCH FROM THE DESIGNER WHICH I THEN SPENT A WEEK 'PERFECTING'.*

OH, JEEZUS! HE'S REALLY GOT HIS NOSE TO THE GRINDSTONE THIS TIME!

* I MUST'VE MADE ABOUT $1.25/HR. ON THAT JOB.

"I FINISHED A LITTLE AHEAD OF DEADLINE, BUT SLOWLY BEGAN TO GET AN UNEASY FEELING IN THE PIT OF MY STOMACH.

"WHAT IF THERE'S SOMETHING WRONG WITH IT -- SOME FATAL FLAW OF WHICH I'M SOMEHOW UNAWARE...?

"I IMAGINED MYSELF TURNING IN THE PAGE...

YOU CALL THIS ART?!! GET OUT OF MY SIGHT, FREELANCE SCUM!! YIKES! RIP! SHRED! DESTROY!

"SO BEFORE I SUFFER HUMILIATION AND DEFEAT AT THE HANDS OF SOME EDITOR, I'LL RUN THE COVER PAST JACK!

"SUDDENLY, I GOT A BRILLIANT IDEA!

BRAINSTORM! HEY! I KNOW! I'LL SHOW TH' COVER TO JACK!

"AFTER ALL, JACK ABEL IS A SEASONED PROFESSIONAL... WELL RESPECTED... EXPERIENCED. SURELY HE WOULD SPOT ANY "TRAGIC FLAWS" IN MY ARTWORK!

SOMETIMES I WONDER WHY I SPEND LONELY NIGHTS...

"WHAT'S MORE, I KNEW FROM SITTING NEXT TO HIM FOR A COUPL'A YEARS THAT JACK WAS ALSO KIND... WISE... SENSITIVE... IF THERE WAS A PROBLEM WITH MY DRAWING, HE'D BREAK THE NEWS TO ME GENTLY... MERCIFULLY!!

JACK WORKED ON VARIOUS "FREELANCE" ASSIGNMENTS OR DOODLED FOR AMUSEMENT.

"SO I SHOWED IT TO JACK...HE LOOKED IT OVER THOUGHTFULLY FOR A MOMENT OR TWO...

HMMMM...

"THEN HE SAID..."

...PUT SOME HAIR ON THE GIRL'S ARMS...

"PUT...SOME...HAIR... ON...THE GIRL'S ARMS...?

"I REPEATED HIS WORDS AS THOUGH I HADN'T HEARD HIM CLEARLY.

YEAH...,THAT WAY WHEN YOU SHOW IT TO THE EDITOR, HE'LL NOTICE THE HAIRY ARMS RIGHT OFF THE BAT!

EDITORS GENERALLY LIKE TO MAKE YOU CHANGE SOMETHING, TO VALIDATE THEIR POSITION, OR EXERCISE THEIR OWN AUTHORITY...SO TO SAY...

NO SLAVE TO FASHION

NOTE: JACK WRAPPED TAPE AROUND HIS #3 WINSOR & NEWTON FOR MORE COMFORTABLE GRIP

TH' IDEA IS, THAT'S AN EASY THING TO FIX. CHANCES ARE, THEY'LL JUST SAY "TAKE TH' HAIR OFF THE ARMS AND IT'LL BE FINE..."

"SO I SAT BACK DOWN AT MY DRAWING TABLE AND WITH MY CROWQUILL BEGAN ADDING THOUSANDS OF TINY BLACK HAIRS TO THE FOREARMS OF THE SPACEGIRLS FROM MICHAEL KALUTA'S STARBURST SERIES...

Take Jack Abel to ANDREW'S

*APOLOGIES TO MIKE KALUTA

"LATER WHEN I 'WALKED TH' LAST MILE' TO THE EDITOR'S OFFICE TO TURN IN THE PAGE, I REMEMBER FEELING IT WAS A STROKE OF GOOD LUCK THAT THE EDITOR'S GIRLFRIEND JUST HAPPENED TO BE IN HIS OFFICE VISITING HIM AT THE TIME.

PERHAPS HE'LL GO EASY ON ME SINCE SHE'S HERE.

" AFTER STUDYING THE COVER FOR WHAT SEEMED LIKE A VERY LONG TIME, HE SAID...

... NICE JOB... I ESPECIALLY LIKE THE WAY YOU DRAW FEMALES!

JIM SOMEONE

HE DIDN'T MAKE ME CHANGE A THING! MAYBE JACK WAS WRONG?

"THANKYOU!" I BLURTED OUT, GRATEFUL THAT NOT ONLY DID HE NOT RIP ME TO SHREDS--BUT I DIDN'T EVEN HAVE TO CHANGE ANYTHING!!

"ON MY WAY OUT, I NOTICED HIS GIRLFRIEND HAD REALLY HAIRY ARMS.

MAN! JACK AIN'T NEVER GONNA BELIEVE THIS!

THANKS, JACK! "WRITE IF YA GET WORK!"HANG BY YER THUMBS!"

THE END

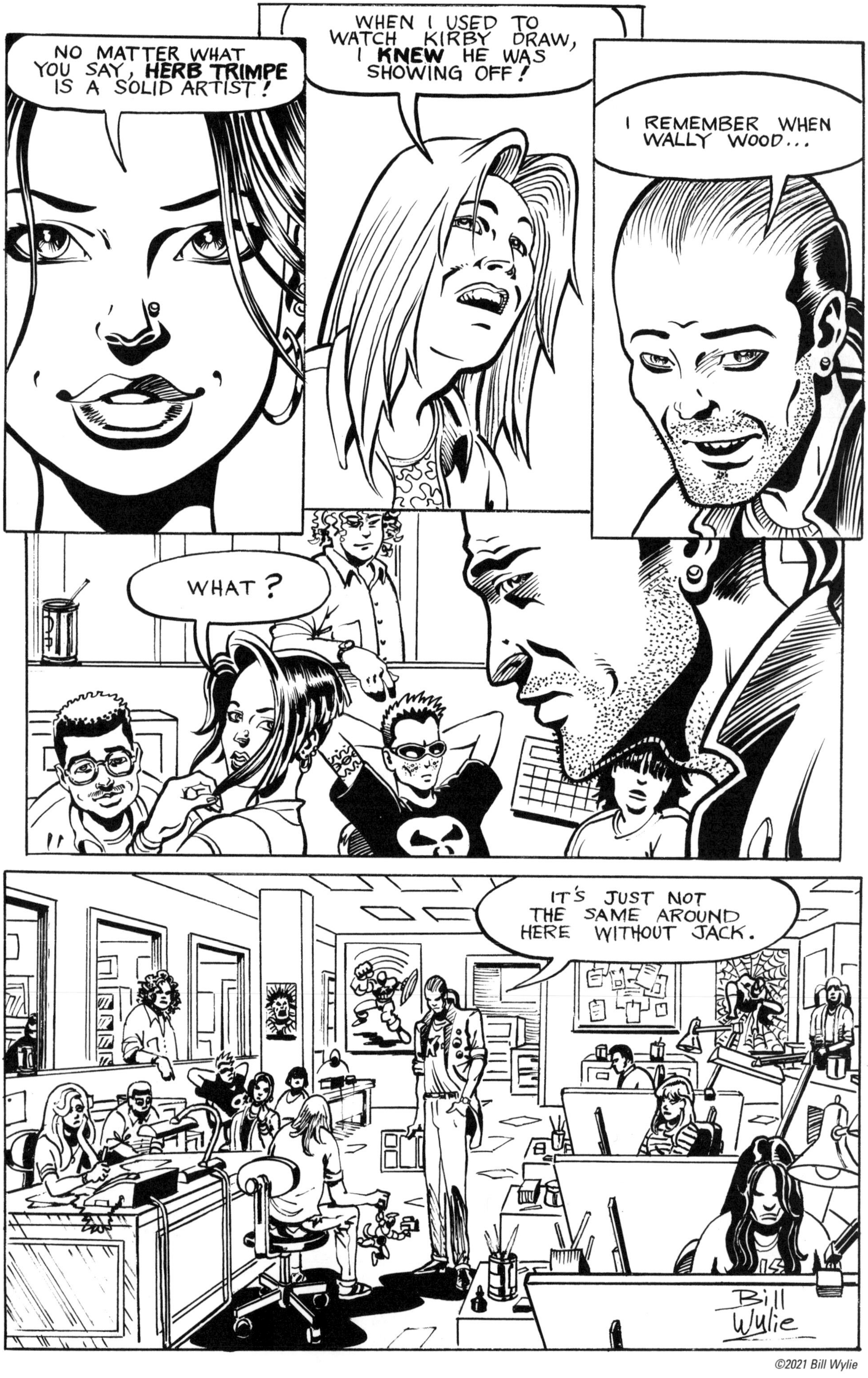
NO MATTER WHAT YOU SAY, HERB TRIMPE IS A SOLID ARTIST!
WHEN I USED TO WATCH KIRBY DRAW, I KNEW HE WAS SHOWING OFF!
I REMEMBER WHEN WALLY WOOD...
WHAT?
IT'S JUST NOT THE SAME AROUND HERE WITHOUT JACK.
Bill Wylie

I FIRST MET JACK IN '83

BY *DON HUDSON*

It WAS EARLY SUMMER, AND I'D BEEN CHOSEN TO BE AN INTERN TO START THAT FALL. I WAS AS *NERVOUS* AS A *CAT* SITTING IN JIM SHOOTERS OFFICE AND TALKING TO HIS SECRETARY.

SHE STARTED BLATHERING ABOUT HOW MUCH *FUN* I'D HAVE AND HOW *GREAT* THE JOB IS AND SO FORTH.

BLAH BLAH BLAH...

*B*UT AFTER MEETING SHOOTER AND GETTING THIS JOB, I COULDN'T PAY *ATTENTION.*

THEN SHE SAID *"LETS GO BY THE BULLPEN!" THAT* GOT MY ATTENTION!

I MUST HAVE BEEN THE *BIGGEST* FAN GEEK BECAUSE I RECOGNIZED SO MANY FACES! I WAS BROUGHT TOWARDS THE BACK WHERE I FIRST MET *JACK ABEL.*

*T*HE MOMENT SHE SAID HIS NAME I RECALLED HIS CREDITS: FROM *THE AVENGERS* TO *THE HULK* AND THOUSANDS MORE.

I THOUGHT, "THIS GUY IS SOMEONE TO REMEMBER."

WE WERE INTRODUCED, THEN HE SAID:

DID YOU KNOW THERE WAS A *FOOTBALL PLAYER* NAMED DON HUTSON BACK IN THE FORTIES?

GREATEST PLAYER WHO EVER *LIVED.*

I FOUND OUT RIGHT AWAY THAT HE WAS INTO *SPORTS.*

I WENT HOME AND READ ALL MY JACK ABEL BOOKS AND THOUGHT OF HIM.

I'D NEVER FORGOTTEN HOW JACK MADE ME WELCOME. IT WAS MY *FIRST* DAY AT MARVEL, AND I'D MET SOMEONE WHO KNEW MY NAME, AND KNEW ME *WELL.*

ONE DAY, JACK TOLD ME AND 'LITTLE JOE' RUBINSTEIN THAT HE HAD GONE TO HIGH SCHOOL WITH *TONY BENNETT!* HE SAID BENNETT WASN'T ANYTHING SPECIAL THEN. JACK SAID HE COULD'VE BECOME A SINGER *HIMSELF,* MAYBE!

I MISS YOU, JACK!

— BOB McLEOD

54

bob mcleod

JACK ABEL GRUMPY GOURMET

ADAM PHILIPS 1997

BACK IN 1985, WHEN I WAS AN ASSISTANT EDITOR AT MARVEL COMICS, I WOULD GO TO LUNCH A COUPLE OF TIMES A WEEK WITH MY BOSS, JIM SALICRUP, AND JACK ABEL. AT THE TIME, JACK HAD A DESK IN THE BULLPEN, THOUGH HE WASN'T ON STAFF.

ONE PLACE WE LIKED WAS A GREASY SPOON CALLED THE SUNLIGHT CAFE.

JACK ALWAYS WENT FOR A HEARTY MEAL, LIKE SOUP AND AN ENTRÉE SUCH AS BEEF STROGANOFF.

THIS WAS JACK'S REACTION WHEN HE SAW ME EATING SOMETHING WITH AVOCADO.

YOU LIKE THAT STUFF? I CAN'T STAND IT. I TRIED IT ONCE, WHEN I WAS IN THE NAVY. I PUT SOME IN MY MOUTH, SPIT IT OUT, AND SAID 'WHAT THE HELL IS THIS?! IT TASTES LIKE CRAP!'

DID YOU EVER TRY IT AGAIN?

NO, AND I DON'T INTEND TO.

WELL, THAT WAS JACK. HE WAS A GROUCHY, SWEET GUY. HE COULD ALSO BE QUITE GENEROUS. HE SOLD ME A BUNCH OF PAGES HE HAD INKED A THREW IN A GREAT ROMANCE COVER HE HAD PENCILLED AND INKED.

HE NEVER THOUGHT HE WAS MORE THAN AN ADEQUATE INKER, AND ALWAYS DENIGRATED HIS WORK WITH PENCILLERS LIKE GENE COLAN OR CURT SWAN.

AFTER I LEFT MARVEL, I SAW JACK ONLY ONCE IN A WHILE, WHEN I WOULD STOP BY FOR A VISIT. BY THEN HE HAD BECOME MARVEL'S PROOFREADER. I THINK THE LAST TIME WE SPOKE HE WAS COMPLAINING ABOUT AN EDITOR'S INABILITY TO SPELL 'VIETNAM.'

ANYWAY, I WISH I'D SEEN MORE OF HIM IN RECENT YEARS. HE WAS A GREAT OLD GUY... A REAL SALT OF THE EARTH... I MISS HIM.

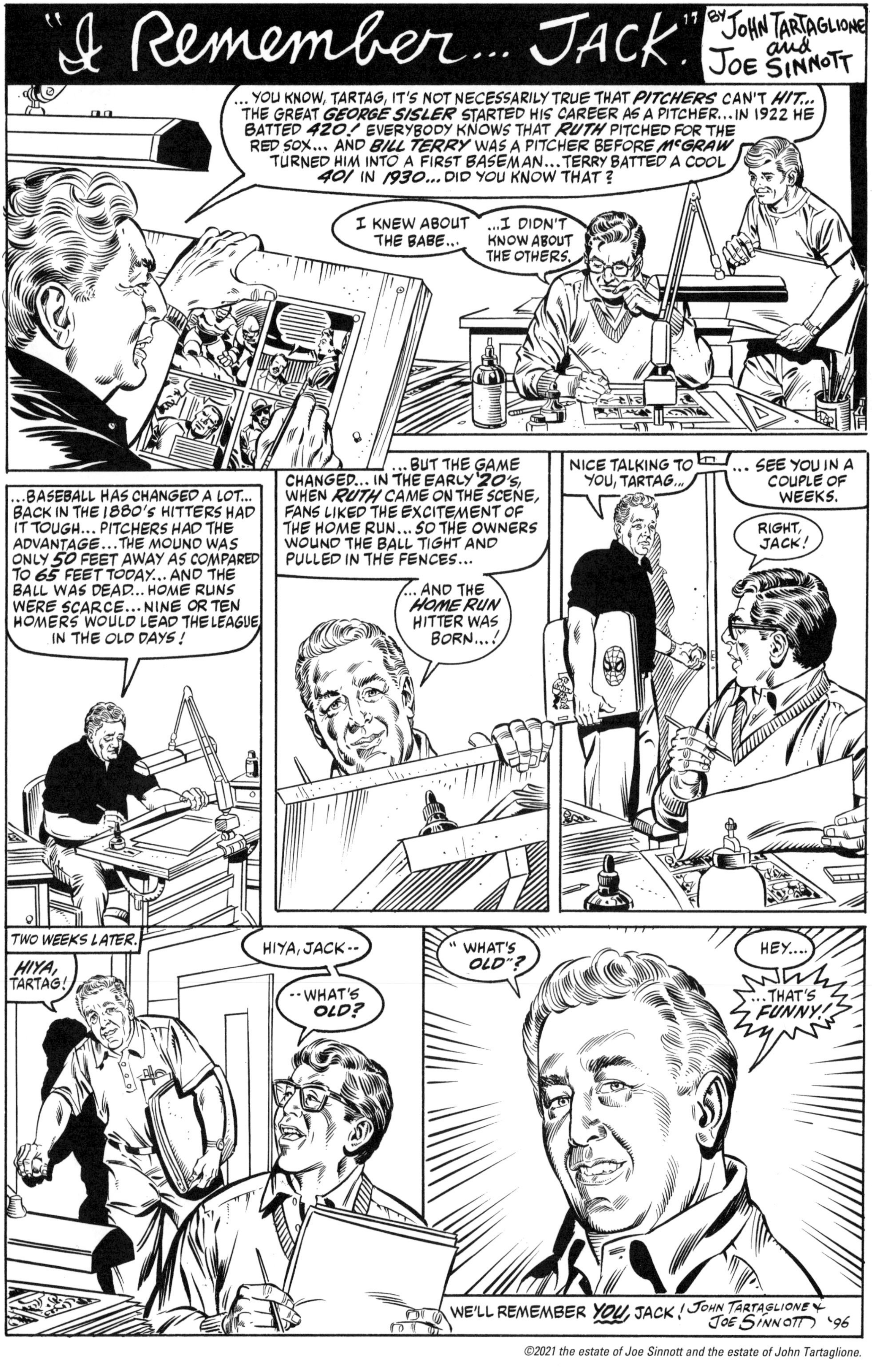
"I Remember... Jack."[17]
BY JOHN TARTAGLIONE and JOE SINNOTT
... YOU KNOW, TARTAG, IT'S NOT NECESSARILY TRUE THAT PITCHERS CAN'T HIT... THE GREAT GEORGE SISLER STARTED HIS CAREER AS A PITCHER... IN 1922 HE BATTED 420! EVERYBODY KNOWS THAT RUTH PITCHED FOR THE RED SOX... AND BILL TERRY WAS A PITCHER BEFORE McGRAW TURNED HIM INTO A FIRST BASEMAN... TERRY BATTED A COOL 401 IN 1930... DID YOU KNOW THAT?
I KNEW ABOUT THE BABE...
...I DIDN'T KNOW ABOUT THE OTHERS.
...BASEBALL HAS CHANGED A LOT... BACK IN THE 1880'S HITTERS HAD IT TOUGH... PITCHERS HAD THE ADVANTAGE... THE MOUND WAS ONLY 50 FEET AWAY AS COMPARED TO 65 FEET TODAY... AND THE BALL WAS DEAD... HOME RUNS WERE SCARCE... NINE OR TEN HOMERS WOULD LEAD THE LEAGUE IN THE OLD DAYS!
... BUT THE GAME CHANGED... IN THE EARLY '20'S, WHEN RUTH CAME ON THE SCENE, FANS LIKED THE EXCITEMENT OF THE HOME RUN... SO THE OWNERS WOUND THE BALL TIGHT AND PULLED IN THE FENCES...
... AND THE HOME RUN HITTER WAS BORN...!
NICE TALKING TO YOU, TARTAG...
... SEE YOU IN A COUPLE OF WEEKS.
RIGHT, JACK!
TWO WEEKS LATER.
HIYA, TARTAG!
HIYA, JACK --
-- WHAT'S OLD?
"WHAT'S OLD"?
HEY....
...THAT'S FUNNY!
WE'LL REMEMBER YOU, JACK! JOHN TARTAGLIONE + JOE SINNOTT '96

Back in 1970...
NATIONAL PERIODICAL PUBLICATIONS, Inc. (DC COMICS) had an artist's room at its offices on the 20th floor of 909 Third Ave.

I came in every day and sat mostly at the drawing table opposite the door.

One day, I walked in and found sitting at "my" place an artist I hadn't met. On his ("my") drawing table he'd placed uninked SUPERGIRL pages. The pencils were fuzzier than I'd expected~ the lines, softer-- graphite, more smudged ... but still recognizable as the artwork of WIN MORTIMER.

They were beautiful, but I couldn't imagine how they could be inked.

As I said: I had not yet met

Jack Abel

Hi. Hello.

You're Win Mortimer?

NO.

Oh... I...

Oh.

I'm Jack Abel.

Oh... I...

Oh.

Jack and I had two other tense moments between us over the years. But I believe he considered us to be friends.

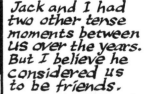

I know I did.
Sal Amendola

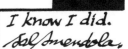

MORT TODD'S COMIC ART HISTORY 2096

GREETINGS, STUDENTS!

SCHOOL OF COMIC ART!

GOOD MORNING, DR. LOBE!

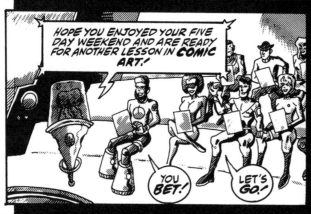

HOPE YOU ENJOYED YOUR FIVE DAY WEEKEND AND ARE READY FOR ANOTHER LESSON IN COMIC ART!

YOU BET!

LET'S GO!

YOU'LL REMEMBER WE WERE COVERING ARTISTS IN THE SECOND HALF OF THE 20TH CENTURY... HOW 'BOUT A POP QUIZ?

AWWWWWW

DON'T WORRY, YOU WON'T BE GRADED! LOOK ON YOUR LC DESKS AND YOU'LL SEE A PANEL FROM THE EARLY 1970'S... OBVIOUSLY, IT WAS PENCILED BY CURT SWAN... BUT WHO INKED IT?

EASY! MURPHY ANDERSON!

IS THAT ALL?

OOH! OOH!

YES, KAYTEL?

THE BACKGROUNDS ARE BY JACK ABEL! I CAN TELL BY THE WAY THE TREES ARE DISTINCTLY EMBELLISHED. BESIDES, HE INKED OVER SWAN IN EARLIER ISSUES!

CORRECT!

RONCO, CAN YOU TELL ME ANYTHING ELSE ABOUT JACK ABEL?

UMM... YEAH!!

HE INKED THE FIRST APPEARANCE OF WOLVERINE IN THE INCREDIBLE HULK!

-- AND HE WAS THE 'GARY MICHAELS' THAT INKED GENE COLAN'S EARLY IRON MAN IN TALES OF SUSPENSE!

RIGHT!!

--BUT JACK ABEL WAS ALSO A PROLIFIC PENCILER IN HIS OWN RIGHT BEFORE INKING THOUSANDS OF PAGES FOR MARVEL AND DC!

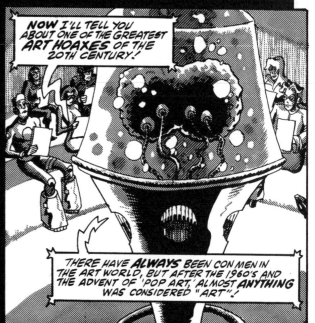

NOW I'LL TELL YOU ABOUT ONE OF THE GREATEST ART HOAXES OF THE 20TH CENTURY!

THERE HAVE ALWAYS BEEN CON MEN IN THE ART WORLD, BUT AFTER THE 1960'S AND THE ADVENT OF 'POP ART,' ALMOST ANYTHING WAS CONSIDERED "ART"!

mort todd

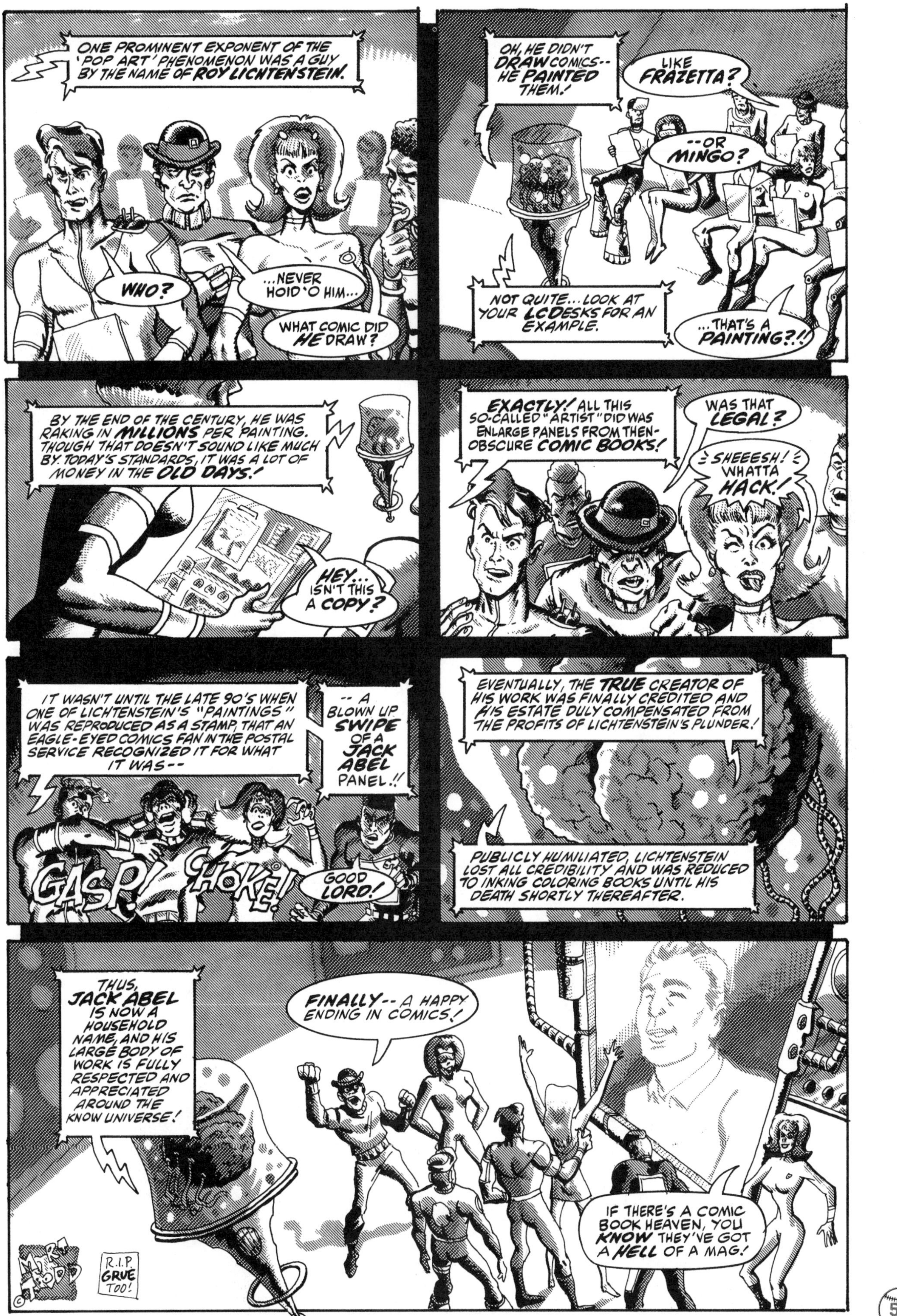
ONE PROMINENT EXPONENT OF THE 'POP ART' PHENOMENON WAS A GUY BY THE NAME OF ROY LICHTENSTEIN.
WHO?
...NEVER HOID 'O HIM...
WHAT COMIC DID HE DRAW?
OH, HE DIDN'T DRAW COMICS-- HE PAINTED THEM!
LIKE FRAZETTA?
--OR MINGO?
NOT QUITE... LOOK AT YOUR LCDESKS FOR AN EXAMPLE.
...THAT'S A PAINTING?!!
BY THE END OF THE CENTURY, HE WAS RAKING IN MILLIONS PER PAINTING. THOUGH THAT DOESN'T SOUND LIKE MUCH BY TODAY'S STANDARDS, IT WAS A LOT OF MONEY IN THE OLD DAYS!
HEY... ISN'T THIS A COPY?
EXACTLY! ALL THIS SO-CALLED "ARTIST" DID WAS ENLARGE PANELS FROM THEN-OBSCURE COMIC BOOKS!
WAS THAT LEGAL?
SHEEESH! WHATTA HACK!
IT WASN'T UNTIL THE LATE 90'S WHEN ONE OF LICHTENSTEIN'S "PAINTINGS" WAS REPRODUCED AS A STAMP, THAT AN EAGLE-EYED COMICS FAN IN THE POSTAL SERVICE RECOGNIZED IT FOR WHAT IT WAS--
-- A BLOWN UP SWIPE OF A JACK ABEL PANEL!!
GASP!
CHOKE!
GOOD LORD!
EVENTUALLY, THE TRUE CREATOR OF HIS WORK WAS FINALLY CREDITED AND HIS ESTATE DULY COMPENSATED FROM THE PROFITS OF LICHTENSTEIN'S PLUNDER!
PUBLICLY HUMILIATED, LICHTENSTEIN LOST ALL CREDIBILITY AND WAS REDUCED TO INKING COLORING BOOKS UNTIL HIS DEATH SHORTLY THEREAFTER.
THUS, JACK ABEL IS NOW A HOUSEHOLD NAME, AND HIS LARGE BODY OF WORK IS FULLY RESPECTED AND APPRECIATED AROUND THE KNOW UNIVERSE!
FINALLY-- A HAPPY ENDING IN COMICS!
IF THERE'S A COMIC BOOK HEAVEN, YOU KNOW THEY'VE GOT A HELL OF A MAG!
R.I.P. GRUE TOO!

GOOD OL' JACK ABEL

MEMORIES... THERE WAS A HAPPY NEW YEAR'S EVE PARTY AT SYD SHORE'S HOME...

WHEN JACK HAD HIS DRAWING TABLE IN NEAL ADAM'S STUDIO ON 48TH STREET I'D STOP BY AND VISIT WITH HIM WHEN I WAS "IN TOWN".

JACK INKED "OUTLAW KID" THAT I PENCILLED FOR MARVEL IN THE '70'S.

AND WHEN DC ASSIGNED ME TO "FREEDOM FIGHTERS" I ASKED THEM TO ASSIGN JACK TO DO THE INKING.

WE WERE A TEAM FOR QUITE A RUN. JACK WAS A FAVORITE.

DICK AYERS

A FABLE FROM THE FOGGY MEMORY OF **TERRY AUSTIN** — FORMER BOY CARTOONIST!

①nce upon a time.... WAY BACK IN THE **OLDEN DAYS** (WE CALLED 'EM THE **SEVENTIES**) THERE EXISTED AN **ENCHANTED KINGDOM** IN A FAR AWAY CITY CALLED **NYC** ...

THE OFFICES OF **CONTINUITY ASSOCIATES!**

FROM NEAR AND FAR, **HOPEFULL YOUNG SUPPLICANTS** WOULD ARRIVE TO SIT AT THE FEET OF THE **COMIC ART MASTERS**, **NEAL ADAMS, DICK GIORDANO** -- AND THAT CRUSTIEST OF LOVABLE CRUMUDGEONS, **JACK ABEL** ...

LI'L MARSHAL ROGERS
LI'L BOB WIACEK
LI'L LARRY HAMA
LI'L CARL POTTS
LI'L RICH BASILE
LI'L BOB McLEOD
LI'L ME
LI'L MIKE NASSER
LI'L JOE RUBENSTEIN

JACK RULED OVER HIS **HUMBLE OFFICE SPACE,** STEADILY LABORING IN THE MIDST OF **YOUTHFUL PRANKS** AND **SWIRLING NONSENSE,** LISTENING TO **DANNY STILES NOSTALGIA RADIO PROGRAM** AND OCCASIONALLY PAUSING TO RELATE A **STORY** OR **FIVE** ...

AND THEN DANNY'S SUBSTITUTE INTRODUCES THE SONG "TAKE THE 'A' TRAIN" BY SAYING, "AND NOW, THE POPULAR FAVORITE: 'TAKE A TRAIN!'" HEH!

FLOONT! WAK! SMEK!

LUNCHTIME -- A KINGLY REPAST! DISPATCHED ACROSS THE STREET ARMED WITH **JACK'S SANDWICH ORDER,** JUST AS THE ELEVATOR DOORS WERE **CLOSING,** I'D HEAR **JACK'S PARTING ADMONITION** ...

REMEMBER-- **NO FxxKING MAYONNAISE!!!**

IT SEEMS THAT JACK **HATED** MAYONNAISE ...

BEING A LAD OF **LIGHTNING QUICK WIT,** I'D QUIP ON MY RETURN: "I GOT YOU **DOUBLE MAYONNAISE** JUST LIKE YOU **SAID,** JACK," AND HE WOULD GRACIOUSLY **REPLY** ...

THAT'S **IT,** AUSTIN -- YOU'RE GOIN' ON MY **SHIT LIST!**

SEIZED BY INSPIRATION WHILE ON A TRIP HOME TO MICHIGAN, I DREW UP AN **ACTUAL SHIT LIST** FOR JACK'S **WALL,** COMPLETE WITH A HUGE **PAD** OF NUMBERED **PAPER** ATTACHED....

MEN! WOMEN! BOYS! GIRLS! SMALL FURRY ANIMALS! MAYONAISE! MICHAEL NASSER! ARE **YOU** ON THE CELEBRATED (WHOOPIE!) **JACK ABEL SHIT LIST** AS SEEN ON TV!

PICTURED ABOVE = THE MAN WHOSE SPIRITUAL MESSAGE HAS BROUGHT NEW HOPE TO MILLIONS!

ACCEPT **NO** SUBSTITUTIONS!

	(SHIT FROM LAST PAGE)
#1	#13023
#2	#13024

PRESENTING IT TO JACK UPON MY RETURN, HE SEEMED GENUINELY **AMUSED** AND **PLEASED,** AND GRANTED ME A GREAT **HONOR** ...

YOU GET TO SIGN IT **FIRST,** KID, 'CAUSE YOU'LL ALWAYS BE **#1** ON **MY** SHIT LIST!

BY THE WAY, YOU MISSPELLED MAYONNAISE!*

* A PRECURSOR TO JACK'S LATER CAREER AS A PROOFREADER.

IN THE **YEARS AHEAD,** ALL OF JACK'S VISITORS WERE SIMILARLY INVITED TO **SIGN IN,** RESULTING IN THE **DOCUMENTATION** OF A ROLE CALL OF **COMICS HISTORY** OVER THE LAST COUPLE OF **DECADES** ...

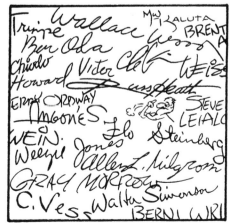

IN A STRANGE WAY JACK'S SHIT LIST BECAME A LIST OF **JACK'S FRIENDS,** OF WHICH THERE WERE **MANY** ... AND JACK, I'M MIGHTY PROUD TO HAVE HAD MY NAME ON **THAT** LIST!

P.S. JACK TAUGHT ME THE CARTOONIST'S TECHNIQUE OF THE **RAZOR-BLADE SKIP** ... TO THIS DAY, I CAN'T USE THIS TECHNIQUE WITHOUT THINKING OF JACK ...

JACK, THIS SKIP IS FOR YOU!

©2021 Terry Austin.

61

terry austin

JACK ABEL AND THE HAM SANDWICH

BY MARK GRUENWALD
TOM PALMER – FINISHES
SUSAN CRESPI – LETTERS

575 MADISON AVENUE... EARLY 1982....JACK ABEL, MIKE CARLIN, AND I SHARED A 10' BY 12' OFFICE...

JACK

ME

MIKE

ONE DAY...

OOPS! I FORGOT TO TAKE LUNCH TODAY!

SNACK TRUCK SHOULD BE AROUND SOON.

AND...

AW, MAN! ALL THEY HAD LEFT WAS THIS HAM AND CHEESE SANDWICH. I DON'T EAT HAM!

THEN JUST TOSS IT!

I'VE GOT A BETTER IDEA.

WHILE JACK'S AWAY FROM HIS BOARD, I'LL SLIP THE HAM IN HIS TABORET!

WON'T HE BE SURPRISED WHEN HE GOES FOR HIS INKBRUSH TOMORROW!

THE NEXT MORNING....

HI, JACK!

HI, MEN!

YOU, TOO, MARK.

HE'S NOT OPENING IT!

DON'T WORRY. HE'S BOUND TO OPEN THAT DRAWER SOONER OR LATER!

....WORKING TOGETHER ONE MORE TIME.

HUBBA HUBBA!

"HUBBA HUBBA," THAT'S WHAT JACK ABEL USED TO SAY TO ME, A SMIRK SHINING IN HIS BOYISH BLUES.

POLITELY, BUT WITH THAT SAME SLY SMILE, HE WOULD ADD THAT WAS THE COMMENT MEN OF HIS DAY USED TO DESCRIBE A SEXY LADY.

INEVITABLY, MOMENTS LATER HE WAS TELLING ME ABOUT THE FOXY CHICK HE WAS MARRIED TO.

NOT ONLY WAS HIS WIFE A LOOKER, EVEN AFTER 46 YEARS, BUT HE'D BRAG ABOUT HER COOKING AS WELL.

ENDING HIS CONVERSATION, AS ALWAYS, HE'D INFORM ME WHAT A LUCKY MAN HE WAS.

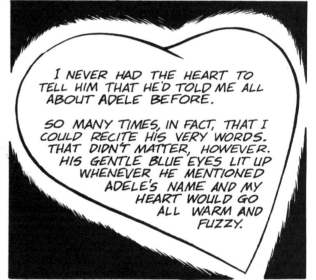

I NEVER HAD THE HEART TO TELL HIM THAT HE'D TOLD ME ALL ABOUT ADELE BEFORE.

SO MANY TIMES, IN FACT, THAT I COULD RECITE HIS VERY WORDS. THAT DIDN'T MATTER, HOWEVER. HIS GENTLE BLUE EYES LIT UP WHENEVER HE MENTIONED ADELE'S NAME AND MY HEART WOULD GO ALL WARM AND FUZZY.

DOES LOVE LIKE THIS REALLY EXIST? OR WAS HE A VOICE FROM THE PAST WHO SPOKE LONG DEAD WORDS LIKE HUBBA HUBBA.

I ONCE READ THAT KINDNESS TRAVELS BRIEFLY THROUGH ONES LIFE. WHEN YOU RECOGNIZE IT, YOU SHOULD HOLD ONTO IT, NEVER LET IT GO.

I AM BLESSED TO HAVE KNOWN JACK ABEL.

ONLY ONE THING LEFT TO BE SAID.

HUBBA HUBBA, MR. ABEL.

WORDS   LYSA HAWKINS
PICTURES   M. KRAIGER

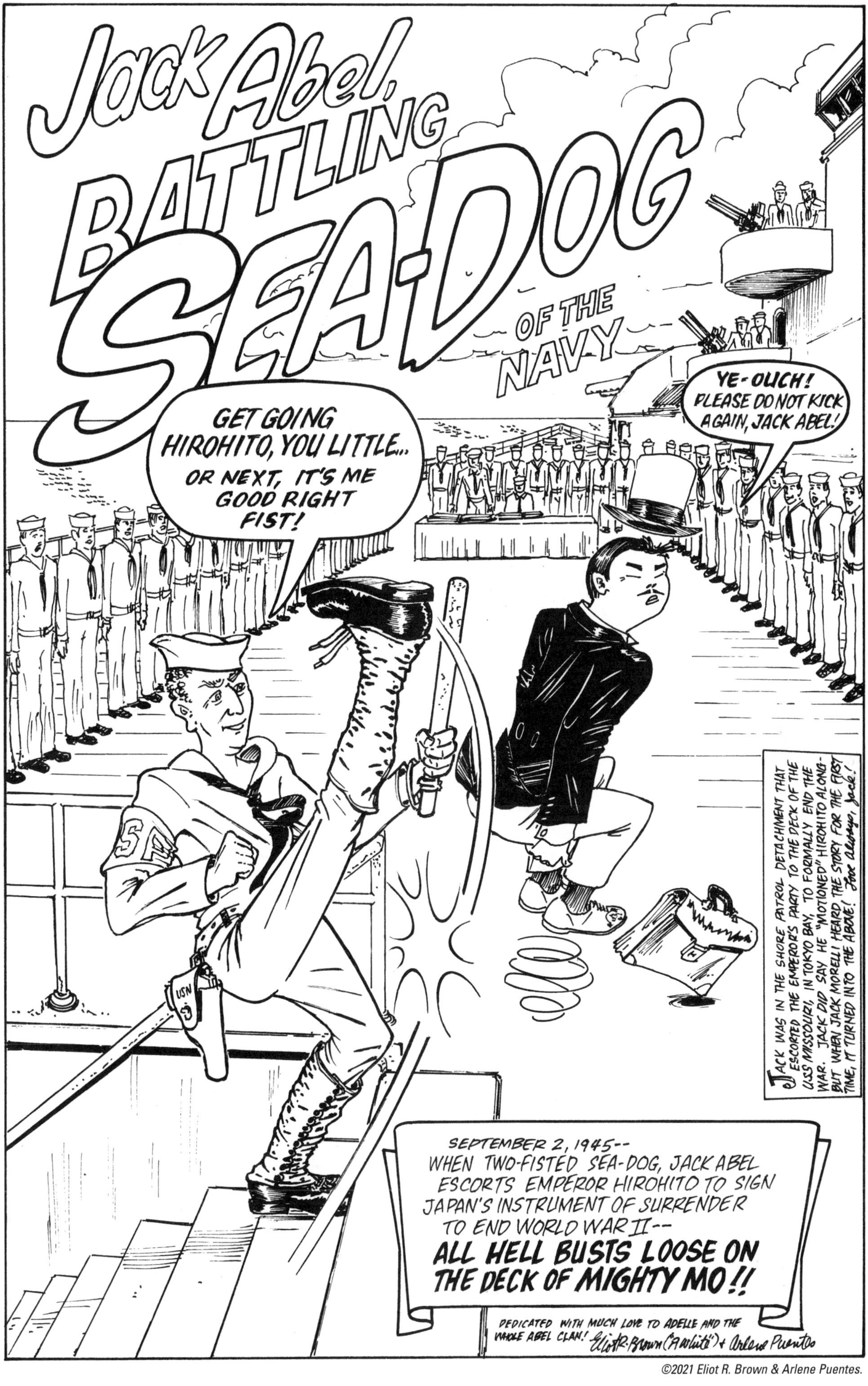

Jack Abel, BATTLING SEA-DOG OF THE NAVY
GET GOING HIROHITO, YOU LITTLE... OR NEXT, IT'S ME GOOD RIGHT FIST!
YE-OUCH! PLEASE DO NOT KICK AGAIN, JACK ABEL!
JACK WAS IN THE SHORE PATROL DETACHMENT THAT ESCORTED THE EMPEROR'S PARTY TO THE DECK OF THE USS MISSOURI, IN TOKYO BAY, TO FORMALLY END THE WAR. JACK DID SAY HE "MOTIONED" HIROHITO ALONG-BUT WHEN JACK MORELLI HEARD THE STORY FOR THE FIRST TIME, IT TURNED INTO THE ABOVE! Love always, Jack!
SEPTEMBER 2, 1945-- WHEN TWO-FISTED SEA-DOG, JACK ABEL ESCORTS EMPEROR HIROHITO TO SIGN JAPAN'S INSTRUMENT OF SURRENDER TO END WORLD WAR II--
ALL HELL BUSTS LOOSE ON THE DECK OF MIGHTY MO!!
DEDICATED WITH MUCH LOVE TO ADELLE AND THE WHOLE ABEL CLAN!
USN

My VIEW OF JACK--

AT AN AGE WHEN MANY FREELANCERS FADE INTO
DARKEST. SETTLING IN AT THE MARVEL BULLPEN, JACK
SOON REALIZED HE WAS SURROUNDED BY PEOPLE WHO
TO MENTION SPORTS TRIVIA), JACK HAD THE STRENGTH TO
VERY DEFINITION OF "COURAGE." GO AHEAD, LOOK UP COURAGE

OBSCURITY, JACK GOT A SECOND CHANCE WHEN THINGS LOOKED
OVERCAME HIS HANDICAP, FOUND A NEW BEGINNING, AND
LOVED HIM. A SOFT-SPOKEN MAN OF ENDLESS WIT AND TALENT, (NOT
PROCEED WHEN OTHERS WOULD HAVE GIVEN IN. HE'S THE
IN THE DICTIONARY--YOU'LL FIND A PICTURE OF JACK.

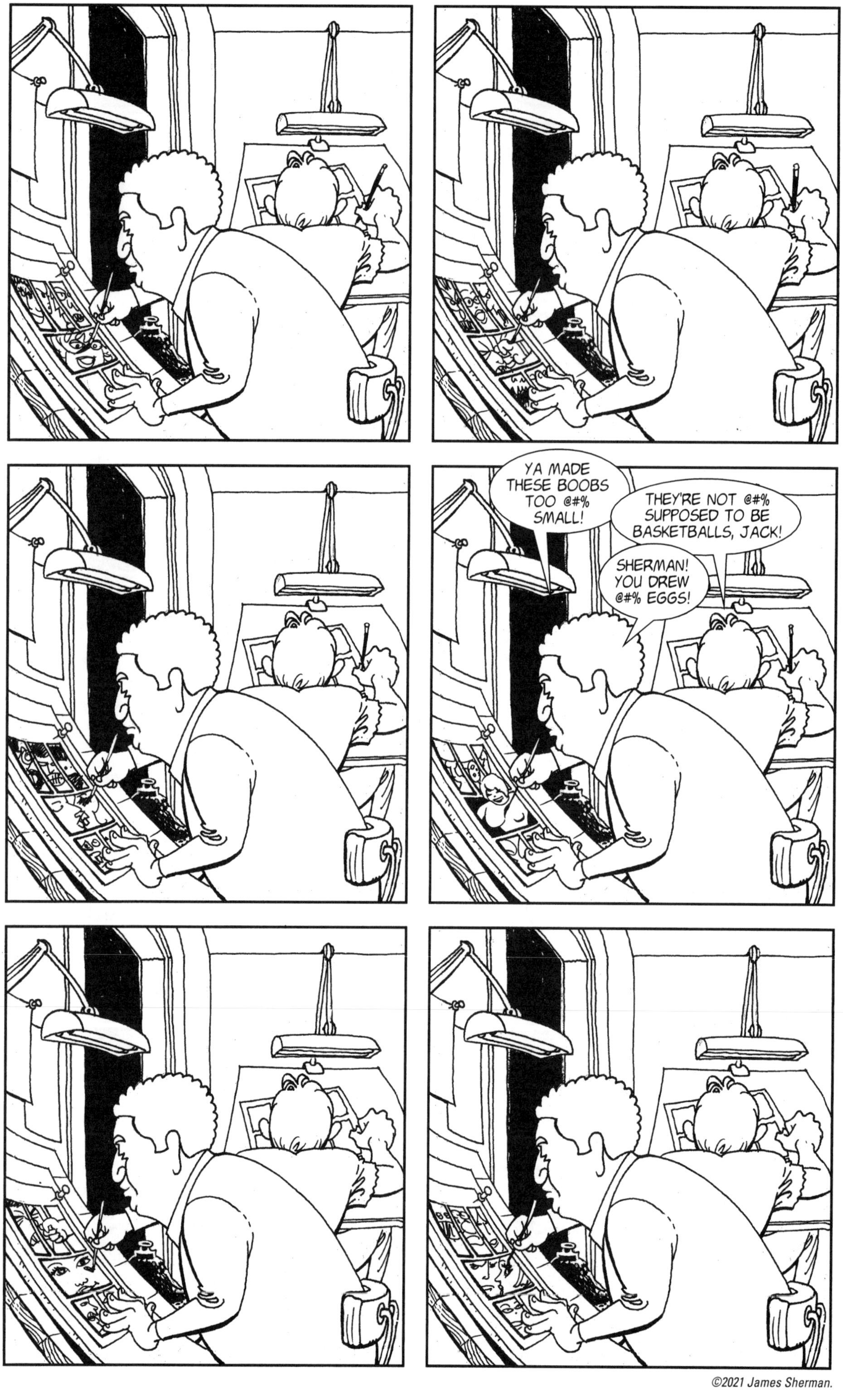
YA MADE THESE BOOBS TOO @#% SMALL!
THEY'RE NOT @#% SUPPOSED TO BE BASKETBALLS, JACK!
SHERMAN! YOU DREW @#% EGGS!

UNCLE JACK

WRITTEN AND DRAWN

BY

SOJOURNER & FLOYD HUGHES

©1996

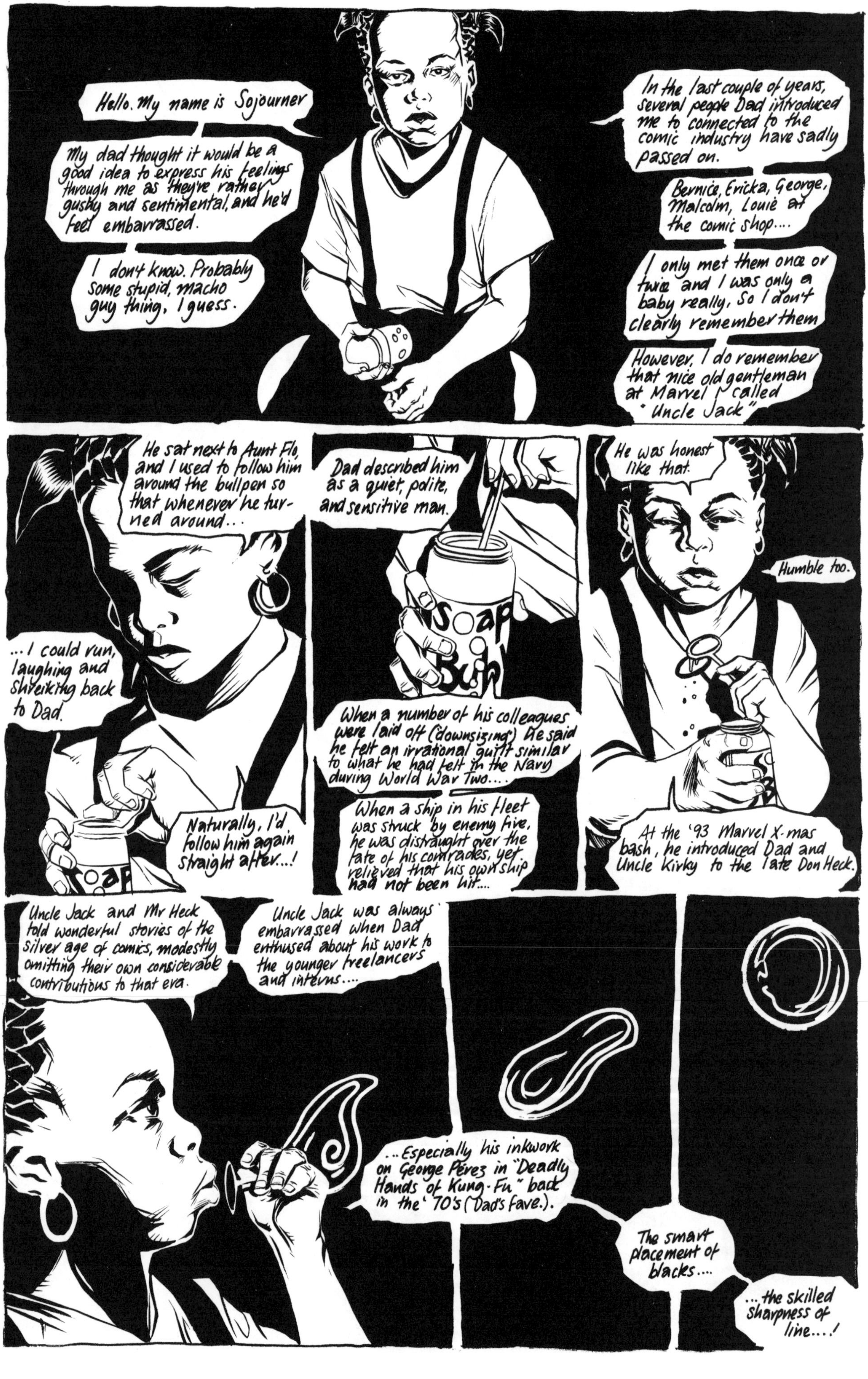
Hello. My name is Sojourner
My dad thought it would be a good idea to express his feelings through me as they're rather gushy and sentimental, and he'd feel embarrassed.
I don't know. Probably some stupid, macho guy thing, I guess.
In the last couple of years, several people Dad introduced me to connected to the comic industry have sadly passed on.
Bernice, Ericka, George, Malcolm, Louie at the comic shop....
I only met them once or twice and I was only a baby really, So I don't clearly remember them
However, I do remember that nice old gentleman at Marvel I called "Uncle Jack"
He sat next to Aunt Flo, and I used to follow him around the bullpen so that whenever he turned around...
...I could run, laughing and shreiking back to Dad.
Naturally, I'd follow him again straight after...!
Dad described him as a quiet, polite, and sensitive man.
Soap Bub
When a number of his colleagues were laid off (downsizing) he said he felt an irrational guilt similar to what he had felt in the Navy during World War Two....
When a ship in his fleet was struck by enemy fire, he was distraught over the fate of his comrades, yet relieved that his own ship had not been hit....
He was honest like that.
Humble too.
At the '93 Marvel X-mas bash, he introduced Dad and Uncle Kirky to the late Don Heck.
Uncle Jack and Mr Heck told wonderful stories of the silver age of comics, modestly omitting their own considerable contributions to that era.
Uncle Jack was always embarrassed when Dad enthused about his work to the younger freelancers and interns....
...Especially his inkwork on George Peres in "Deadly Hands of Kung-Fu" back in the '70's (Dad's fave.).
The smart placement of blacks....
...the skilled sharpness of line....!

... but I digress...

Apart from comics, Dad and Uncle Jack discussed, Music, Art, Literature, Religeous/ Racial / Class and Sexual politics; plus Parenting, Grandparenting and of course, Baseball.

My Dad thinks it's sad that I'll not get to know Uncle Jack when I'm older.

He was a sweet, gentle guy with a sharp mind and a wonderfully subtle sense of humour, which I would have appreciated on another level.

Dad and I last saw Uncle Jack about a week or so before he passed away..., which was a week before my fourth birthday.

Uncle Richard told Dad, who turned to me and said "Honey. Uncle Jack has gone away. We won't see him at Marvel anymore."

Dad knows that in a year or so from now, I will probably have forgotten Uncle Jack, so maybe in a few years from now (If I ever bother to read any of his stuff) this might trigger a memory, or perhaps a smile....

These thing are hard to explain to a three year old, and I still don't quite understand....

Neither does Dad.

...I hope so.

Anyhow, I'd better wrap this up. Dad thinks it's getting too soppy and emotional.

Goodbye Uncle Jack..

...I'll...., sorry, We'll miss you—

Now if you'll kindly excuse us...

We have soap in our eyes.....

MEMORIES OF JACK

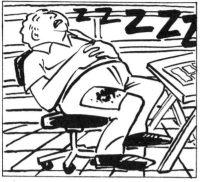

THANKS, JACK! YOU TAUGHT US ALL HOW TO DO IT!

LIKE MOST KIDS, MY LITTLE BROTHER AND I LOVED COMIC BOOKS. OF COURSE, WE LIKED THE SUPERHEROES, THE CLASSICS ILLUSTRATED, THE WESTERNS...

THEN WE DISCOVERED THE WAR COMICS. THE DC BOOKS SEEMED TO BE THE BEST.

THEY HAD THE BEST ARTWORK. THERE WERE STRIPS BY MASTERS LIKE KUBERT, HEATH, NOVICK, DRUCKER, TOTH, GRANDINETTI, GLANZMAN...

IN OUR FIGHTING FORCES THERE WAS A FEATURE CALLED GUNNER AND SARGE. STORIES ABOUT TWO MARINES AND THEIR K9 CORPS DOG, PVT. POOCH.

THOSE STORIES WERE INKED WITH A VERY STRONG, CONFIDENT LINE. THAT WAS MY FIRST TASTE OF JACK ABEL'S WORK.

YEARS LATER I RECOGNIZED THAT LINEWORK OVER GENE COLAN'S PENCILS ON MARVEL'S IRON MAN.

THE INKER CREDIT READ GARY MICHAELS, BUT SURE ENOUGH, IT WAS JACK.

I MET JACK SOON AFTER I MOVED TO NEW YORK IN THE EARLY SEVENTIES TO GET INTO COMICS. WHEN I MENTIONED THOSE OLD GUNNER AND SARGE STORIES, HE'D HOLD UP AN INVISIBLE TOMMY GUN AND SAY...

BUDDA BUDDA!

THAT CARTOON SOUND EFFECT BECAME OUR SPECIAL GREETING.

WE ONLY GOT TO WORK TOGETHER ONCE. HE INKED MY PENCILS ON A SHORT-LIVED TITLE FROM A SHORT-LIVED COMPANY.

ATLAS COMICS
THE BRUTE

LATER I'D RUN INTO JACK AT CONTINUITY ASSOCIATES, WHERE HE HAD STUDIO SPACE. SHORT VISITS BECAME LONG ONES AS JACK DREW FROM HIS INEXHAUSTIBLE FOUNTAIN OF KNOWLEDGE...

SWEET LITTLE SAX SOLO.

SURE, HE USED TO PLAY WITH MIFF MOLE AND HIS LITTLE MOLARS.

JACK SEEMED TO KNOW EVERYTHING ABOUT CLASSIC JAZZ...

...BASEBALL, HISTORY, OLD MOVIES...

YOU KNOW, THAT WAS DIRECTED BY ABNER BIBERMAN...

...REMEMBER? HE PLAYED YOUNG TOADFACE IN GUNGA DIN.

THE LAST TIME I SAW JACK HE WAS PROUDLY DISPLAYING A SNAPSHOT OF HIS GRANDDAUGHTER.

HEY AL, WANNA SEE MY NEW GIRLFRIEND?

IN THE COMICS BIZ, AND I'M SURE IN OTHERS, IT'S NOT ALWAYS THE BEST KNOWN GUYS THAT ARE THE BEST GUYS...
BUDDA BUDDA, JACK!
—ALAN WEISS '96

73

Alan Kupperberg's:

"TEN THINGS I LEARNED FROM JACK ABEL"

© 1996

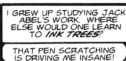

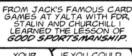

WHY JACK ABEL WAS SO TIRED!

75

JACK ABEL - THAT CRAZY OLD FART.
by Steve Bunche '96

I FIRST MET JACK ABEL IN 1990, WHEN I FIRST WENT TO WORK IN THE MARVEL BULLPEN. ANYONE WHO KNEW JACK WILL TELL YOU THAT HE WAS ONE COLORFUL OLD SOMBITCH AND TO RECAP ALL THE POSSIBLE JACK ANECDOTES WOULD FILL UP A WHOLE BOOK.

SO, FOR THE SAKE OF BREVITY, HERE ARE MY FOUR FAVORITE ASPECTS OF THE BULLPEN'S BELOVED "CRAZY OLD FART".

♫ GROOVE IS IN TH' HAAAAART!!!

POP MUSIC SINGER. HE WAS INTO THE MUSIC OF THE KIDS, MAN!!!

ORAL HISTORIAN (AKA "THE NEVER-ENDING STORY TELLER").

HE ACTUALLY TOLD THIS ONE.

...DURING WORLD WAR TWO, I KNEW SOME DUMB SCHMUCK WHO GOT CIRCUMCIZED (AS AN ADULT!) AND THEN WENT ON LEAVE TO SCREW SOME HOOKER BEFORE THE SURGERY HEALED!!! WHAT A STUPID BASTARD! HE CAUGHT THE GOD-DAMNDEST CASE OF VD YOU EVER SAW!!!

HEY! WHY ARE YOU CRINGING? WHATTAYOU, A PUSSY???

MORE CRAP TO PROOF-READ.

GRAND-MASTER OF GIRL-WATCHING.

♫ ZUM ZUM ZUM...

AAH, YES... THE GLORY OF NATURE AT ITS VERY BEST... ≥HUBBA HUBBA!!!≤

COVER GAL!

LOVING SOUL WHO REVELLED IN THE DIVERSITY OF THE INDIVIDUAL. OY, YOU SHOULDA SEEN THE FUNERAL!!!

YO. REST IN PEACE AN' SHIT!!!

ELECTRIC MAYHEM

FOR HIS KICKASS INKS ON BOOKS LIKE LEGION OF SUPER-HEROES, THE INCREDIBLE HULK AND THE TOTALLY EFFIN' EXCELLENT TOMB OF DRACULA, JACK DESERVES A STATUE IN HIS HONOR BUT THAT AIN'T GONNA HAPPEN.

BESIDES, WHO WANTS TO SPEND ETERNITY COVERED IN PIGEON-SHIT???...

THE BULLPEN MISSES YA, OLD WHITE-HAIR. NO ONE TOLD TY COBB STORIES LIKE YOU DID. HOPE YOU'RE HANGIN' WITH MANTLE. — MUCH LOVE, EL BUNCHO.

WITH ALL DUE RESPECT TO JACK ABEL, WE INTERRUPT THESE MEMORIES TO SALUTE ANOTHER FALLEN COMRADE... A MAN WHOSE TALENTS WERE AT LEAST THE EQUAL OF THE LATE MR. ABEL...

A TRIBUTE TO GARY MICHAELS

BY *Mark* EVANIER

ILLUSTRATED BY *Aragonés*

LETTERING BY STAN SAKAI

THE YEAR WAS *1965* AND, IN MY OLD NEIGHBORHOOD, THE COMIC BOOK FANS ENGAGED IN ONLY THE MOST LOFTY AND ENLIGHTENED DEBATE...

MARVELS SUCK!

DC BITES!

THE DC ARTISTS ARE THE WORST!

DC RULES!

OH YEAH? *MARVEL* RULES!

THE BIGGEST MARVELITE IN TOWN WAS A KID NAMED *KEVIN.* ONE DAY, KEVIN WENT TO THE NEWSSTAND AND FOUND A COMIC THAT CHANGED HIS LIFE...

SOMEONE NEW DRAWING IRON MAN?

THE COMIC WAS *TALES OF SUSPENSE #73* (JAN., 1966) AND IT FEATURED THE FIRST *IRON MAN* STORY DRAWN BY THE TEAM OF ADAM AUSTIN AND GARY MICHAELS. KEVIN WAS IN LOVE...

THIS...

...IS THE BEST ART *EVER* IN A COMIC BOOK!

AS FAR AS HE WAS CONCERNED, THE "WHICH COMPANY RULES" ARGUMENT WAS SETTLED...

LOOK AT THIS!

BEST ART EVER!

BETTER THAN ANY LOUSY DC GUYS!

FOR WEEKS, KEVIN WAS INSUFFERABLE ON THE SUBJECT. THEN, ONE DAY, AN ITEM IN A FANZINE SHATTERED HIS WORLD...

OH, KEVIN...WE JUST FOUND OUT SOMETHING...

WHAT?

"ADAM AUSTIN" IS REALLY *GENE COLAN!* "GARY MICHAELS" IS A PEN NAME FOR *JACK ABEL!*

THEY'RE TWO DC ARTISTS!

NO! NO!

I'D BETTER PHONE NEW YORK! I MUST WARN STAN!

IT SHATTERED EVERYTHING THE YOUNG LAD BELIEVED IN. THE NEXT DAY, HE SOLD OFF EVERY COMIC BOOK HE OWNED...

STAN...HOW COULD YOU DO THIS TO ME?

COMICS SALE

YES, "GARY MICHAELS" WAS ACTUALLY JACK ABEL. HIS ACCOMPLISHMENTS WERE MANY, BUT I WILL ALWAYS BE GRATEFUL TO HIM FOR ONE ABOVE ALL... HE CAUSED KEVIN TO SHUT THE HELL UP.

WE MISS YOU, JACK!

Mark, SERGIO & STAN

"WHEN I WAS A KID BACK IN THE 60'S, I WAS A BIG COMIC BOOK FAN. I FIRST NOTICED *JACK ABEL'S* WORK IN *TALES OF SUSPENSE*, INKING *GENE COLAN'S* PENCILS ON *THE INVINCIBLE IRON MAN*. HE WAS USING A NOM DE PLUME AT THE TIME FOR BUSINESS REASONS. BUT IN A FEW MONTHS I SAW HIS REAL NAME IN THE CREDITS FOR *IRON MAN* AND LATER STILL IN THE THE *SUPERMAN* FAMILY OF TITLES."

"I PROBABLY ALSO SAW HIS WORK ON *GUNNER AND SARGE*, A WAR SERIES I READ INFREQUENTLY. THOSE STORIES USUALLY DIDN'T HAVE CREDITS, SO I DIDN'T KNOW WHO DID THEM AT THE TIME. THE POINT IS, WHENEVER I SAW JACK'S PENCILING OR INKING, I ENJOYED IT."

"I WAS AN ASPIRING CARTOONIST MYSELF, SO I PICKED UP ON HOW THINGS WERE DRAWN IN THE COMICS. I ESPECIALLY LIKED THE WAY JACK INKED LEAVES ON TREES. I THOUGHT THEY LOOKED PARTICULARLY REAL. SO I TRIED TO DRAW TREES THAT WAY."

"YEARS LATER, WHEN I FIRST STARTED TO WORK FOR *MARVEL COMICS*, I MET JACK AND STARTED INKING BACKGROUNDS FOR HIM OCCASIONALLY. THAT INCLUDED, OF COURSE, TREES."

NICE TREES, BUB.

MY BARK IS BETTER THAN MY BITE.

"OVER THE YEARS I LEARNED A LOT ABOUT INKING FROM JACK. I ALSO LEARNED ABOUT A LOT OF OTHER INTERESTING SUBJECTS FROM HIM, ESPECIALLY WHEN A BUNCH OF US WOULD HAVE LUNCH AT A LOCAL DINER."

...DURING DiMAGGIO'S HITTING STREAK...

"WHENEVER I THINK OF JACK, A SMILE COMES TO MY FACE. I REMEMBER THE TALKS WE HAD AND THE LAUGHS WE SHARED. I'M GLAD I GOT TO KNOW HIM AND I'LL SURE MISS HIM."
— JOE ALBELO

♪ MONA LISA, MONA LISA, MEN HAVE NAMED YOU... ♪

joe abelo

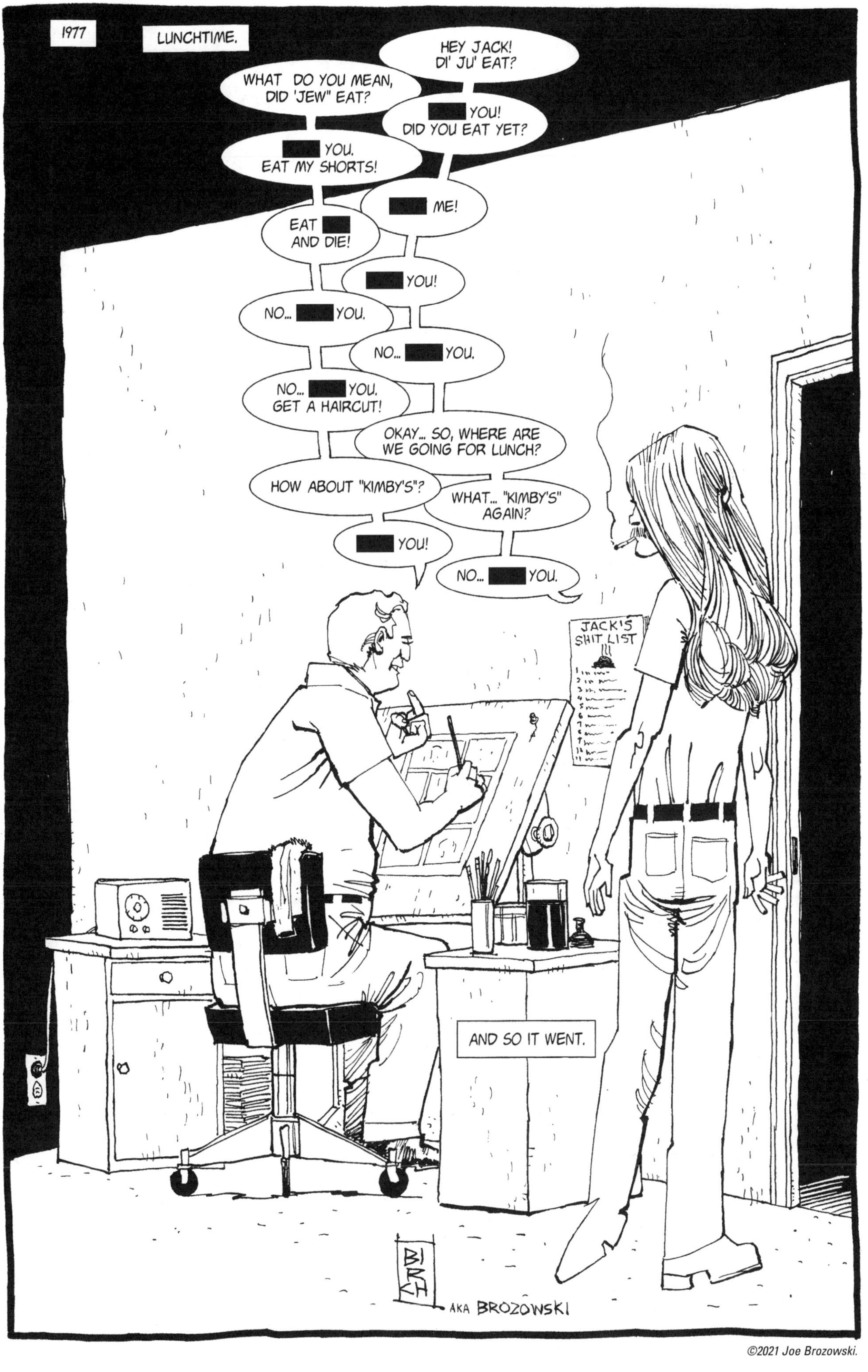
1977
LUNCHTIME.
HEY JACK! DI' JU' EAT?
WHAT DO YOU MEAN, DID 'JEW" EAT?
[redacted] YOU! DID YOU EAT YET?
[redacted] YOU. EAT MY SHORTS!
[redacted] ME!
EAT [redacted] AND DIE!
[redacted] YOU!
NO... [redacted] YOU.
NO... [redacted] YOU.
NO... [redacted] YOU. GET A HAIRCUT!
OKAY... SO, WHERE ARE WE GOING FOR LUNCH?
HOW ABOUT "KIMBY'S"?
WHAT... "KIMBY'S" AGAIN?
[redacted] YOU!
NO... [redacted] YOU.
JACK'S SHIT LIST
AND SO IT WENT.
BIRCH
AKA BROZOWSKI

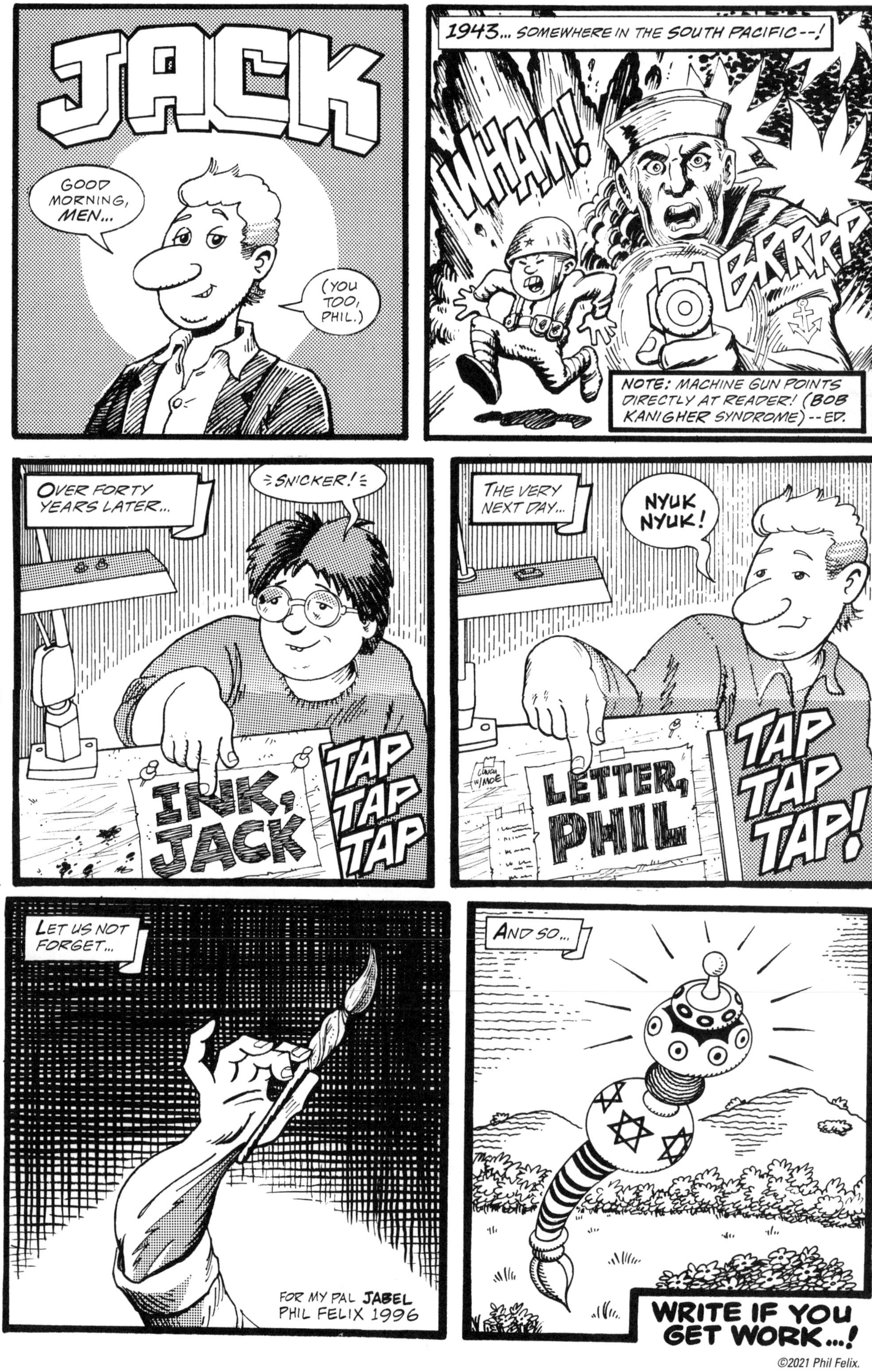
JACK
GOOD MORNING, MEN...
(YOU TOO, PHIL.)
1943... SOMEWHERE IN THE SOUTH PACIFIC--!
WHAM!
BRRRP
NOTE: MACHINE GUN POINTS DIRECTLY AT READER! (BOB KANIGHER SYNDROME) --ED.
OVER FORTY YEARS LATER...
SNICKER!
INK, JACK
TAP TAP TAP
THE VERY NEXT DAY...
NYUK NYUK!
LETTER, PHIL
TAP TAP TAP!
LET US NOT FORGET...
FOR MY PAL JABEL
PHIL FELIX 1996
AND SO...
WRITE IF YOU GET WORK...!

JACK ABEL

JACK...ABLE ABEL. SILVER HAIRED, SILVER TONGUED RACONTEUR, SLICK MASTER EMBELLISHER OF THE COMICS PAGE, WOULD NO DOUBT BE EMBARRASSED AND AMAZED THAT HIS PASSING WOULD GIVE CAUSE FOR THIS BOOK'S TRIBUTE. HE WAS ALWAYS MODEST AND SELF-EFFACING ABOUT HIS ABILITIES AS AN ARTIST, BUT IN A HUMOROUS MANNER. HE WAS WARMLY REGARDED AND GREATLY RESPECTED BY HIS PEERS TO A DEGREE I BELIEVE HE WAS FOR THE MOST PART UNAWARE.

FOR SOME YEARS JACK HELD OFFICE SPACE AND COURT AT NEAL ADAM'S OLD STUDIO IN MIDTOWN MANHATTAN WHICH WAS A KIND OF STOPOVER FOR ARTISTS AND WRITERS AFTER BUSINESS HOURS. FREE COFFEE, FREE GOSSIP AND A CHANCE TO UNWIND BEFORE HEADING HOME. AND JACK. HIS STORIES AND JOKES. HIS FAMOUS SH*T LIST TO PERUSE DETAILING WITH WRY HUMOR THOSE PEOPLE AND THINGS HE TOOK EXCEPTION TO. JACK. ALWAYS WILLING TO PUT DOWN PEN OR BRUSH FOR A NIP DOWNSTAIRS TO EVERYBODY'S FAVORITE IRISH PUB, P.J.'S, FOR A GLASS OR TWO.

IT WOULD BE TRITE BUT NONETHELESS TRUE TO SAY THAT JACK WILL BE SORELY MISSED BY THE INDUSTRY AND FRIENDS HE ENRICHED BY HIS PRESENCE.

LOVE YOU, JACK—

GRAY MORROW

My Last Conversation With Jack.

by Kyle Baker

I was back in town on a visit. I'd moved away years ago.

"Hey Jack."

No answer. I sat down to work.

"I'm a little board."

"You know, I didn't recognize you with the hair."

I didn't have the heart to tell him he'd said the same thing to me the day before.

"How's it goin', Jack?"

"Not so good."

"You'll be okay."

"I had another stroke."

"You told me."

He'd told me yesterday. And he'd told me a month before that, the last time I was in town.

"I did, huh? I forget things now. I'm pretty bad off."

"You told me. I heard. But you're better, things are looking up!"

"I still can't— I'm not what I was."

"Yes, but look how far you've come! You're walking, you went through the physical therapy—"

"Physical therapy's the worst."

"You told me. And you made it! Not many guys could come back the way you've done! You'll be great! You're lucky you're—"

"GOD DAMN IT NO! I'm sick of everybody telling me how lucky I am! I don't feel lucky! I feel like shit! Everybody keeps telling me, lucky, lucky—Bullshit! I'm not lucky, it's terrible what's happened to me!"

"Fine Jack. It's terrible. You're right."

I guess I was rude to him, but I'd heard that damn depressing story three times already, and I didn't see the point of sitting sympathetically through it again when he wasn't even going to remember it. I wanted to tell him, you're here now, you're alive now, it's all any of us have. None of our lives turn out the way we wanted, we have to be happy with whatever we get. I wanted to tell him, but I figured he'd just yell at me again. He wouldn't get it.

"You know, after all these years of marriage...I still find my wife to be the sexiest woman in the world...Does that seem sick to you?"

"I think it's wonderful, Jack."

view from the willy b.

Cannon Street, the Lower East Side of New York City, 1941. It's already hot and sticky on this mid-July morning. White smoke curls from the funnel of a passing tug down at the east end of this tenement-lined street, where it meets the river. In harsh contrast to the hazy blue sky above the water looms the mighty steel and concrete framework of the Williamsburg Bridge.

Stickball. In the era, New York's street game of choice. Dirty-faced kids from different backgrounds, but with the same "Baldy Bean" summer haircuts, scrapped knees, and baloney-skin-thin sneakers, wage passionate contests that rival any World Series—every day. Laundry waves from the fire escapes like pennants from a slightly more famous façade in the Bronx. The voices of women loudly discussing the injustice of meat prices at the local delicatessen across great distances out of open windows may as well be the cheering and jeering of ardent fans. Taxi and truck horns blare like cow calls from the bleachers. A pitcher from Essex Street nervously rolls a well-worn red rubber ball, known as a Spaldeen or Pinky, through his fingers. And with good reason. The best slugger on the Lower East Side is twisting Mom's old discarded mop handle, wrapped with black, gummy, cloth tape, in his fists as he strides to the sewer cap. Young Jackie Abel eases into his stance. Legs wide apart, hands held high and back, chin nearly resting on his left shoulder. Relaxed. Just like his idol, Joe D.

Almost reluctantly, the pitcher releases the ball. Instantly, Jackie's crystal blue eyes recognize it. *His* pitch. He effortlessly triggers his swing. Minimal stride, hips ahead of hands, head down, lots of wrist. Power—the union of strength, speed, and timing. After the initial, delicious *"THWOP"* of pine distorting rubber, it is as if the city falls silent. The combatants crane their necks and roll their wide eyes to follow the path of the little red rocket. A ball belted the distance between three sewer covers is considered a colossal wallop, but this Ruthian blast may be the rare one that reaches the corner. Can it still be rising? Holee! It might even make the river! Then, the seemingly impossible happens. Something that no one there that day would ever forget, no matter how old they might grow. As the rosy comet finally begins its downward arc, it strikes the top of a girder on the lower section of the bridge. It ricochets around a bit before hopping down to the next level, dancing along, and hopping down again. All of Cannon Street holds its breath, waiting for the tiny orb to culminate the spectacle with a daring Brodie into the East River. Refusing at the last possible instant, however, it wedges instead in a triangular intersection of rivet-lined steel. The slack-jawed silence holds a second longer before being shattered by exploding clouds of pigeons, taking to the air from rooftops like celebratory fireworks. Only then does the din of the city return. Boys jump and howl and throw their hats, then everyone runs to tell someone who wasn't there. But the ball stays. Oh, how it stayed.

There it remained, looking down like a sentinel, as a boy turned all too quickly into a man. It saw Jackie claim

to be older than he was in order to enlist in the Navy, and not miss World War II. It watched as he endured a brutally frigid boot camp in Samson, N.Y. It waited while he went overseas and defended his country, so very far from those carefree days of stickball. While he was away, it sadly looked on as Cannon Street itself was plowed under to make room for a housing project. Would nothing be the same when he returned?

Jack's heart would be. It saw him come home to have his "cup of coffee" with the St. Louis Cardinals, and barely miss making the team. It watched him pursue his other passion—art—and graduate from the Cartoonists and Illustrators School. The ball was there when he married his sweetheart, his treasured Adele.

It watched Jack perfect his craft and work for all of the major companies, and with all the legendary names of comic art. It was there as he thrilled in all those Yankee championships, too. It faded a shade on the day the Bambino died, glowed in salute when DiMaggio retired, and pulsed with excitement when Mantle first came up. It witnessed Jack's pride and joy when his beloved children, Gary and Randy, were born. It was there while he helped to build Marvel Comics into the giant of the industry and amass a body of work that would influence generations of professionals to come. It saw Jack amass something else, too. Something more truly the measure of a man. An army of friends who loved him for all of the wonderful things he was: open, honest, compassionate, humorous, thoughtful, generous, and just... *interested.* Interested in you, in new things, in everything. No generation gap with Jack. No gaps at all.

That little red ball was there for the difficult

Below: *Portrait of Jack Abel by fellow one-time Continuity associate Joe Rubinstein.*

Illustration ©2021 Joe Rubinstein.

times, too. It withstood wind and rain as Jack suffered the first of his strokes. Blessed with graceful dexterity of hand, keen intellect, photographic memory, and tremendous strength and pride, he now fought daily to regain what had always come so naturally. It watched him as he bounced nearly all the way back. Although his sharp mind and astounding memory returned fully, his deft and powerful hand, to a degree, did not. Closing the book on his 30-year career as a top freelancer, Jack took an office job at Marvel as an assistant editor, and later as proofreader. On occasion, he even played softball on the company team, displaying some of the old skills. He still drew every day, too, but, as time wore on, more for the love of it and for his friends than for a living. But the things that made Jack *Jack* remained a constant, and for the next decade and more, he was a big part of what made Marvel so *marvelous*.

Then the ball nearly fell. A second severe stroke clouded his mind and damaged his formidable heart. The doctors conferred, and the scenario was written. It was agreed that the end of the story was at hand. But those who knew Jack can testify that for all of his wonderful traits, he could at times be, well... *stubborn*. This was one of those times.

In an industry where courage, strength, character and determina-

Right inset: *Photo collage of New York City's Williamsburg Bridge by B. Abbott.* **Below:** *Portrait of Jack Abel by Sal Buscema.*

You'll be missed, Jack!

tion of a fictitious nature are written about daily, it is amazing how many don't recognize it when these traits tower before them in reality. How Jack staged a two-out, bottom-nine rally once again, no one will ever know. How he kept his sense of humor while suffering from the realization of who he was to who he had become, no one will ever know. How he struggled to the

office, through all types of weather, in a body which had all but abandoned him, no one will ever know. But Jack knew. He knew he loved comics, and the people who made them.

And so the ball did not fall. And it did not witness only suffering in this time. These extra innings were a particularly sweet time for Jack. He had been saved for one last glory, one last jubilation. It was now that Jack would meet his granddaughter, a fresh little life that breathed such infinite delight into his now waning one—Kelly.

In 1996, Jack left us. Fittingly, it was at his post, still drawing a little bit each day, at the company he helped to build, in the industry he loved. And what of the red rubber ball? Is it is still at its post, looking down on us from the Willy B.? Well, when I close my eyes, I can see it as clear as day. And I can see the twinkling of crystal blue eyes, too. I see my friend Jack.

— **J. Morelli**

paying tribute to jack abel

a brief interview with compiler rick parker

To give us the full story behind this Jack Abel tribute, CBA Bullpen thought it best to get a short interview—conducted via e-mail in February and March, 2004—from longtime former Marvel staffer and cartoonist extraordinaire, Rick Parker, the gent who first put all of these contributions together back in 1996. After reviewing all the lovely testimonials and heartfelt remembrances—sincere as they are—your editor was puzzled: Just how did the compiler (our pal Parker) plan in '96 to see the tribute book published?

CBA Bullpen: *Where are you originally from, Rick, and when were you born?*
Rick Parker: I was born in Miami, Florida, in 1946, and I grew up in Savannah, Georgia.
Bullpen: *When did you get interested in comics?*
Rick: My grandmother used to read me the funny pages when I was little.
Bullpen: *Growing up, what were your favorite books?*
Rick: I liked *Uncle Scrooge*, EC's horror comics, and the early *MAD* comics and magazines. I also loved the comics devoted to Walt Disney's animated films, and other animated cartoons like *Tom and Jerry*, *Popeye*, *Road Runner*, *Bugs Bunny* and *Elmer Fudd*, etc.
Bullpen: *When did you first consider a career in art? (Please describe when you started drawing, if you drew your own comics, and dreams and aspirations)*
Rick: I was fascinated from the very beginning by drawing and illustration. I enjoyed coloring and drawing, and wanted to be an artist "when I grew up." My father used to give me—when I was about six or seven—the cardboard laundered shirts used to be packed in after they were pressed. We always had a lot of paper and pencils around the house and I seemed to have plenty of time on my hands to draw. I saw artwork by Wally Wood and Jack Davis, and thought that I might do something like that when I got older.
Bullpen: *Were you involved in comics fandom?*
Rick: No, I never collected comic books or joined any clubs, but I did try to see every horror movie I could and dressed up on Halloween every year.
Bullpen: *How did you get a job in the field?*
Rick: I met a girl—June Braverman—who was a freelance letterer for Marvel when we were both in graduate school at the Pratt Institute, in 1973, in New York City. She took me up to the offices at 575 Madison Avenue and introduced me to some of the people there. I thought it seemed like a nice place to work if I ever needed a job. About three years later, I answered an ad in *The New York Times* and was hired by [Marvel bullpenner] Danny Crespi to do lettering corrections on staff.
Bullpen: *When did you first meet Jack Abel?*
Rick: It was after Jack came to Marvel to work as a proofreader. I think it was about 1981 or thereabouts, before Marvel relocated to 28th Street in '82.

Bullpen: *What does Jack mean to you?*
Rick: Like many others before and after me, I instantly fell under Jack's spell because of his basic humanity and good-heartedness. As mentioned by others in this tribute, his warmth, wit, charm, sense of humor, encyclopedic mind, and seemingly boundless knowledge of practically everything—coupled with his ability as a raconteur and experiences in the comics business and familiarity with its fascinating practitioners—made his company impossible to resist. I simply could not get enough of him.
Bullpen: *What was the Marvel Bullpen like?*
Rick: When I started in 1977, it was a relatively small and convivial kind of place where everyone wished you a good weekend

Above: *Poor Rick Parker meets his fate. This is what the wise-guy artist sent us when we asked for a portrait from Rick.*

Below: *Sample of Rick Parker's art from his memorable stint on the Marvel comic book,* Beavis and Butt-Head. *Courtesy of the artist.*

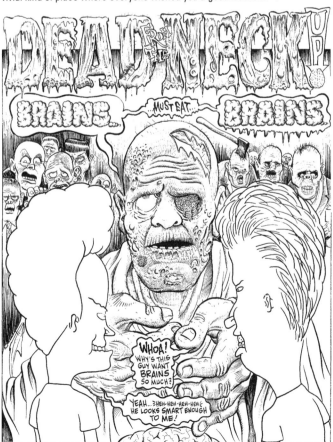

Beavis and Butt-Head ©2021 Viacom International, Inc.

rick parker

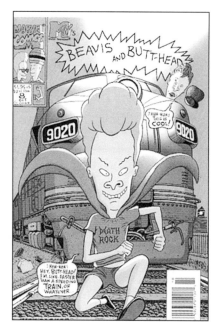

when you left on Friday. "Big John" Verpoorten was the man in charge in those days and he assigned all the artwork. Mary McPherran handled secretarial. Marie Severin and George Roussos oversaw the coloring. John Tartaglione was in charge of art corrections. Danny Crespi was the production manager and handled cover lettering, and Morrie Kuramoto did paste-ups and mechanicals. Nora Maclin set up the covers. Jim Novak and I took care of the lettering corrections. Stu Schwartzburg shot the stats. Stan "somebody-or-other" was their typesetter. Stan Lee was in his office down the hall and Archie Goodwin, Len Wein, Sol Brodsky, Roy Thomas, Marv Wolfman, Rick Marschall, and a few others handled editorial. Herb Trimpe and Don McGregor came in and out a lot, and we all loved seeing those two.

Bullpen: *Please describe your work in comics.*

Rick: I started out on staff doing lettering corrections and lettered practically every title they published at one time or another, and that continued for my first 15 years there. I lettered the *Hulk* and both the Sunday and daily *Spider-Man* newspaper strips, and a lot of the early *Epic Illustrated* material. I began doing a few pieces of artwork about 1984, and I got my big break when assignment as artist for *Beavis and Butt-Head* came along in 1993.

Bullpen: *How did you hear about Jack's death and how did it affect you?*

Rick: I knew that Jack's health was on the decline and was still devastated when he died. I always knew there would be no one else like him again in my life and tried to see as much of him when I could.

Bullpen: *When did the idea of a tribute comic book come up?*

Rick: After his death, I soon realized everyone I met had a Jack Abel story, and these were talented creative people. Naturally, I wanted to coax them into putting these tales down on paper and I soon realized they were a lot more than just Jack Abel stories. I tried to find out who he had been buddies with and contact every one I could. I'm sure I missed many, but I did what I could.

Bullpen: *Did you have a specific plan to see the tribute book published? And what happened?*

Rick: Naive person that I am, I naturally assumed Marvel or DC would publish it. I thought it would provide some great insights into the comic art business and the people who worked there. I thought they might realize the public rela-

tions value or something like that. Terry Stewart of Marvel declined, but promised $10,000 toward publishing costs. I wish I'd taken a check right there on the spot.

Emboldened by Terry's generous offer, I went up to see Paul Levitz at DC Comics (where Jack had worked for many years), but Paul didn't think it was the right thing for DC to do, apparently. He did make a few helpful suggestions about who to approach concerning publishing (and I now wish I had taken notes). Reality set in. I had been devoting quite a bit of time to this endeavor. My contract with Marvel had just been cancelled around then. Marvel was cutting way back on publishing. Hundreds were losing their jobs and hitting the streets, so I reluctantly turned my attention to becoming a free-lancer again in order to try and support my young family. The project languished after that for a very long time. Finally I photocopied the whole batch of pages and forwarded copies to Adele Abel, Jack's widow.

Bullpen: *Why were some of the pages' dimensions comic-book size and others regular letter-size? What was to be the original format?*

Rick: I let people work at a size that is comfortable to them.

Bullpen: *What do you think of the final results?*

Rick: I knew one day someone would want the material. It's funny now how much has changed in the comic art world. That world described so well by the contributors doesn't exist anymore. It's a pleasant, romantic, and fading memory. I'm very thankful that so many talented artists gave their valuable time (and all for no compensation) to this unusual project and I'm very pleased with their work. I'll bet Jack would be, too.

Bullpen: *How long did you work on staff at Marvel? What were the circumstances behind you leaving the company?*

Rick: I was on staff from 1977 until they cancelled my contract in '96, when they essentially lost interest in publishing and cancelled all licensed material.

Bullpen: *What have you done since working at Marvel and what's up today?*

Rick: I've illustrated quite a few stories for DC's *Big Book* series. I did some writing and drawing for the *Kid Death and Fluffy* comic from Event. I contributed quite a bit of material to *Harpoon*, a full-color humor magazine of political and social satire. I drew a few covers for *Cracked* and learned computer coloring and lettering. I illustrated several children's books that we are still trying to get published. Currently, I'm freelancing illustration work and illustrating *The Road To Hell,* a new creation by Dwayne McDuffy and Matt Wayne.

Bullpen: *Do you miss Jack? What would you say his greatest contribution to comics was? How should he be remembered?*

Rick: I believe Jack was a great humanitarian. I think he would have been flattered that all his buddies took the time to do those great pages and I'm positive that he would have gone over the finished product with a fine-toothed comb, and let me know the details concerning each error he found there. If only I was to be that lucky!

Bullpen: *What would you like to be doing in the future? Any ideas for a* magnum opus?

Rick: I would like to continue to write and illustrate children's books and do as much drawing as I can. I'm gearing up for a big autobiographical thing someday soon. I am a big admirer of the work of R. Crumb. He has shown us all the way.

becton on abel

BASEBALL… Especially the New York Yankees. Regardless of who was wearing those pinstripes, they were Jack's demigods. Anyone tryong to compare any other team's players — especially the Brooklyn Dodgers — whew!

GOLF… Every weekend, if the weather was good, he'd drag his butt over to the local golf course, hit a little white ball… and then chase it! *Why?*

POKER… Jack had a small clique of buddies — myself included — who would play cards. I usually lost. He'd always, at least, break even. The first time I played cards with Jack, he pulled a straight flush, sitting in his own chair, in his own apartment. Hell, I even think he was the *dealer!* The old bastard!

OLD FILMS… Well, they were old to me! Jack would recall seeing them like they were new, like those with his favorite actress, Alice Faye. He told me once how, when being surveyed on who was his favorite actor, he replied, "George Raft!" just for a goof!

JACK + ADELE

Becton 016

Above: *Portrait of a storyteller. Jack Abel as remembered by James Fry.*

Below: *Jim Salicrup cartoon of the artist at rest. Jack Abel at his post.*

©2021 Jim Salicrup.

SALICRUP

Jack Abel: CBA All-Star!

COMIC BOOK ARTIST
ALL★STARS

MARVEL/DC
PENCILER
& INKER

JACK ABEL

003-4

JACK ABEL
PENCILER • INKER
BORN: 7/15/27 • DIED: 3/6/96
BIRTHPLACE: BROOKLYN, NEW YORK
CARTOONISTS & ILLUSTRATORS SCHOOL ('51)

J.A. LEARNED HIS INKING TECHNIQUE FROM HIS TEACHER & LIFE-LONG INFLUENCE JERRY "THE JOKER" ROBINSON!

MEMORABLE WORK:

CAPTAIN HUNTER
DC COMICS

PROFESSIONAL COMIC BOOK/STRIP ART HIGHLIGHTS

YEARS	PUBLISHER	FEATURES/GENRES
1950	VICTOR FOX	Blue Beetle
Early 50s	ST. JOHN'S	Romance, horror strips
1952-53	FICTION HOUSE	Horror strips
1952-56	MARVEL COMICS	Horror, Western strips
1956-70	DC COMICS	Innumerable strips — pencils & inks — for editor Robert Kanigher's war titles: Our Army At War, Our Fighting Forces, All-American Men of War, Star Spangled War Stories, and G.I. Combat. Also worked on Sea Devils, Adventure Comics (Legion of Superheroes, Supergirl), Challengers of the Unknown, etc.
1966	MARVEL COMICS	As "Gary Michaels," inked Tales of Suspense (Iron Man),
1967	TOWER	T.H.U.N.D.E.R. Agents (NoMan)
Early '70s	WOOD STUDIOS	over Gene Colan ("Adam Austin") pencils
'70s-'90s	MARVEL COMICS	Worked on Wallace Wood's Overseas Weekly newspaper strips, Sally Forth and Shattuck, as well as other comic book assignments as freelancer working out of Woody's studio. You name it, Jack inked almost every title at one time or another at the House of Ideas. Also worked on-staff as proofreader. Memorable work includes Amazing Adventures (Killraven), The Avengers, Gunhawks, Godzilla, Hulk, Iron Man, Ka-Zar, Master of Kung Fu, Red Wolf, and Tomb of Dracula
'70s-'80s	DC COMICS	Enormous volume of work during Jack's second tenure as freelancer, including DC Comics Presents, Firestorm, Flash, Freedom Fighters, Justice League of America, Karate Kid, Superboy, Teen Titans
1971	SKYWALD	The Heap
1975	ATLAS/SEABOARD	The Brute

Captain Hunter ©2004 DC Comics

Collect 'em All!

Trading card data compiled with reference to Who's Who of American Comic Books, 1st edition.

COMIC BOOK ARTIST™ BULLPEN was published between 2003–04 by RetroHouse Press, c/o Jon B. Cooke, P.O. Box 601, West Kingston, R.I. 02892 USA. Jon B. Cooke, Editor. Vol. 1, #3/4, Feb.–Mar. 2004.

"Abelisms": The Art of Jack-Speak

NIGHT CLUB

One of Jack Abel's most endearing habits was to draw up visual puns in cartoon form to share with his co-workers. Rick Parker kindly contributed the actual Abel sketch at left. Below, excerpted from his submission within, cartoonist Kyle Baker recalls one such instance. Left ©2021 the estate of Jack Abel. Below ©2021 Kyle Baker.

"I'm a little board."

Special thanks to Adele, Gary & Randi Abel for their participation & approval!

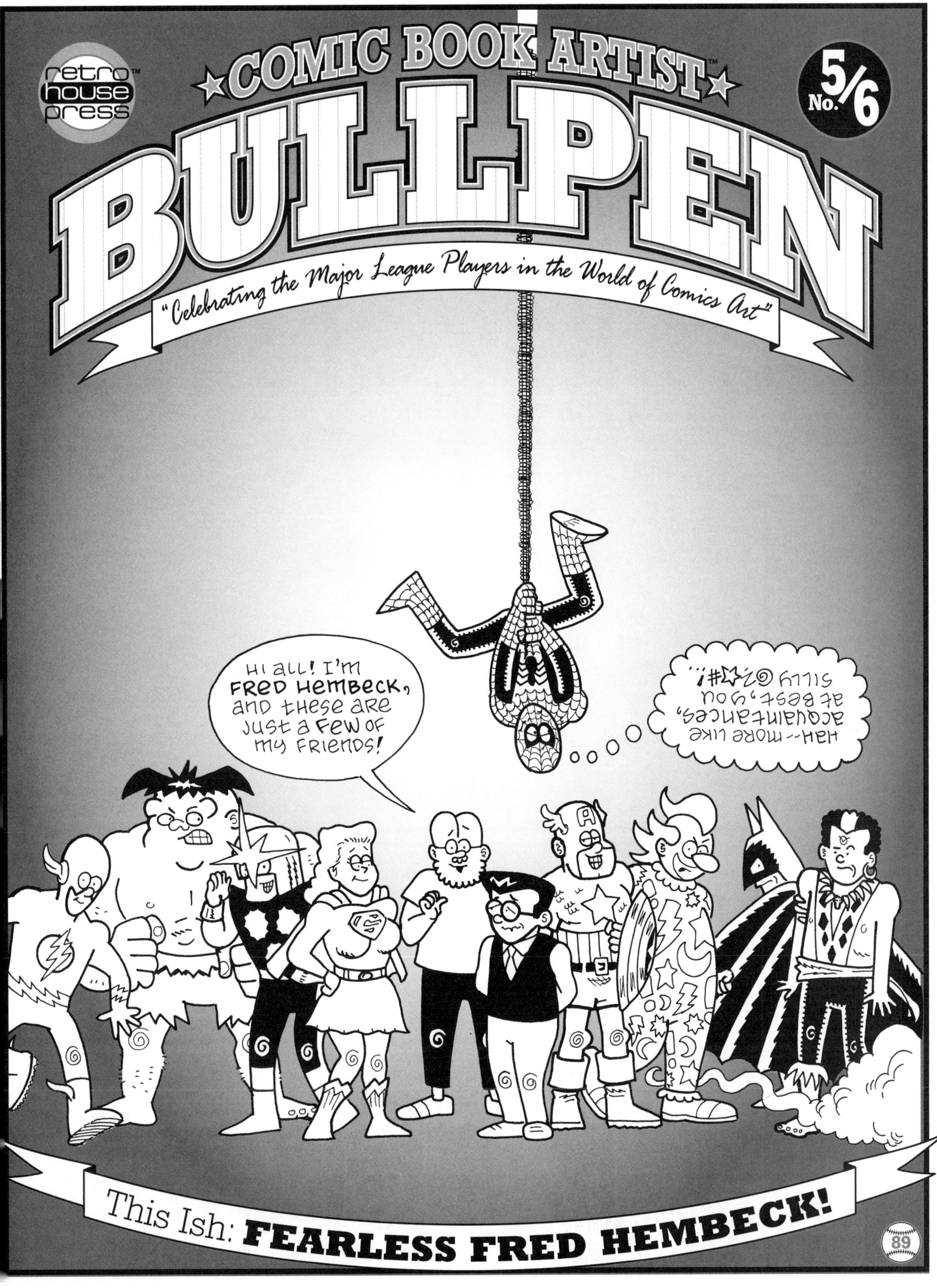

retro house press
COMIC BOOK ARTIST
BULLPEN
No. 5/6
"Celebrating the Major League Players in the World of Comics Art"
Hi all! I'm FRED HEMBECK, and these are just a FEW of my friends!
HAH--MORE LIKE ACQUAINTANCES, AT BEST, YOU SILLY @Z☆#!..
This Ish: FEARLESS FRED HEMBECK!

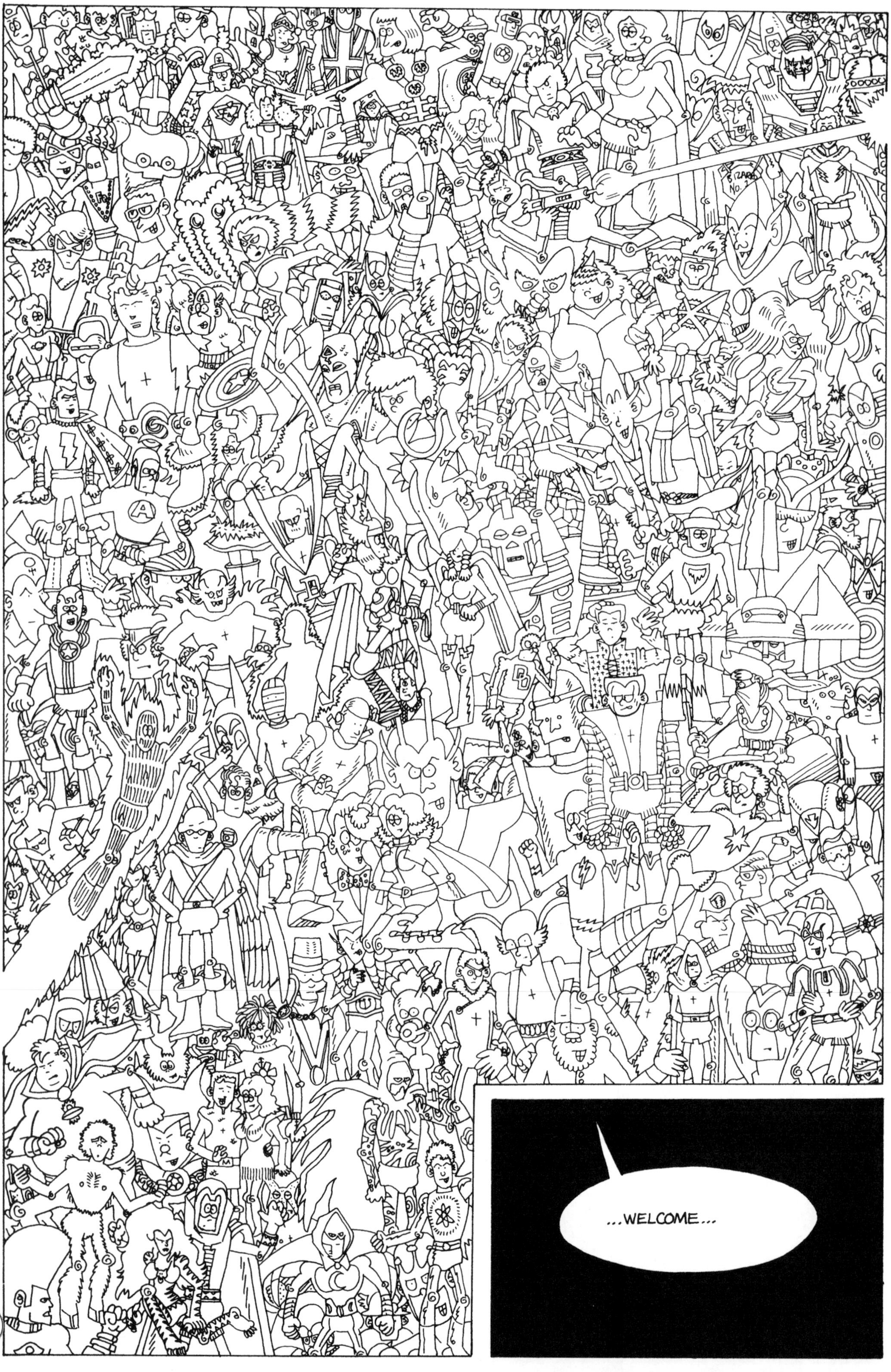
...WELCOME...

★COMIC BOOK ARTIST★
BULLPEN
HEMBECK

There's simply no doubt about it: Fred Hembeck is a *bone fide* institution in American comic books. He's been an aficionado, a player, an anecdotal historian (if ever there was such a thing), and the best example of a fan professional ever to come along in this field. How many other funnybook creators have actual comics named for—and starring!—themselves? Hembeck is renowned not only as a cartoonist of some pretty damn funny material; he's also a recognizable, long-running character within his work, wooly beard, helmet o' hair, 'n' all!

Needless to say, I've been long fascinated with Fred's career because of his unique stature in this wacky biz, so this retrospective is quite overdue. And, regardless of his long-running—and very welcome—contributions to my other magazine, *Comic Book Artist* (where he has shared "Dateline: @*!?#" strips since our second issue, back in 1998), I fervently believe that the cartoonist's accomplishments beg closer examination. Not only is the guy's work intelligent, funny, and just plain solidly entertaining, but Fred has also got an insightful grasp on the history of comics, one that goes beyond super-heroes, and into appreciation for other genres, ones too often neglected and dismissed. His is an important voice in our medium.

On a personal note, I gotta confess I love Hembeck not just because he puts up with my insufferable demands to send a new strip under ungodly deadlines, but because—as I

learned when conducting the following interview (and by mirroring myself in his significant body of work since that time)—the dude loves so much of the strange and eclectic in comics and in popular culture as yours truly. Maybe it's because we both grew up in the great Empire State (Fred on Long Island, myself in Westchester County), exposed to the same media… *Soupy Sales, Wonderama, Million Dollar Movie,* the Miracle Mets, Chuck McCann… and we never lost our respective affections for those great comics of our youth, the ones outside the DC and Marvel super-hero pantheons. Who knew there was another hapless fan out there as devoted as I to the delights of Bob Bolling's *Adventures of Little Archie*? Or the bizarre super-heroics of Joe Simon's Harvey Comics "Thriller" line of in the mid-'60s? Or Al Wiseman's superbly artful take on *Dennis the Menace*? Plus the Mighty Hembeck also digs *Saturday Night Live,* Steve Ditko, *National Lampoon, Herbie,* underground comix, Alan Moore, *American Flagg!,* and that winner of *FOOM*'s create-a-character contest, the unforgettable Humus Sapiens! Fred is a kindred spirit of my geek within.

Natch, we hope you enjoy this long overdue glimpse into the life and work of our good friend, and be sure to check out Fred's wonderful website, <www.hembeck.com>, where you'll find an astonishing array of rarely-seen material.

— **The editor.**

HEMBECK

What to say about Fred George Hembeck? Certainly the cartoonist has created his own unique niche in the comics world, going so far as making his own bearded caricature a recognizable funnybook character alongside any number of Spandex-clad four-color heroes. He may also be as close to a professional comic-book fan as they get, given the content of Fred's innumerable "Dateline" strips over the decades. So here's hoping we give the indomitable Hembeck (who has been a part of the CBA family since 1998) his proper due. This interview was conducted on January 8, 2004, and Fred copy-edited the final transcript.

CBA Bullpen: *Where are you originally from, Fred?*
Fred Hembeck: I grew up on Long Island, in a small town called Yaphank. It's about 60 miles out from New York City, in a rural part of Long Island. I lived there for my first 21 years.
Bullpen: *Do you have any brothers or sisters?*
Fred: No, I'm an only child.
Bullpen: *What's the ethnicity of the name Hembeck?*
Fred: German.
Bullpen: *Does it mean anything?*
Fred: Not that I know of. I just know there aren't very many of them in this country, maybe two or three. It's a very obscure name. There are very few relatives on this side of the Atlantic.
Bullpen: *What's your mother's ethnic background?*
Fred: Scotch/Irish, but she was born in this country. Baker was her last name. My dad was born in Germany and came over in the early 1920s.
Bullpen: *Did he speak with a thick accent?*
Fred: Yes, pretty much. It was still an accent by the time he was an older guy. He was one of about seven or eight children, but only two of them ever made it over to this side of the world. His sister lived in New Jersey, so that's why I don't have any real relatives in the U.S.
Bullpen: *What did your father do for work?*
Fred: My mom and dad both worked at the Suffolk County

Interviewed by Jon B. Cooke

FOREVER!

Infirmary. My dad worked in the kitchen as a cook, and my mother worked as a registered nurse's helper.

Bullpen: *They both had the same place of employment?*

Fred: Yes, pretty much.

Bullpen: *So you had a middle-class life?*

Fred: Probably these days you would call it lower middle-class, but the fact was they only had one child, so it never seemed like we were wanting in any way. It was certainly middle-class to me.

Bullpen: *Was the neighborhood you grew up in pretty suburban, somewhat typical?*

Fred: I grew up in the Yaphank Estates. [*laughter*] Of course, it sounded much better than it really was, but it was a new development that had just gone up a few years before we moved in (about 1959 or so). But, yes, it was suburban, with not a lot of thoroughfare traffic. You only drove there if you lived there.

Bullpen: *You were born in 1953?*

Fred: Yes, '53.

Bullpen: *Did your parents have any creative inclinations?*

Fred: No, not really.

Bullpen: *Did they read a lot?*

Fred: My dad was always one to read the newspapers. We used to have three newspapers in the house at all times every day for years, so he was into that stuff. But he was never much for fiction.

Bullpen: *The New York City papers?*

Fred: We got *The New York Daily News*, *Long Island Newsday*, and what used to be called *The Long Island Press*.

Bullpen: *What comic strips were in* The Press *and* Newsday?

Fred: Well, *Newsday* actually had the *Ben Casey* strip by Neal Adams, which I didn't like at the time! [*laughter*] The drawing was kind of ugly to me, y'know? It looked too realistic! Years later, I realized my mistake on that one! *The Long Island Press* had *The Phantom, Mandrake,* and a lot of King Features stuff. Of course, *The Daily News* had *Dick Tracy, Little Orphan Annie,* and all those classic strips. Even amongst all that good stuff, my favorite turned out to be Leonard Starr's *Mary Perkins: On Stage,* a sadly underrated strip.

Bullpen: *Did you get the* Sunday Daily News *and see those in color?*

Fred: Oh, yes.

Bullpen: *Did you have a liking for comic strips?*

Fred: Well, the first thing I remember that really stuck in my head was a *Dick Tracy* strip about a baby with a beard or mustache. It was very peculiar and that caught my attention. "What is *this* supposed to be?" I would clip them out and color them. So, yes, I did like the strips, but once I got into comics, I became snobbish towards the strips, a reverse-snobbism, because everybody usually looked down on comic *books* and looked up to the strips, so I decided to do the opposite. [*laughter*]

Bullpen: *Did you have woods around there?*

Fred: Oh, yes. There were lots of opportunities to go out in the woods, set up your tent, run off on your own, do all that kind of stuff that's pretty hard to do these days.

Bullpen: *Were you a Cub Scout?*

Fred: No, I was never a Scout or anything like that. I had a lot of kids my own age who were in the neighborhood, and none of them seemed to join any of the usual organizations, so if they weren't in it, I wasn't in it.

Bullpen: *Were your parents political at all?*

Fred: Not overly so, but they were obviously Republicans.

Bullpen: *What made it obvious?*

Fred: Well, they voted for Nixon. That'll do it. [*laughter*] I wasn't a big fan of Mr. Nixon, though.

Bullpen: *Were they Goldwater Republicans?*

Fred: I couldn't tell you that. That was such a wacky year, after Kennedy got shot, and I don't remember too much what they thought about politically at that point.

Bullpen: *Were they religious at all?*

Fred: No. I never went to Sunday school.

Bullpen: *How would you typify your upbringing? Was it pleasant?*

Fred: It was pleasant, but my parents were a lot older than I. My dad was 50 and my mother 39 when I was born, so they were pretty far removed from me, in terms of age. They also weren't that demonstrative, if you know what I'm saying. So I was a kid who got along and was treated well. They got me all the stuff I needed, but we didn't really have a lot of communication going on between us. So when I was

Above: *1979 unpublished Adam Strange drawing by Hembeck. Courtesy of the artist. Character ©2021 DC Comics.*

Transcribed by Steven Tice

GOOD QUESTIONS.

FIRST OFF, I'M FRED HEMBECK. I'M THE FELLOW WHO **WROTE** AND **DREW** THIS BOOK--LETTERED IT, TOO (EVERYONE **ELSE** RAN SCREAMING)--BUT, MORE PECULIARLY, I ALSO COSTAR AMONGST THE MIGHTY MINIONS OF THE MARVEL UNIVERSE AS A BONAFIDE CARTOON CHARACTER; SORT OF A CROSSOVER FROM REALITY. **WEIRD,** huh?

BUT EXACTLY **HOW** DID THIS ALL BEGIN? WELL, IT ALL STARTED IN A FIVE THOUSAND WATT RADIO STATION IN FRESNO, CALIFORNIA, A SIXTY FIVE DOLLAR PAYCHECK, AND A CRAZY DREA--

OOPS. SORRY. THAT'S THE ORIGIN STORY OF A **DIFFERENT** BLOWHARD. heh.

ME, I WAS BORN THE ONLY CHILD OF FRED AND HELEN HEMBECK BACK IN 1953. AFTER MY KINDERGARTEN TEACHER PRAISED MY ABILITIES, I KNEW ART WAS FOR ME, THOUGH IT WASN'T UNTIL TWO YEARS LATER THAT I DETERMINED EXACTLY **WHAT** SORT OF ART: A LONG FORGOTTEN CO-WORKER OF MY FATHER'S GAVE HIM A LARGE CARD-BOARD BOX OF COMICS FOR ME THAT HIS KID HAD EVIDENTLY OUTGROWN. **NOT ME!** NOT EVEN TO THIS DAY! I SIMPLY **FELL IN LOVE** WITH THE THINGS!

THINGS WERE **REALLY** CLINCHED ABOUT A YEAR LATER--I'D SINCE LEARNED HOW TO BUY MY FAVORITES DIRECTLY OFF THE NEWSSTAND--WHEN THE **THRILL** OF MY **FIRST** MARVEL COMIC-- Fantastic Four #4, TO BE PRECISE--ADDED WHAT LITTLE FUEL MIGHT'VE BEEN NECESSARY IN SOL-IDIFYING MY **DETERMINATION** TO GROW UP TO BE A CARTOONIST.

(NOTICE I **NEVER** SAID **ANYTHING** ABOUT **BECOMING** A CARTOON CHARACTER. **THAT** CAME LATER, MUCH LATER.)

OKAY, SO THE YEARS PASS AS I CONTINUE TO **READ, COLLECT,** AND **DREAM.** IT'S THE LATE SEVENTIES. JUST OUT OF COLLEGE, I TAKE A PORTFOLIO OF STANDARD SUPER HERO ART INTO NEW YORK CITY, ONLY TO BE GREETED BY A COLLECTIVE INDUSTRY-WIDE YAWN.

DISCOURAGED, I WENT HOME TO PREPARE A **SEC-OND** ASSAULT, AND FOLKS, **THAT'S** WHEN MY CAREER BEGAN TO TAKE ON A LIFE OF ITS **OWN!!**

Y'SEE, MY **SINGLE** ATTEMPT AT A **HU-MOROUS ART STYLE** WAS DONE 6 MONTHS EARLIER FOR A COLLEGE FRIEND. NOW, DURING THIS **BLEAK PERIOD,** I FOUND MYSELF UTILIZING THIS STYLE TO WRITE **CARTOON LETTERS** TO ALL THE FOLKS FROM SCHOOL I MISSED, HELPING TO BOTH KEEP MY SPIRITS **UP** AND MY DRAWING HAND **BUSY.**

AND JUST **WHO** WAS STARRING IN THIS COMIC STYLE CORRES-PONDENCE? THAT'S **RIGHT**--GIVE THE FELLOW IN THE BACK A **GOLD STAR**--IT INDEED WAS **ME, "FRED",** TALKIN' RIGHT AT THE READER, NOT AT ALL UNLIKE RIGHT **HERE** AND **NOW!** SAME AS IT EVER WAS.

AND THEN ONE NIGHT, AFTER SPEND-ING MOST OF THE DAY COPYING LIGAMENTS OUT OF AN ANATOMY BOOK, ON A **WHIM** I SAT DOWN AND WHIPPED UP A STRIP FEATURING A TYPICAL MAN ON THE STREET INTERVIEW, ONLY WITH SPIDER-MAN AS THE INTERVIEW**EE** AND **"FRED"** AS THE INTERVIEW**ER.** DRAWING IN MY HUMOROUS STYLE, I FILLED THOSE 9 PANELS WITH **FACTS, OPINIONS,** AND--oh, yeah--**JOKES,** PACKAGED IT UP AND SENT IT OFF IN HOPES THAT IT MIGHT ACTUALLY BE PUB-LISHED IN The BUYER'S GUIDE FOR COMICS FANDOM (NOW The COMICS BUYER'S GUIDE), A WEEKLY TRADE PAPER.

PUBLISHER/EDITOR **ALAN LIGHT** DID INDEED PRINT THAT INITIAL STRIP, AND IT RECEIVED SUCH A **POSITIVE** RESPONSE, I WAS SOON TURNING 'EM OUT **FULL TIME!** THIS SURE **WASN'T** THE WAY THAT I HAD PLANNED THINGS, BUT BEFORE I KNEW IT, I WAS BEING **INVITED** TO WORK FOR **THE BIG GUYS,** MARVEL INCLUDED!

WOW!

NOW, I REALLY DIDN'T **MISS** MY DRAMATIC STYLE--AFTER ALL, I HAD TO **SWEAT** TO ACHIEVE **MEDIOCRITY**--AND ANYWAY, MY NEW **HUMOROUS** STYLE WAS FAR MORE **DISTINCTIVE** (NOT TO MENTION FAR **EASIER!**), BUT **WRITING?** I'D NEVER EVEN **CONSIDERED** SUCH A THING. HOW-EVER, I FOUND THAT IF I DIDN'T HAVE TO CONCERN MYSELF WITH SUCH NICETIES AS **PLOT** AND **CHARACTERIZATION,** INSTEAD JUST SPEWING FORTH MY **THOUGHTS** AND **FEELINGS**--WITH A FEW **LAUGHS** THROWN IN IN AN ATTEMPT TO HOLD PEOPLE'S **ATTENTION**--I'D BE ALL RIGHT.

AFTER DOING WORK HERE, THERE, AND EVERYWHERE--INCLUDING MY **PERSONAL** FAVORITE, The Fantastic Four ROAST--ED-ITOR **JIM SALICRUP** ASKED ME TO COME UP WITH A COMIC STRIP TO RUN IN THE CEN-TERSPREAD OF **MARVEL AGE MAGAZINE,** HUMOROUSLY SPOTLIGHTING ONE OF THE SUBJECTS EXAMINED ELSEWHERE WITH-IN THE PAGES OF MARVEL'S NEWS MAG-AZINE THAT MONTH. THIS **GREAT GIG** BEGAN BACK IN **1984**--MARVEL AGE MAGAZINE #14 BEING THE FIRST--AND, I'M HAPPY TO SAY, WITH ONLY TWO EXCEPTIONS, MY STRIP HAS APPEARED IN **EVERY** ISSUE SINCE!

home, I had a lot of friends around the area, but once it came five, six o'clock, you're in the house, it was either TV or the comic book. I went for both media. Later on, I also got into music.

Bullpen: *TV was always available?*

Fred: Yes.

Bullpen: *You could watch it at your leisure after five o'clock?*

Fred: Yes. After a while, we got two TV sets, and then, of course, there was a choice. You didn't have to watch what everyone else was watching.

Bullpen: *So they weren't necessarily control freaks?*

Fred: No. Well, they were over-protective, but I just went with it, if you know what I mean.

Bullpen: *What do you mean by "over-protective"?*

Fred: Oh, "don't turn on the stove, you might set the house on fire," "don't do this, don't do that…" That kind of stuff.

Bullpen: *Did you go through a period of rebel-lion at all?*

Fred: I guess I did, but it was mild. I just grew my hair long. They didn't particularly like that. That was about 1970, when I was just finishing high school. It was a little late, but even so, it was not necessarily the accepted thing to do in those days.

Bullpen: *So were you alone a lot, as an only child, and not interacting with your parents a lot?*

Fred: Well, my parents were always home. They arranged their schedules so that while one was working, and the other one would be home. I never had a babysitter, because there was always somebody there. I had my maternal grandmother around, too, until I was 13.

Bullpen: *Was she living there?*

Fred: No, but she had her own house for a while, and ended up going to living at Suffolk County Infirmary, where my mom and dad worked, for her last five or six years. She'd come over and visit most every weekend.

Bullpen: *Did you have cousins?*

Fred: Not to speak of. I had one or two cousins who were, like, 45 and 50, that kind of thing, because of my mother's age. There was such a disparity there.

Bullpen: *Did your parents get married late in life?*

Fred: Oh, yes.

Bullpen: *Was it their first marriage respectively?*

Fred: No. In fact, the truth is, it was not a planned situation at all. I came out as a surprise. [*laughter*] No one was expecting it. Apparently, my mom was married for 10 years to this *other* guy, and they were divorced. Because they had had no children, it was assumed that, well, of course, it was be-cause of Helen.

Bullpen: *Of course, it's gotta be the woman!* [laughter]

Fred: Exactly! But they found that wasn't the case. I proved that.

Bullpen: *Did you grow up knowing you were unexpected?*

Fred: No, I didn't. I actually wrote about this at my website. There's an essay there about going to my mom's house, after she passed away (she died about four years before my dad passed away), and my father and I had to get some papers in order to get her final Social Security benefits. We dug out their marriage license and my dad says, "I found it!" I looked at it and noticed the marriage license was dated, like, April 23 (or something), 1953. I said, "Wait a second! *I* was born on January 30, 1953! Ooohhh… du'oh! I get it!"

Bullpen: *How old were you when you found out?*

Fred: This was after my mom died, so this would have been around 1983, so I didn't experience one of those made-for-TV movie moments. I'm like, "Oh, okay. This is cool. Now I get it."

Bullpen: *That's information you didn't need to find out at 12 years old!*

Fred: Right, I had no idea. Although, y'know, looking back, you go, "*Now* I get it." They weren't exactly the happiest couple around, if you know what I'm saying.

Bullpen: *Did they work together?*

Fred: No. I mean, they were in the same building, but not the same department.

Bullpen: *But that's how they had initially met? At work?*

Fred: That's how they initially met.

Bullpen: *Were you a sociable kid?*

Fred: Yes, I was. I was lucky enough to have a *lot* of people my own age living in the neighborhood, and kids next door, too. So I was never really at a loss for peers to play with. Except, of course, nowadays, kids are more likely to do these sleepovers and all that kind of stuff, but back in those days, it was pretty much like, well, at six o'clock everyone goes home and does their thing, right? So I had those hours to kill.

Bullpen: *You've obviously spent a lot of time looking back at those years growing up, through your strip. Have you ever really figured out* why *you became a comic book fan? Did you ever look into the, at least on the surface, the psychology behind it? What makes* you *a fan, as compared to your peers? Y'know, there are comic readers, then you've got your comic fanatics.*

Fred: I really don't know. I sometimes think I know why they appealed to me so much, but then again, I'm not quite sure. I had this ability to draw, so *that* was appealing, I suppose. I don't know why I liked it so much and stuck with it for so long, though.

Bullpen: *What were the circumstances of your getting into comics?*

Fred: Well, it was twofold in some respects: My dad brought home a copy of *Spooky, the Tough Little Ghost*. A fellow he worked with gave it to him, because that guy had a kid who was getting older. I read it and really liked it, and then Dad said, "Oh, okay. Well, he's got some more." So my dad brings home this huge box of comics. Well, that was it! From that moment on— it's like 1959—I was hooked. These were Harvey comics, *Dennis the Menace, Little Lulu*, assorted Dell funny animals… There were only two super-hero comics in the stack, and one was *Jimmy Olsen,* the cover where the king of the marbles was playing marbles on the cover with Superman. That didn't really grab me, believe it or not. It was from, like, '56.

Bullpen: *Had you seen* The Adventures of Superman *on TV?*

Fred: No, not at that point. By the time I watched it, George Reeves was no longer alive. It had to be after '59. But in the second grade, there was a kid who brought in comic books, the Mort Weisinger comics. He was one of the kids who lived around the neighborhood. And these comics were really strange. The thing that got me was the Bizarro character, who was just so peculiar. That whole nutty concept was what initially got me being interested in the titles. I wound up getting my mom to buy me a copy of *Superman Annual*

#2, which had Bizarro in it. I liked it, but it wasn't the same kind of Bizarro, because that very first story had a lot of pathos and emotional type stuff, not the wacky stuff that they'd turn out later. So I didn't buy any more *Superman* comics for about four or five months. Then they came out with Bizarro in his own series and that kind of pushed me over the top. Pretty much from about May of 1961, I started buying my own comic books, and just kept going after that. For about a year before that, my grandmother used to buy me books, but strictly the humor ones. And, of course, I got into the Marvels after that.

Bullpen: *You can pin it down to a month, that that's when you started becoming a fan?*

Fred: Yes, I can, because, oddly enough, the very first comic I went out to buy — not counting that *Superman Annual* — was an issue of *Superman* which told his life story. It started with

Opposite page: *Truncated intro page of* Fred Hembeck $ells the Marvel Universe, *giving autobio info from the cartoonist himself. The one-shot was published in October, 1990. ©2021 Marvel Characters, Inc.*

Below: *The Fab Four made a major impact on the young Hembeck. This* Dateline:@*!?# *page, featuring lyrics from the Beatles' song, "I Wanna Hold Your Hand," was repro'd in Hembeck Series #5 [1981]. Courtesy of F.H.*

his origin. I didn't plan it that way, but it was an absolutely perfect point to jump on board. Then, two months later, DC came out with that *Secret Origins* giant, so I got all the background information I needed within the first two months.

Lyrics ©2021 Sony/ATV Music Publishing LLC, Kobalt Music Publishing Ltd.. Characters ©2021 the respective copyright holders. Art ©2021 Fred Hembeck.

god! That's Johnny Storm!" (because it looked just like Johnny Storm!). So that's when I realized, "Hey, this is the same guy," Jack Kirby.

Bullpen: *Did you draw from an early age?*

Fred: Yes, pretty much. When I was in kindergarten, I had a swell teacher, and at one point she told my mom, "Y'know, your son's a pretty good artist. You really should encourage him." Of course, my mom told me that, and, of course, from that point on, "Well, oh gosh, I'm a good artist. I guess that's what I gotta do." It planted the idea into my head really early.

Bullpen: *So your artistic inclinations were cool with your parents?*

Fred: You know, they didn't say one thing one way or the other. Years later, I'm getting my strip published, and I'm having a couple of books come out. I'm living near Albany, and a fellow who's a reporter from that area calls me up, because he's a comics fan too, and wants to do an article on me. I said, "Sure." So he does the article, it gets printed in the Albany papers, a nice spread, pictures, this, that, and the other thing, color even. Not long after, I drive down to visit my parents. I give a copy of the newspaper to my dad, and I say, "Hey, see? Look, look!" He looks at it for a minute, and then says, "Oh! Interesting… it's a Hearst paper!" [*laughter*] *That* was his comment! So there you go.

Bullpen: *Albany had a Hearst paper.* [laughs]

Fred: Yes. There just happened to be an article about me in there, but hey, let's not quibble about details.

Bullpen: *So there wasn't a lot of support, one way or the other?*

Fred: There wasn't discouragement; there wasn't encouragement. There just *was*. Nobody beat me. I can honestly say that. Nobody screamed at me too often (except for me to get my hair cut).

Bullpen: *But you weren't necessarily a bad kid?*

Fred: Nah, I was a wimpy guy, pretty much, but *always* joking.

Bullpen: *Were you liked in school?*

Fred: Pretty much, but I wasn't the most popular kid around. I probably did better in elementary school, if you know what I mean. I got to high school and developed a little bit of acne, so that threw me off. I was a sensitive kid, and that condition made me more shy than I had been. I was doing pretty good up until seventh grade. In retrospect, I got more introverted. Although I still was comfortable with my long-time friends, I was really quiet around people who *weren't* my friends.

Bullpen: *Were you known as a cartoonist in school?*

Fred: I was known as an *artist*. I didn't really do the cartooning that much. Bear in mind my graduating high school class was about 180 (which I thought was a lot, but people tell me that's not so).

Bullpen: *Were you dating at all?*

Fred: Oh, no. I wasn't participating in any of those kinds of teenage rituals. I waited for college for that, and even then, I had to work that into the schedule!

Bullpen: *Did you go to movies a lot?*

Fred: Depends on what period you're talking about. Late in my teens, my friends and I had nothing else to do, so we would go out to movies. But when I was growing up, not so much,

Bullpen: *You were hooked!*

Fred: Yes.

Bullpen: *Did you go to summer camp?*

Fred: Yes, one year I went to day camp. I didn't like it.

Bullpen: *What year was that?*

Fred: I was reading comics, so it had to be second or third grade. The best part was coming home and going to Heisenbuttel's general store, where I bought all my comics. That was my comic-book store.

Bullpen: *Did you trade comics with kids in the neighborhood?*

Fred: I did that twice, when I first started, because I really wanted this one comic, *World's Finest,* with "The Caveman from Krypton." But after I traded for that, I didn't want to let go of any of *my* comics, so there was just no point.

Bullpen: *Did you recognize different artistic styles?*

Fred: I suppose I did, but it took me a while to put together that that Challengers portion in *Secret Origins* was by the same guy who drew *The Fantastic Four,* y'know, a book I discovered about a year later. The first time I noticed something like that was when there was this farmer's market area we used to go to that sold old comics, and at one point there they were selling all these old Harvey 3-D comics, including *Captain 3-D,* for really cheap prices. I bought one, and on the splash page they had little headshots of the characters, and I go, "My

although there was a period when I was trying to watch as many movies on TV as I possibly could.

Bullpen: *Did you have much exposure to 1950s pre-Code comics at all?*

Fred: Not the 1950s books. My dad had relatives in New Jersey, and we'd occasionally go over there, and—because my cousin was about 15 years older than me, as she was in her 30s, at that point—she had some comics down in the basement. She let me pretty much take what I wanted. The material was from the late '40s to the early '50s. There was stuff like *Betty and Veronica #1,* a handful of Fawcett *Captain Marvel* comics, a single issue of *Marvel Mystery Comics,* and some Lev Gleason *Daredevil* and *Boy Comics,* but no horror comics, and only one or two other super-hero titles. So that gave me some perspective. This was in 1963 or '64, so I had a taste of that golden-age material at a young age when it wasn't really otherwise available, but I didn't see the EC stuff.

Bullpen: *Were you impressed with the C.C. Beck material?*

Fred: Yes. I enjoyed *Captain Marvel Adventures* a lot, and enjoyed the Lev Gleason/Charles Biro stuff as well. I was very much impressed by that stuff.

Bullpen: *Did you enjoy all the different genres? The war comics, for instance?*

Fred: When I was growing up, I was never really much for funny animals. I went through an initial phase buying the Harvey comics, as well as the Dells and Gold Keys, but once I developed a big taste for super-heroes, I put those other genres aside. Of course, the big exception was the funny kid comics, which were *Little Lulu, Dennis the Menace,* and *Little Archie* (which, to this day, is are pretty much my favorites). The war comics I'd buy on and off. For a couple years, I'd buy them, then I'd get sick of them, then they'd hook me up again. I'm talking about the DC ones, mainly. Not *Sgt. Fury,* because that was really a super-hero comic book, so I always bought that.

Bullpen: *Did you continue to buy* Little Lulu *and* Dennis the Menace *through the '60s?*

Fred: Up until about 1965 or so, longer than any of the other humor comics. I bought the regular (teenaged) *Archie* titles, too.

far more realistically than most characters would in any other comics. Henry and Alice Mitchell occasionally lost their tempers and stuff along those lines, and they just seemed more like genuine parents.

Bullpen: *As a kid, I remember being impressed by the lengthy specials, where Dennis would go off to Washington, D.C., or Hawaii, and there would be a whole issue devoted to his trips.*

Fred: Oh, definitely.

Bullpen: *Did you get into Marvel immediately when they started coming out?*

Fred: No, I got into Marvel about a year or so into it, actually. I avoided all those monster books, the Atlas titles. My friends who had those *Superman*s, had those, too, but I said, "Nah! I don't want to deal with those things." They looked dark, they looked ugly, so I just didn't want to get into them.

In 1962, I had a mild case of scarlet fever, and I wasn't

Bullpen: *Do you look back at the original* Dennis the Menace *by Al Wiseman, for instance, as being impressive?*

Fred: Oh, yes, definitely.

Bullpen: *What made it so?*

Fred: Wiseman captured the era better than pretty much anything else I can think of, as far as the illustrations went… It really looked like a 1950s suburban world in those books. The stories were clever, written by Fred Toole, and they also managed to capture a semi-realistic relationship between parents and kids that you didn't really see in the other comics. Dennis would always exasperate his parents, and they'd would react

Left inset and bottom: Advertising art by Fred Hembeck, drawn in 1990 for an upstate New York firm. Courtesy of F.H. ©2021 the respective copyright holder.

Below inset: For the Kingston Freeman, *a local newspaper, Fred wrote and drew a short-lived strip,* The Caped Consumer, *which appeared in the weekly* Today's Homeowner *supplement in 1978. Courtesy of Fred Hembeck and ©2021 the respective copyright holder*

able to go to school. I'd go to the doctor every couple weeks—the only time I got out of the house—and I was missing my comics. Well, as it turned out, the place where I bought the comics had this big rack right near the front window. So I was getting desperate. One day, on my suggestion, my mother parked right in front of that window and she went in, held up, pretty much at random, one comic after another, and I'd shake my head yes or no (because she certainly didn't know what which ones I wanted or needed). So after I said yes to a couple of standard DCs, she held up this cover with this really strange-looking logo. It looked almost like something out of a circus. It was *Fantastic Four* #4. I didn't really know what to make of it, and I thought, "Oh, what the heck," and gave it a thumbs-up. She brought it out, and pretty much ever since then I've loved Marvel Comics.

Bullpen: *The return of the Sub-Mariner, baby!* [laughter]

Fred: Yes, exactly! I got that comic, but I thought he was the good guy. I was convinced that the big ugly guy made out of orange clay had to be the bad guy! [laughter]

Bullpen: *You say you were known as an artist in school. What were you drawing?*

Fred: Just anything, really. When they had art classes, they'd go, "Oh, look at what Fred drew." I didn't pump out that much stuff, but you know how kids look around and see stuff. I would copy out of the comics… I *still* copy out of the comics.

Bullpen: *Did you do actual stories?*

Fred: No, I was too lazy for that. It was a whole lot easier to just draw a guy standing there. Who wanted to draw backgrounds? For years, I didn't want to draw girls. That was too difficult to even think about. I couldn't do those ankles!

Bullpen: *Did* MAD *magazine make an impression on you?*

Fred: It took a while, but *MAD* magazine came along about 1964 in my life, and for about a year or so, I just couldn't get enough of it. The funny thing about *MAD* magazine, though, is that if you read it for about a year-and-a-half, you think it's the greatest thing ever, and then you realize that the jokes are pretty much all the same. So I kept buying it until, like, 1971 or so, but the only ones I really remember is are from 1964–66. Which are the best ones, y'know! Just because.

Bullpen: *Mad had their finger on juvenile delinquency pretty well there for a while. Remember the "Crust" painting by Kelly Freas?*

Fred: Oh, yes, definitely! That was during my "good" period.

Bullpen: *So when the Warrens came out, did you clue into* Creepy *and* Eerie?

Fred: Yes, I did. I started off reading *Famous Monsters of Filmland.* I went through a Universal monsters phase, too. That was pretty big at that point, in '64, and I watched all those movies on TV, and then I'd buy the magazine, and got into all the classic monsters.

Bullpen: *Were you able to get all the New York stations on Long Island?*

Fred: Yes, definitely. We received the three networks — ABC, NBC, and CBS — as well as the independent stations, channels 5 [WNEW], 9 [WOR], and 11 [WPIX]. We even got Connecticut stations occasionally.

Bullpen: *So you watched* Creature Features?

Fred: Exactly, for a while.

Bullpen: *Do you remember when WOR played* King Kong *endlessly?*

Fred: Oh, yes! *The Million Dollar Movie!* That's when channel 9 took one movie and played it repeatedly, all week. That's where I learned to love the monster movies and Abbott and Costello. I used to watch certain movies over and over, at least the parts I enjoyed.

Bullpen: *WOR used to play* The Bowery Boys *a lot, too, didn't it?*

Fred: *The Bowery Boys,* yup.

Bullpen: *Did you go to the 1964–65 New York World's Fair?*

Fred: Several times with my family. Of course, it was a big thing for my school class to go, at that time. I guess we were close enough to Flushing, where the Fair was located. It was about 50 miles away, maybe less.

Bullpen: *Did you go to the beach in the summertime, too?*

Fred: Yes, but not to Jones Beach. We went to Smith Point, which was nearby.

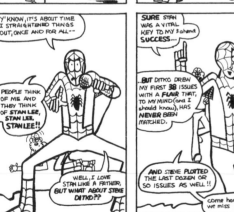

Bullpen: *Did you like growing up in Long Island?*

Fred: Oh, yes! It's tough for me to understand people who've never gotten to go to the beach. I've never been a swimmer, but you don't have to be; you just go out in the waves and frolic around.

Bullpen: *When did you graduate high school?*

Fred: Nineteen seventy-one, from Longwood High School.

Bullpen: *Did the '60s have an effect on you within the neighborhood at all?*

Fred: I was big into the '60s because I also avidly followed the music scene.

Bullpen: *When did music come into play?*

Fred: 1964. I believe it was the ninth of February.

Bullpen: *Do ya think? Was it courtesy of CBS and Ed Sullivan, on a Sunday night?* [laughter]

Fred: *"Yeah-yeah-yeah"!* [laughs] Before that, I was like, "Ahhh, music; that stuff is no good." I never even cared about it. I can distinctly remember that I never paid any attention to it, instead I kind of mocked it. But from that February day on, it was all different. I was really into the scene. I followed all the magazines, started reading *Rolling Stone* magazine from, like, #19. That made me a radical in my house. Nobody else was reading *Rolling Stone,* at that point. I subscribed to it because you pretty much had to. Distribution was pretty limited. Occasionally, the covers were a little on the outré side for Yaphank, if you know what I'm saying.

Bullpen: *For CBA Bullpen's younger readers, we'll have to specify that it was the American television debut of the Beatles that sparked you, right?*

Fred: The Beatles, yes! I forgot to mention that. [laughter] *Rolling Stone* would have Abbie Hoffman on the cover in those days, not just Britney Spears and the Olsen twins, so it was a way different era for that, too.

Bullpen: *What was it that you can see that caused the Beatles to be such a sensation with America's youth?*

Fred: I don't know. They just sounded so fresh, so incredibly joyful. It was something I'd never heard before. I mean, I was familiar with Elvis, the "Teenie-Weenie, Itsy-Bitsy, Yellow, Polka-Dot Bikini," and "Puff, the Magic Dragon," but outside of that, I didn't know much about pop music at all. *Now* I know, because I went back and listened to a lot of the earlier stuff. I just love music and, to this day, two things that get me really choked up are a 1964 Marvel comic book or a Beatles record. There's just nothing better than those two things.

Bullpen: *One of the great joys as editor of* Comic Book Artist — *something virtually nobody else sees — is to get a submission from Fred Hembeck, turn the page around and* [Fred laughs] *to see, written in pencil, a list of songs you listened to while you laid out and finished the piece. Do you always do that?*

Fred: Over the last couple of years I've done that. I never did that until recently. I don't know why I decided to do that… just to demarcate time, I guess. Sometimes I write a joke or something on the back, too. You never know.

Bullpen: *Did you pursue music yourself?*

Fred: No, I never really had an interest in playing an instrument.

Well, I should say, just before the Beatles, I went to see *The Music Man,* the 1963 Robert Preston movie, and it so impressed me that I came out of the theater desperately wanting to learn how to play the trombone.

Bullpen: *Be the 76th trombone?* [laughter]

Fred: Exactly. Well, it turned out I was a zero. [laughter] After about a month, the music teacher said, "You don't have the right kind of lips for this. Why don't you try the saxophone?" [laughter] So I wound up in the fourth grade, playing saxophone in the band, but I didn't like to practice, so whenever the band would play, I would just push the buttons and make-believe I was play-

ing. That lasted almost a year, and afterwards, that was the end of it for me. I loved music, but the idea of practicing never appealed to me. I suppose I should have played the piano or guitar, but it just never happened.

Bullpen: *If you had grown up in the '80s, would you have been called a slacker?* [laughter]

Fred: I guess so! That was kind of a Milli Vanilli moment in my life.

Bullpen: *So did you expand your musical tastes? Did you get into the Rolling Stones and the Kinks?*

Fred: Oh, yes.

Bullpen: *How far did it go? Did it go into the Yardbirds and the blues at all?*

Fred: I never got into the blues, but I liked soul music, Motown, all the Top Forty, and then—in 1967 or so, when the heavy stuff was coming out—Jimi Hendrix, Cream, Donovan, Jefferson Airplane, I got into all that stuff. I enjoyed that even without the drugs, actually.

Bullpen: *Did you do drugs?*

Fred: No, not at that point. I'm not going to say what happened later on in college, but I think you know what I'm saying. But not when I was growing up in the '60s.

Bullpen: *But you certainly got the artistic after-effects of the psychedelic age, so to speak? A contact high?*

FantaCo

Below: *Fred Hembeck and frequent '80s collaborator, Marvel writer Bill Mantlo, pitched a 10-page fantasy story to* Epic *magazine. Alas, the tale didn't make the cut but did finally appear in* Hembeck Series #5 [Feb. '81], *pubbed by Fantaco Enterprises (logo above).* **Opposite:** *Covers for the entire* Hembeck Series [1980-83] *published by Fantaco Enterprises of Albany, New York. All are courtesy of and ©2021 Fred Hembeck.*

Fred: Yes, exactly. I empathized with the whole thing. I was fascinated by the whole culture, none of which was anywhere near *me*, except when *Rolling Stone* magazine arrived in the mailbox.

Bullpen: *Abbie Hoffman was on the cover of* Rolling Stone?

Fred: For a time, I was actually an expert on the Chicago Seven trial. I read the transcripts, like a thousand pages worth of court documents. Even in college I did a report on it. I figured, "Hey, why not? I'd just read it a few years earlier."

Bullpen: *Virtually a generation of kids truly loathed President Richard Milhous Nixon…*

Fred: Nooo… [*laughter*] Is this a trick question? I was *there*. In retrospect, yeah, he was bad, but I guess he had some good points, but when you were living through those days, he didn't

seem like he had *any*. Plus, he had every young man's fate in his hands. I wasn't eager to go out into the jungle and get shot, and I *was* around that draft age. Luckily for me, it turned out that I was in the last of the draft lotteries. I don't even remember my number, because it was that high, it was in the 150s or something, and they only took up to #10 or so that year.

Bullpen: *Did you know friends who went to Vietnam?*

Fred: You know, I never did, oddly enough.

Bullpen: *Do you think they escaped the draft because of college deferments?*

Fred: Well, they were mostly my age, and that was the same year. So I just lucked out, and, of course, I was in that class of 180, as opposed to the people who go to schools with 50,000 graduates per class and stuff. There were a couple of people who went to Vietnam in my town who got killed, but no one I really knew well, though.

Bullpen: *What was your ambition in high school?*

Fred: To be a cartoonist and draw *The Fantastic Four*.

Bullpen: *New York City wasn't that far away, right? Did you ever go down to DC or Marvel as a kid in the late '60s or early '70s?*

Fred: From grade three on, I didn't really have any friends around who were into comics, so I kind of had to go it alone. (I had friends, but they weren't into comics.) I somehow managed to convince a few friends to get into them years later around the time Barry Smith was drawing *Conan the Barbarian*, and *Shazam!* was coming out, as was *Swamp Thing*. We're teenagers by then. So we went into the city one day and decided, "Let's go up to Marvel Comics!" "Okay!" We got into the elevator, went up to the right floor, and then chickened out! We never got out of the elevator, because we didn't know what we were going to say. [*laughter*] So that was as close as I got until I actually tried to go up there to get a job later on.

Bullpen: *Did you ever seek out professionals to get advice on how to become a comic book artist?*

Fred: Not before I actively put together a portfolio. There just wasn't anybody around where I lived that I knew of, anyway. If I had known Frank Springer lived down the road, I might have gone over to his house.

Bullpen: Did *Frank Springer live down the road?*

Fred: Not necessarily, but I knew he lived on Long Island somewhere, so that's why I threw his name out there. He could have been relatively nearby. I know he didn't live in Yaphank, but he probably would have been the most likely person, since I'd heard he lived in Suffolk county.

Bullpen: Long Island *is* a long island! Jack Kirby once lived there.

Fred: Yes, but most of the artists stayed up close to the city. I lived out in the boonies.

Bullpen: *So how did you do in school, academically?*

Fred: Fine, until they made me take math and science in seventh grade. I was really sailing through elementary school with the As and Bs, and then it I got to junior high, and all of a sudden, science and math got real hard. I suddenly found out my brain doesn't work that way. I always did well in English and social studies, terrible in foreign languages, which was German, which I took because I thought my dad could help me. But I found out after about the second time I brought home my homework, he looks at it and goes, "Oh, I spoke a different dialect than they have here." [*laughter*] And that was the end of my help for the next five years.

Bullpen: [Laughs] *Was your dad just bailing?*

Fred: No, he was telling the truth. Just because you speak English, doesn't mean you could tell everyone all the rules of the English language. So, if you transfer that to German, that was what we were dealing with. Of course, math was not good and science was not good, but I got through high school. Barely, as

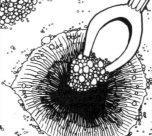

far as those classes go, but I got out.

Bullpen: *So you had acne and were having problems with science and math. Not too many great memories of high school, or was it okay?*

Fred: It was okay. I had a bunch of friends. Nothing really horrible happened. I mean, it could have been better, but it could have been a lot worse, too, if you think about it. It was okay. Elementary school was better, but that's the general rule, isn't it? Why not? So was college.

Bullpen: *Did you fear the draft?*

Fred: I did. By the time I got to that age, the draft was winding down, and you knew it wasn't going to happen, but just a couple years before, you're thinking, "Hey, they gotta really cut this war out! This is *not* working." But there wasn't an imminent threat, let's put it that way.

Bullpen: *Was the transition to college immediate? Did you start the September after you graduated?*

Fred: Yes, I did.

Bullpen: *Where did you go?*

Fred: The State University of New York, at

Farmingdale, for a two-year hitch. That was on Long Island, 30 miles away from my house. I drove there, a 60-mile round-trip each day. I took the course, "Advertising Art and Design," which was a course that Len Wein took about five years earlier. (I remember reading that somewhere in one of those comic book feature pages. "Oh, look, I'm going to the Len Wein course. I'm gonna write *Swamp Thing!*") [*laughter*]

Bullpen: *What was your experience?*

Fred: It was good. I probably learned more in those two years than I had in a long time, as far as art went. I had a number of pretty good teachers. I had one teacher named Raphael DeSoto, who I later learned had been a pulp artist who did covers for *The Shadow* and titles along those lines, although I didn't really realize that until midway through the first year and I came across his name in one of Jim Steranko's *Mediascene* articles, one of the early issues. DeSoto was a little old man at that point. I did well in his class, because it was illustration. In the other classes, where it was more technical, I didn't

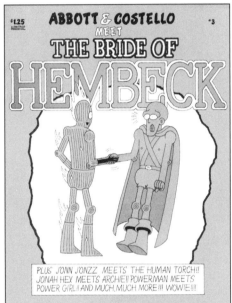

Dr. DITKO
MASTER OF THE MYSTIC ARTWORK

do quite as well. I did okay, but it I was better off when it was just me with a pen, as opposed to me with an airbrush.

Bullpen: *Were you into fanzines at all?*

Fred: Yes. I got into them in about 1967, and was pretty intense for a couple of years. But then, when the end of high school was coming up, I got less into that kind of thing, and I went away from it almost until the *Steranko History of Comics* came out again in 1971 or '72. I still have a pile of them down in the basement from those old days.

Bullpen: Rocket's Blast/Comic Collector?

Fred: *Rocket's Blast/Comic Collector,* some of the ditto-zines, like Dwight Decker's *Freon,* and some of the big name ones like *witzend,* the very first one I ever bought.

Bullpen: *Where did you buy* witzend?

Fred: I bought it through the mail. Back in those days, you'd stick a dollar in an envelope and hope for the best. You pretty much bought everything by Scotch-taping quarters to index cards and sending them off for 'zines and stuff. A lot of Tony Isabella/Mark Evanier stuff. I even for a while there had a pen pal relationship with ol' Tony, who would write to anybody who

would ask. He was writing a column for every 'zine out there. He probably got tired of it, but for a few months, we corresponded.

Bullpen: *Did you make contributions to the 'zines?*

Fred: Yes, that happened. I sent in several drawings, a couple of covers, a handful of articles, some of which were pretty flaky if you read them now.

Bullpen: *What were they about?*

Fred: Actually, I stumbled across one a few months ago which was about why comics are not immature, or something like that. It was like, "Methinks thou doth protest too much, Fred…" That kind of deal. [*laughter*]

Bullpen: *Did you always remain appreciative of* Little Archie *and John Stanley into your adolescent years?*

Fred: Yes. Sometime around '67 or so, I had my one and only purge of my comic collection, and I got rid of almost all my Harveys, most of my funny animals, and the majority of my "big" Archies, but I held onto all three of the titles we're talking about here. I wouldn't get rid of those, so I must have realized their superior quality by then, known by then their superior value. (I now wish I hadn't got rid of those other ones mainly just because of nostalgia, but at least I certainly knew which ones to keep.)

Bullpen: *So to this day you're appreciative of that material?*

Fred: More so now than ever. I've got all those oversize *Little Lulu* hardcovers. In fact, one of the most exciting things I can remember being announced was when they said they were going to come out with those hardcovers. That's the one bit of comic book news that I can remember from the '80s that really got me excited.

Bullpen: *Did Russ Cochran publish those* Lulu *reprints?*

Fred: Yes, he did.

Bullpen: *Are they chronological?*

Fred: They're chronological, but he published them backwards. I guess he knew if he started with the very first

material, which was a bit crude, that might put some potential customers off. So they started with the newer stuff and then went backwards. But they didn't start at the very end, so there's actually some issues that haven't been reprinted. They could actually do more, but I guess it didn't sell well enough for anyone to go back and finish up.

Bullpen: *What is it about* Little Lulu *that holds true?*

Fred: Well, John Stanley, the writer, has perfect comic timing. Everything is set up in such a way that the situations just play out naturally, and the humor just builds and builds. The amazing thing is he would begin a story without any idea how he was going to end it, but you would never know that from reading the material! So it's hard for me to put a finger on what makes his work so good, but it's great stuff, it really is. *Little Archie,* of the three, is the only one where sentimentality comes into the mix. You don't really find that in the other two, but Bob Bolling in *Little Archie* does that exceptionally well at times.

Bullpen: *It's funny how resonant* Little Archie *is, y'know? As a kid, I was not at all interested in the "big" Archie stuff, but* Little Archie *had adventure, with the character put in a sense of real danger, where you actually worried about the kid.*

Fred: Exactly. The characters seemed more real. They weren't just going through the same situations just for the sake of tired jokes over and over again.

Bullpen: *Did you have exposure to the more sophisticated stuff, shall we say? The undergrounds?*

Fred: Yes. I got into the undergrounds there for a while. Before *Rolling Stone*, there was this thing called *Eye* magazine. You

might have heard of it because at one point they had a Marvel mini-comic on the front of one issue. *Eye* ran for about a year, and it was a monthly the size of *Life* magazine, and it started out as a radical magazine and ended up like *Cosmopolitan*, because it wasn't doing well, so it was changed by [*Cosmo* editor] Helen Gurley-Brown.

Bullpen: National Lampoon *art director Michael Gross worked on this mag.*

Fred: Yes, I remember reading about that, yup. One issue had an article on Marvel Comics, and it had a little mini-comic stapled to the front that was a condensed version of that John Romita issue of *Amazing Spider-Man* [#42, Nov. '66] where John Jameson, the astronaut, is on the loose. They used to include a poster stapled into the center of each issue, and on the backside of the poster in real small print, they would have reports on what was happening in different towns—Los

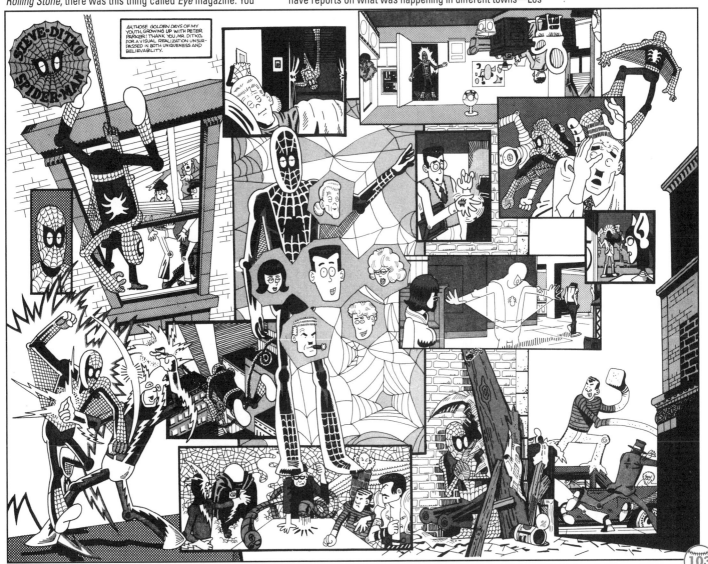

Angeles, New York, San Francisco—and they had a little blurb there about Robert Crumb, and that was the first time I ever heard of Crumb. It piqued my interest because they had a little picture along with it there. So I was fascinated by that.

In fact, this leads to a semi-embarrassing story: When I was in ninth grade, my Earth science teacher was a pretty cool guy, and he took the class into New York City on a field trip to see *2001: A Space Odyssey* on a big, gigantic screen. So after we saw the movie, he says, "Okay, you guys can go run around the city if you want, for a while." [*laughter*] You can't really do that *now*, I wouldn't think. But, back then it was, "We'll meet you back here at the bus in an hour." So I go up to this little shop, and I see, "Oh, look! There's that magazine they were talking about in *Eye* magazine!" *The East Village Other*, right? So I buy it. This is like 1968. I buy a copy for, like, a quarter, and take it back with me on the bus. Then some of the kids looked through it, as I passed it around. But the comics are kind of, you might say, *rude*. The tough guys in the back are going, [*tough guy voice*] "Hey, Hembeck! You bought *this*? Oh, man!" [*laughter*] Compared to what you can see now, it wasn't that bad, but there were certain words in there you weren't exactly seeing anywhere else in those days. You can say them in your new magazine, but not the old one! [*laughter*] So that always stuck with me, getting that oddly earned smidgen of respect from unexpected quarters. Then, not long after, I ordered a copy of *ZAP Comix* #3 through the mail.

Bullpen: *Was that through an ad?*

Fred: Yeah, through an ad by a guy named Eric Fromme. (That's the name of some famous writer [Erich Fromm], I later learned.) I knew *ZAP* was some sort of a risqué thing, so when it arrived, I got it out of the mail, and took it downstairs into the basement where there was no access except through an outside door. I looked at it, and there was that S. Clay Wilson stuff, and it horrified me! To this day, I've since developed a taste for most of the original underground artists, but S. Clay Wilson, he still scares me. I mean, I love Crumb and the Kim Deitch stuff — I love a *lot* of the stuff — but I never got into good ol' S. Clay.

Bullpen: *Well, it really is disturbing material, isn't it?*

Fred: A whole bunch of pirates and a whole bunch of weird things.

Bullpen: *And cut-off penises!*

Fred: Cut-off penises were bad enough, but they also had nails being pounded through them with hammers! [*laughter*]

Bullpen: [*Pirate voice*] *"Arrr, emasculation on the high seas, matey!"* [laughter] *Were there any head shops near home to buy comix?*

Fred: No, but I wound up amassing a collection of about a hundred of them through the mail, periodically. I bought the ones that either had good artists or a fair amount of sex, because when you're a teen, you *gotta* get that stuff!

Bullpen: *But, of course! You said you stopped buying* Mad *in '71. Is that when you started buying* National Lampoon? [*Fred gives insight into evolving humor mag tastes in his "Teen Fred" strip in CBA V1, #24, April '03.—Ed.*]

Fred: Yes. A friend had a copy, the one with their parody of *MAD* magazine which provoked me into taking a look, and it was pretty funny. You never knew what was going to be in an issue from month to month, as opposed to *MAD*, which was always pretty much the same. Which is not to knock *MAD*, because they had a lot of good stuff, when you think about it, but I needed more variety in those days.

Bullpen: *In the '60s, did you have exposure to the surfing and drag strip cartoon magazines?*

Fred: I bought one or two *Drag CARtoons* when they had Batman on the cover. I also actually bought the two *Wonder Wart-Hog* magazines that came out from those same publishers.

Bullpen: *Because it was a super-hero?*

Fred: Yes, but I really wound up liking them for their own sake, though.

Bullpen: *How about* Help!?

Fred: I never bought *Help!* off the newsstand, although I saw it once. I was a little too young for that and thought it was an adult magazine, so I didn't buy it, because frankly, I didn't really

Above: Fred's first mainstream appearance was in the form of a comic-strip letter of comment in Iron Man #112 [July '78].

Below and inset: Fred also briefly assisted artist Bob Layton, helping with backgrounds for either Marvel Premiere #47 or 48, *and a single page of* Iron Man #117 [Dec. '78], *where he sneaked in his own name—and those of other friends—in the panel reproduced at right. TM & ©2021 Marvel Characters, Inc.*

understand it. I have a couple of issues now, but… Actually, one of the few things in my house that I bought that disappeared, and I think I know why, was a collection of the *Goodman Beaver* strips called *The Executive Comic Book*. It was a paperback, and on the front cover they drew Goodman Beaver as if he were Superman, flying in the air with the same color costume. So I got my mom to buy me this when I'm nine or 10 years old. Then I went home and read it, and the story that always sticks in my mind, everybody says it's Goodman Beaver at the *Playboy* mansion, but it's all the Archie characters, and they're all naked! So I had that in my collection for a while, and then it strangely disappeared. I think someone else took a look at it. So a couple of years later, by the time I got involved with the undergrounds, I managed to put those in a place where they were not likely to be found, or at least mixed them in with stuff like the *Hulk*s. Now, the *Hulk*s never disappeared…

Bullpen: *So were those two years of college it for your higher education?*

Fred: No, because then I went on to another two years of college. Farmingdale was a two-year school, and then after that I transferred. Because you know, I wouldn't have to go to work too soon. You just wanted to do another two years. All of my friends were going to four-year colleges, so what am I doing just two years for, right? Plus, I'm living at home. I didn't want to do *that* anymore. All of my friends went off to college and had a great time, but I'm driving back and forth to my parents' house every day.

Bullpen: *Did you have your own car?*

Fred: Yes.

Bullpen: *What was it?*

Fred: Ah… a blue one? [*laughter*] It was the car that my parents used to have.

Bullpen: *"A blue one"!* [laughs]

Fred: Hey, you asked, buddy.

Bullpen: *Not mechanically inclined, Fred?*

Fred: No, not at all.

Bullpen: *Were you athletic at all?*

Fred: Mildly, I would say. I always liked to play baseball, but I was never good on any teams in school. In seventh grade, I tried out for the baseball team, but didn't do well. In the ninth grade, my best friend decided to join the football team and he was really good, but he didn't want to do it alone, so he conned the rest of us into joining the team, but none of us were any good. I was an end. You know, the end is the guy who runs out and catches the ball? I never caught the ball, not even in practice, but all I could do was run. Not that I was that fast, but I wasn't big enough to do anything else. Practicing all the time just wasn't for me. My friend ruined his knee for that.

I play volleyball to this day, so I like to play. I've always preferred to play with my friends. I get uptight when I'm under pressure with people I don't know, because they're going to hassle me if I screw up, and I will, trust me. But if I'm just

Above: *How many comic book creators can boast to have an actual comic containing their name in the title? Well, Fred's got two—Fred Hembeck Destroys the Marvel Universe [July '89] and Fred Hembeck $ells the Marvel Universe [Oct. '90]—and you can read the back story behind the former in Fred's essay in* Comic Book Artist *V.2, #4, available as a PDF from TwoMorrows. The latter features mostly reprints of F.H.'s* Marvel Age *centerspread strips. ©2021 Marvel Characters, Inc.*

Inset left: *Certainly one of Fred's biggest breaks came courtesy of then Marvel head honcho Jim Shooter when the cartoonist received an assignment to write and helm the one-shot* Fantastic Four Roast *[May '82]. TM & ©2021 Marvel Characters, Inc.*

Above: *The original version of Fred Hembeck Destroys the Marvel Universe had the boyhood mentor of House of Ideas editor-in-chief Jim Shooter—a thinly-veiled caricature of DC's late uber-editor Mort Weisinger—serve as a villain (of sorts) for the book. After the book was completed, apparently Marvel's powers-that-be sobered up and demanded wholesale changes to the storyline. For complete "before-&-after" looks at the one-shot, be sure to visit www. hembeck.com. TM & ©2021 Marvel Characters, Inc.*

Above: *Fred sure has a knack for "Hembeck-izing" classic comic book covers, such as these early '60s "80-Page Giant"! Contact our man Fred via his website—or we'll forward any letters, of course— if you're interested in owning your own Hembeck to hang on the wall! (Me, I'll be nagging him for a Superman #233!) Courtesy of and art ©2021 Fred Hembeck. Characters, cover design ©2021 DC Comics.*

playing with people I know, I'm relaxed and I play better.

Bullpen: *Was October of '69 important to you in terms of baseball?*

Fred: Oh yeah! I was a big Mets fan. Definitely! The Mets were the one thing my dad and I had in common. I still like the Mets to this day.

Bullpen: *Don't like the New York Yankees?*

Fred: Hate the Yankees!

Bullpen: *Now, the Mets were a relatively new team, obviously, in '69. Why the Mets? Just because the Brooklyn Dodgers had moved out of town?*

Fred: I don't know. My dad didn't really care for the Yankees, and I guess he didn't want to deal with any of the other teams. Again, I had a friend (the same buddy who introduced me to comics) who was into Strat-O-Matic games. That got me interested in baseball, so I just naturally fell into the Mets.

Bullpen: *What was Strat-O-Matic?*

Fred: It was a game where they take the stats for the previous year of all the Major League baseball players, put them on cards, and then you roll dice and, depending on what numbers come up, you do what it says on the card for the particular player in that particular situation. It's all based on the actual stats of any given player.

Bullpen: *So it was Dungeons*

and Dragons for real *American boys, right?* [laughs]

Fred: Yes, it's still around. In fact, a year or so ago, Keith Hernandez was going on and on about it during one of the Mets broadcasts, because they were having a big convention. "Oh, yeah, I used to love that! I'm going to the con today!"

Bullpen: *That was huge for a while with my older brothers.*

Fred: They had ads in the comics for it, too.

Bullpen: *Were you into G.I. Joe?*

Fred: I was never into G.I. Joe. Aurora race cars and Aurora monster models, those were the things I liked. I never got into little dolls for boys.

Bullpen: *And you had the* real *glue back then!* [laughs]

Fred: [*Slyly*] Yeahhhhh… [*laughter*]

Bullpen: *How am I gonna describe how you said that?* [laughs]

Fred: I never thought to actually sniff the glue. We just didn't do any of that… we didn't know.

Bullpen: *When did you do your first* bona fide *comics story? Did you do that at a young age?*

Fred: Nope. I drew my first one in college. My last two years in college were spent at the State University of New York in Buffalo.

Bullpen: *That's quite a distance from Long Island.*

Fred: Five hundred miles. There you go, buddy! Yes, sir! Driving home in those snowstorms in December wasn't much fun, but otherwise I loved it. Well, I was away from home for the first time in my whole life, right? I already had two years of real college under me, so I could just goof around for the next two years! Well, I didn't really expect to, but the second series of courses that I took was a bit more relaxed. It wasn't as specific. With advertising art and design, they tell you specific stuff to do. The Buffalo people were more like, "*You* figure out what to do." That kind of attitude. So I figured out how to goof off instead. So I learned a lot more those first two years, but that's okay, because that's what I needed. But the last year was pretty much devoted to doing a final project. So I said, "I'll do a comic strip!" I did an 11-page story, an adaptation of a story I read in a science-fiction paperback. I can't remember what it was now. I don't know what I was thinking, because the originals were like 20" x 40"! They didn't even do it that big in the '40s. [*laughter*] But I had it shrunk down, and I got an A in the course, so that was good.

Bullpen: *Was it realistic?*

Fred: Yes, it was a realistic style.

Bullpen: *Who would you say was your biggest influence?*

Fred: Neal Adams. You can see it in my art every day, can't cha? Come on, you know it's true! [*laughter*] When I was in my last year of high school, I worked hard at joining the clones. I still have downstairs a whole sketchbook filled up by me using a brush, just redoing pages and pages of *Green Lantern/Green Arrow* and *Batman* by Neal Adams. I got those teeth down just right. That Neal Adams profile with the gritted teeth. Man, I can still do that!

Bullpen: *"I can still draw those gums."* [laughs]

Fred: Right, exactly!

Bullpen: *Obviously you got over your thinking of Neal's work as grotesque, as you did with Ben Casey?*

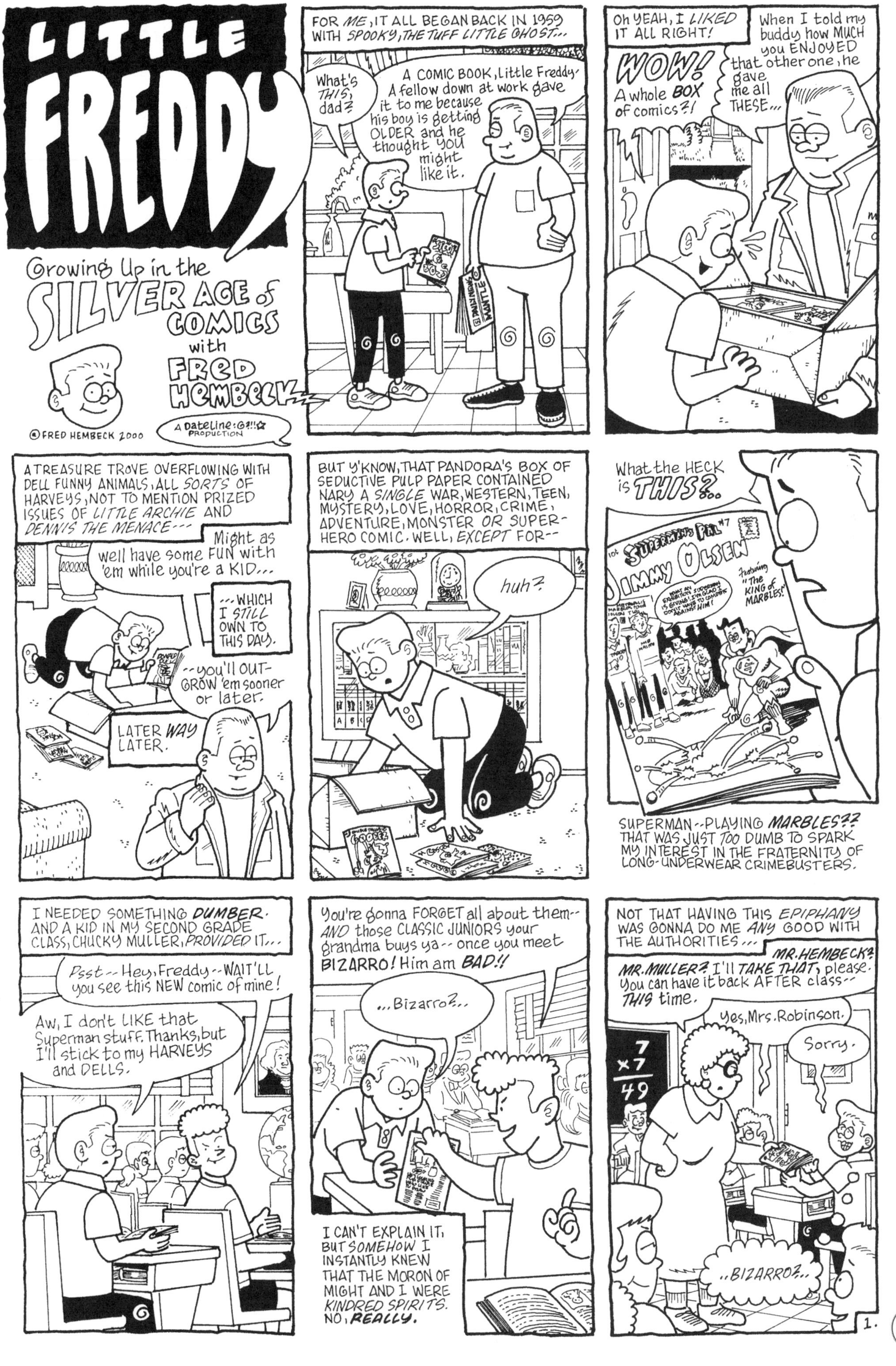
LITTLE FREDDY
Growing Up in the SILVER AGE of COMICS with FRED HEMBECK
©FRED HEMBECK 2000
A Dateline:@!!☆ PRODUCTION
FOR ME, IT ALL BEGAN BACK IN 1959 WITH SPOOKY, THE TUFF LITTLE GHOST...
What's THIS, dad?
A COMIC BOOK, Little Freddy. A fellow down at work gave it to me because his boy is getting OLDER and he thought YOU might like it.
Oh YEAH, I LIKED IT ALL RIGHT!
When I told my buddy how MUCH you ENJOYED that other one, he gave me all THESE...
WOW! A whole BOX of comics?!
A TREASURE TROVE OVERFLOWING WITH DELL FUNNY ANIMALS, ALL SORTS OF HARVEYS, NOT TO MENTION PRIZED ISSUES OF LITTLE ARCHIE AND DENNIS THE MENACE---
Might as well have some FUN with 'em while you're a KID...
---WHICH I STILL OWN TO THIS DAY.
--you'll OUT-GROW 'em sooner or later.
LATER. WAY LATER.
BUT Y'KNOW, THAT PANDORA'S BOX OF SEDUCTIVE PULP PAPER CONTAINED NARY A SINGLE WAR, WESTERN, TEEN, MYSTERY, LOVE, HORROR, CRIME, ADVENTURE, MONSTER OR SUPER-HERO COMIC. WELL, EXCEPT FOR--
huh?
What the HECK is THIS?...
SUPERMAN'S PAL JIMMY OLSEN
Featuring "The KING of MARBLES!"
SUPERMAN--PLAYING MARBLES?? THAT WAS JUST TOO DUMB TO SPARK MY INTEREST IN THE FRATERNITY OF LONG-UNDERWEAR CRIMEBUSTERS.
I NEEDED SOMETHING DUMBER. AND A KID IN MY SECOND GRADE CLASS, CHUCKY MULLER, PROVIDED IT...
Psst--Hey, Freddy--WAIT'LL you see this NEW comic of mine!
Aw, I don't LIKE that Superman stuff. Thanks, but I'll stick to my HARVEYS and DELLS.
You're gonna FORGET all about them--AND those CLASSIC JUNIORS your grandma buys ya--once you meet BIZARRO! Him am BAD!!
...Bizarro?...
I CAN'T EXPLAIN IT, BUT SOMEHOW I INSTANTLY KNEW THAT THE MORON OF MIGHT AND I WERE KINDRED SPIRITS. NO, REALLY.
NOT THAT HAVING THIS EPIPHANY WAS GONNA DO ME ANY GOOD WITH THE AUTHORITIES...
MR. HEMBECK?
MR. MULLER? I'll TAKE THAT, please. You can have it back AFTER class--THIS time.
Yes, Mrs. Robinson.
Sorry.
7 ×7 49
...BIZARRO?...
1.

THE *SEED* HAD BEEN *PLANTED.* AND ONE DAY, NOT LONG AFTER, STARING AT ME FROM THE COMICS SHELF OF *HEISEN-BUTTEL'S* GENERAL STORE, LIKE A FLOWER *RIPE* FOR THE PICK-ING, WAS A COPY OF THE *ALL-MENACE* EDITION OF THE *SUPERMAN ANNUAL* SERIES -- NUMBER TWO, FOR THOSE KEEPING SCORE -- FEATURING --

BIZARRO!

MOM! MOMMY! YOU'VE *GOTTA* BUY ME THIS COMIC -- YOU'VE JUST *GOTTA!?* PLEASE?

Are you SURE, Little Freddy? That's not the sort of book you USUALLY read?...

oh yeah -- ME am SURE!

sigh I'm beginning to think things would've been better for ALL of us if Big Freddy had just brought home a B·B GUN for the boy...

YES!

IT WAS *ANOTHER* FALSE START, THOUGH --SEEMS THIS REPRINT OF THE ORIGIN OF SUPERBOY'S --*NOT MAN'S*-- IMPERFECT DUPLICATE -- WAS PLAYED FAR MORE FOR *PATHOS* THAN FOR *LAUGHS.*

...and in the end, Bizarro SACRIFICES him-self to RESTORE a blind girl's SIGHT...

What's FUNNY about THAT?

SO, ONCE AGAIN, I TURNED MY BACK ON DC COMICS --SAVE FOR A *SINGLE* ISSUE OF *OUR ARMY AT WAR* (#106) THAT I BOUGHT PRIMARILY DUE TO PEER PRESSURE.

...All my friends seem to LIKE these war comics?...

BUT *I* NEVER DID. APPARENTLY, VIEW-ING TOO MANY EPISODES OF *SGT. BILKO* AT A TENDER AGE FOREVER *RUINED* MY APPRECIATION OF THE *FINER* POINTS OF MILITARY LIFE. BESIDES...

"Meet Lt. Rock"...

WHAT'S an "ell tee"?

NOT ONLY DID THE SARGE'S (TEMPORARY) PROMOTION *FLUMMOX* ME, IT WAS A RARE ROCK ESCAPADE *NOT* ILLUSTRATED BY THE LEGENDARY JOE KUBERT!

WHO KNOWS? I MAY'VE SHIED AWAY FROM NATIONAL PERIODICAL PUBLICATIONS *FOREVER* AFTER THAT, IF IT HADN'T BEEN FOR *ONE LITTLE THING*...

Guess WHAT, Freddy? They've given Bizarro his *OWN* series!!

YEAH! Well, I BOUGHT a comic with Bizarro in it, and it was anything BUT funny.

Oh, but *THIS* is!

Just take a look at some of the REALLY stupid things he does!

..heh, heh... Hey, this IS pretty goofy!...

Yeah, and check out Bizarro Lois "tidying" house with her RUBBISH DISPENS--

MR. MULLER! MR. HEMBECK!!

um...

...Us am in TROUBLE, huh?..

..heh..

THEY *CONFISCATED* COMIC BOOKS IN GRADE SCHOOL BACK THEN, SO I HAD NO CHOICE BUT TO HEAD OUT LOOKING FOR MY *OWN* COPY...

ONLY *INSTEAD* OF FINDING THE ISSUE OF *ADVENTURE COMICS* THAT KICKED OFF THE (ULTIMATELY SHORT-LIVED) *TALES OF THE BIZARRO WORLD*, #285, I STUMBLED UPON A COPY OF *SUPERMAN* #146, FEATURING--

"The Story of Superman's Life"? Huh. This just MIGHT be worth reading...

YOU KNOW WHAT THEY *SAY*-- TIMING IS *EVERYTHING!*

AND FROM *THERE*, IT JUST GOT *BETTER!* HAVING ADDED *EVERYBODY* WEARING A BRIGHT COSTUME PUBLISHED UNDER THE DC BANNER TO MY *MUST-BUY* LIST, ANY QUESTIONS I MIGHT'VE HAD ABOUT THESE STRANGE AND WONDERFUL PEOPLE WERE *ANSWERED* BUT A FEW SHORT WEEKS LATER IN --

"SECRET ORIGINS"! COOL!!

I TELL YA, THEY *MUST'VE* SEEN ME COMING!

ARCHIE--*BIG* ARCHIE--AND HIS GANG WERE NEXT, LEAVING BUT *ONE* BONE OF CONTENTION BETWEEN CHUCKY AND ME...

"Moomba Is Here"? Yeah, but undoubtedly your dime *ISN'T*-- here, that is.

HEY!

3.

The ONLY thing that ASTONISHES me about that book is how much you PAID for it! Honestly, the monster's have IDIOTIC names, the art looks CRUDE, and the ENTIRE line is mostly colored GREY, BROWN, and a shade of YUCKY GREEN. I'd have to be SICK in the head before I bought one of *THOSE!*

WHICH IS *EXACTLY* WHAT IT TOOK, AS IT TURNED OUT, FOR ME TO ACTUALLY *TRY* A MARVEL COMIC.

(GRATUITOUS SIDENOTE: OKAY, OKAY, SO A STRAY ISSUE OF *KID COLT, OUTLAW*--#101--SOMEHOW FOUND IT'S WAY INTO MY NASCENT COLLECTION, MAKING *IT* TRULY MY INITIAL ATLAS (SOON TO BE MARVEL) COMIC.

..ewww...

BUT THERE WAS THIS *ONE* STORY IN IT ABOUT A DESPICABLY SLEAZY OVERWEIGHT BADMAN DRAWN BY *DICK AYERS* THAT--I'M SORRY--JUST GAVE ME THE CREEPS. THOSE *SICKLY* HUES *DIDN'T* HELP ANY. YECH!)

IN EARLY 1962, A MILD CASE OF *SCARLET FEVER* FOREVER *CHANGED* THE TRAJECTORY OF MY LIFE. ORDERED QUARANTINED FROM EVERYONE BUT MY FOLKS, I HAD ONLY *ONE* OVERRIDING CONCERN--

What about my COMICS ??

FORTUITOUSLY, THE COMICS SHELF AT HEISENBUTTELS WAS LOCATED *ADJACENT* TO A LARGE DISPLAY WINDOW, INSPIRING A *FOOLPROOF* PLAN.

QUICK! GET THAT PARKING SPACE OUT FRONT!

Okay, Little Freddy, OKAY-- calm down.

MOM WOULD GO IN, HOLD UP A COMIC IN THE WINDOW AT RANDOM, AND I WOULD GIVE AN *AFFIRMATIVE* OR *NEGATIVE* NOD FROM THE SAFETY OF OUR CAR REGARDING IT'S PURCHASABILITY. *SIMPLE*, REALLY.

...The THINGS I DO for that boy! ?...

A FEW "NOS", A COUPLA "YES" NODS-- I DISTINCTLY RECALL GIVING AN ISSUE OF *BLACKHAWK* THUMBS UP-- AND *THEN*, JUST BY CHANCE --OR WAS IT *FATE*?-- MOM HELD UP THIS *CURIOUS* LOOKING COMIC---

..."THE FANTASTIC FOUR"?...

THE LOGO LOOKED *PECULIAR*-- *SILLY*, *ALMOST* CIRCUS-LIKE, BUT IT *INTRIGUED* ME. IN A SPLIT-SECOND, I MADE MY DECISION:

YES!

Here you are.

LEMME SEE THOSE!!

Now, where IS that one?..

ah.

FANTASTIC FOUR #4. STAN *LEE*, JACK KIRBY, FRED HEMBECK--TOGETHER FOR THE *FIRST* TIME. BUT, AS YOU'VE *PROBABLY* SURMISED, *NOT* THE LAST TIME.

NEAT!

I GREW UP IN A SMALL TOWN ON LONG ISLAND BY THE NAME OF YAPHANK, BUT ON THAT LATE WINTER AFTERNOON, I FOUND A *NEW*-- AND DARE I SAY, *BETTER*?-- PLACE TO SPEND MY CHILDHOOD: *THE MARVEL UNIVERSE.*

SPOOKY *SPARKED* MY INTEREST, BIZARRO *SUSTAINED* IT, AND THE F.F. *CLINCHED* IT. FACE IT, I'M A *BORN* COMIC READER IF EVER THERE WAS ONE!

Mommy, WHY is the MONSTER one of the GOOD guys, and this nice looking Sub-Mariner a BAD one?

Ask your FATHER, dear.

Because, if not for that G?!☆✦ing BOX of his!?..

END!

Fred: Oh, yes. Oh, definitely. Once I saw Neal's Warren comics, I thought it was stunning stuff. People don't take his *Creepy* and *Eerie* work into account often enough. They always just think of that DC stuff. As good as his *Spectre* and "Deadman" were, the stories he did around the same time in the last couple of the Archie Goodwin issues were just unbelievably good.

Bullpen: *Did you go through a period of getting more into the Marvel stuff and leaving the DC stuff behind?*

Fred: Oh, yes! From pretty much the minute I started reading the Marvel stuff, I was a confirmed Marvel guy, but I wanted to read *everything*, so it wasn't like I looked down on DC. I kept buying DC comics, but just before Carmine Infantino took over, the books were really getting turgid, and I started dropping titles I'd been reading for years. Almost all of them, until next thing you know there's *The Creeper* and *Hawk and Dove*, *Bat Lash* and *Angel and the Ape,* and I started buying them all again. But there was a very bad period just before that, whereas with the Marvels, those I never stopped buying. Maybe I wouldn't like this one particular guy's art, but I knew the story's going to be at least interesting and go on until the next month or whatever. Actually, they were never as bad as some of those DCs from 1966 or '67.

Bullpen: *Did you look at the Julie Schwartz books as perhaps the best of the line?*

Fred: Yes, but even those titles… I even turned my back on *Batman* and *Justice League* for a minute there, because in the last few years, where Bob Kane was still pretending to draw for them and all? And it was like, "I can't take this anymore!" When Mike Sekowsky was being inked by Sid Greene? Sid Greene just came in and inked *everything* for a year and it just hurt my eyes! I mean, he *ruined* the last year of Carmine's *Flash!* I *loved* Carmine's work! Carmine is my DC god. I loved that guy's artwork. I couldn't take it when they took him off *The Flash* and gave it to Ross Andru, because, as good as Ross actually was, it was just too jarring a change.

Bullpen: *So when Carmine took over as editor-in-chief, was there a noticeable change for the better?*

Fred: Oh, definitely. All of a sudden, DC was my favorite company again. One month you had *Secret Six* coming out, then *Anthro*. I mean, that was one year when DC was far more exciting than Marvel. So the pendulum had swung back.

Bullpen: *Actually, Marvel was getting a little tired, right?*

Fred: It was. Truthfully, the year prior to that, my actual favorite company before Carmine took over DC was when Dick Giordano was doing the "Action Hero Line" at Charlton. That year, I just loved those things the most. They seemed to be the brightest and most exciting things out there.

Bullpen: *The year prior to Charlton, was it Tower?*

Fred: Yes, although I still liked the Marvel stuff, but I'm a guy who thinks Marvel peaked in about the spring of 1965. I always thought *Fantastic Four* #40 was the peak, and after that everything just got too serious and all drawn out. Everyone else was, "Galactus and the Silver Surfer!" "No, no, I liked it when they fought Gideon [*FF* #34, Jan. '65], the guy who was really, really rich!" [*laughter*] I *did*! I *loved* that issue!

Bullpen: *Was Jack Kirby a particular favorite?*

Fred: Oh, yeah! Steve Ditko was *the* favorite, but the fact Jack was doing everything else besides *Spider-Man* and "Doctor Strange" was just stunning. I guess by 1965 he wasn't doing *everything* anymore, as they had let him out of his cell and just gave him a couple of books to do. But I loved '64, when he was doing practically everything and Chic Stone was inking every Kirby book. I just have the very best memories of that particular year. To me, that was the peak of Marvel, because the stories all ran one issue, maybe two, but they were concise, and there was a lot of great stuff packed in them. The thing about that Inhumans/Galactus story was, the Inhumans story, which ran for like five issues, ended in the middle of the first Galactus story [#48, Mar. '66]. I was like, "Well, *that* doesn't strike me as good planning!" But no one ever complains about that. Still, I'm buying them every month, I'm going, "Wait a second. Why can't we have that rich guy come back again? I want to see Gideon!" I was so excited when, I

Pages 107–110: *Fred had intended for a colored version of this Hembeck "origin" story to be the opening episode in the resurrected fanzine* The Comic Reader, *but alas, that mag never saw the light of day. Courtesy of and ©2021 F.H.*

This page: *Fred was an early contributor to* The Comics Journal, *as well as any number of late '70s and early '80s fanzines, as evidenced by (left inset) his cover for TCJ #60 [Nov. '80]. During Jack Kirby's fight with Marvel Comics in the mid-'80s, Hembeck produced the editorial page (below) for TCJ [#107, Apr. '86]. Characters TM & ©2021 Marvel Characters, Inc. Artwork ©2021 Fred Hembeck.*

"THE PARTY"   by FRED HEMBECK

remember reading in a newszine while I was in college, going, "Gerry Conway's bringing back Gideon! Oh my god! I can't believe it!" [*laughter*]

Bullpen: *Did that jazz you when you did that 11-page story?*

Fred: Yes, it really did. I thought, "Wow! This is cool! I like doing this!" I had impressed myself.

Bullpen: *When was the last time you looked at it?*

Fred: Years ago, I printed one page in one of my books, so that particular one sticks out in my mind. That was the best page, obviously. The rest I can't remember.

Bullpen: *Was the work any good?*

Fred: Not that good, no. It seemed like they were good at the time, and as good as I could do, and there were a couple of good panels here and there, and the one page was fairly decent, but you have to look hard for the glimmers.

Bullpen: *Were you swiping?*

Fred: No, not swiping. I said to myself, "No swiping this time, buddy." I had done swipes before, but I thought, "Nah, I've gotta do my own thing here." There might have been a hand here or

there, I don't want to swear to 100% no swiping, but it wasn't a panel from Neal here, a panel from Jim Aparo there. Nothing like that.

Bullpen: *So did it spark you? Did you say, "Hey, maybe I want to do this"?*

Fred: Oh, yes, definitely, but at the time I was staying on in Buffalo, because my girlfriend, who would become my wife, still had a year to go in college. So I hung around an extra year.

Bullpen: *What is your wife's name?*

Fred: Lynn.

Bullpen: *When did you meet her?*

Fred: The last week of my first year in Buffalo, just before summer started. We lived in the same dorm, on the same floor. [*laughs*] So I met her the last week. Hey, I know that doesn't make sense, but that's the way it worked. There was some money left over that they had collected from the people in the dorm, so they took everybody out to have a party. On our floor, one half was the men's side and one half was the women's side, but because we were on the first floor, there was kind of a big room in-between the two wings. Plus, most of the guys on my side were engaged or had girlfriends, so the two sides never mixed. I didn't know any of the people on the other side, and they didn't know us. But then we went out to the party and we just hit it off, and there you go. It's been magic since then!

Bullpen: *What was her major?*

Fred: Psychology, but now she's a programmer for IBM.

Bullpen: *So it's been 27 years together?*

Fred: Well, our 25th wedding anniversary's coming up next year, and we were together five years before that, so I guess that would make 30 years.

I had to hang on an extra year, so I took a temporary job doing some production work, I worked at a grocery store. I delivered flyers door-to-door in little plastic bags for a guy named Jimmy Hendricks (although he didn't spell it the same way as the dead rock star). I got fired from that job, because I was always given a different route, and one time there was too much snow and I didn't want to go door-to-door because it took too long. The good part was, I got all these plastic bags I would put my comic books in, so I'm probably the only person around who has all of his valuable old comic books in plastic bags that have kind of like a hook on them so you can hang them on people's doors. Hey, it was way cheaper than buying mylars through the mail!

Bullpen: *Did you go to any of the early cons in the late '60s? What was your first comic convention?*

Fred: I remember the [Seuling] New York July Fourth con in 1971. Again, this friend of mine who I had gotten into comics recently was interested, but we went to this other guy's house the night before, and there was this party, and we stayed up really late, and my friend got really drunk. I'm going, "Well, *I* want to go to the con tomorrow!" So the next day we finally got out and drove in to the city at about five o'clock, and I remember we walked in late, and there was Russ Heath up there giving a talk. To this day, I've never seen Russ Heath again. It's the oddest thing. "Oh, we missed Russ's talk, but I'm sure I'll see him again someday." Never did. But after that, I started going to them regularly, and went to those first Second Saturdays (or whatever they were), a one-day con in New York Phil Seuling used to host. So, for a while, we went to a lot of those. And, of course, I went to the big Marvel Con [in 1976]. Remember when Marvel threw their own convention? I was in Buffalo then, but came down especially for that event, all three days of it, met a friend there, Charlie Johnson, and we had a really good time. That was my favorite convention experience.

Bullpen: *Did you enjoy the Seuling cons?*

Fred: Yeah, oh yeah! Oh man, I was dazzled by that stuff! Are you kiddin'? As much as I liked comics and the characters,

I was always extremely fascinated by the people *behind* the comics. Since I wasn't going to meet the characters, I figured I could meet the people. It was fun. I talked to Steve Gerber, I talked to Steve Englehart. I would always go up and chat with these guys. Yeah, it was the best thing ever.

Bullpen: *Any particular anecdotes you recall of hanging out with the pros?*

Fred: I didn't hang out *per se*, but they were friendly and generally approachable. I was really enamored with the Marvel writers of the '70s: Englehart, Gerber, Don McGregor, those guys, so I would always go up to them and ask them all kinds of questions, nothing too weird.

One anecdote (which has nothing to do with that) was when I was at one of those Creation Cons with my friend Charlie, who was a big comics fan who I met at Farmingdale. We went into this empty room where there had recently been, I guess, a speech or a panel. And I went up on the podium like I was going to be one of the guests or something, because I was having a little fantasy moment, you know? All of a sudden, these two workers came in, and they thought I was trying to steal the microphone. "No, no! I'm just having fun!" [*laughter*] They let me go. I guess I looked more embarrassed than guilty. Then, ironically, when I finally did become a professional guy, I was too shy to go up there and talk in front of people. I didn't really do that too often at conventions. A few times, but I would get nervous for whatever reason. I liked sitting behind a table and talking to people in the dealer's room, but, because you're looking down from a stage, and people are looking up at you… but then, you can't help but notice that other guys are, like, reading comics and stuff, eating a sandwich… nowadays they're probably playing Game Boy! [*laughter*]

Bullpen: *Didn't a lot of people attend the panels just to take a rest?*

Fred: Yeah, exactly! So I'd be up there talking and I'd think, "I've got them all!" Then I'd look and see that one guy over there reading *Supergirl*. "Oh, man! What—he doesn't like my speech?" [*laughter*] So it would absolutely kill me.

Bullpen: *So what did you do after that 11-page story?*

Fred: For about a year I hung around Buffalo. Finally, I figured,"Okay, you've gotta get something going here." So I decided to put together a portfolio, because I knew that the one story wasn't going to do it. Because it was too big. So, while I was working at these odd jobs, I put together about 30 pages of pencil samples. Of course, I did them fully penciled and inked, which probably wasn't the best way to do it, as I probably should have just penciled them, but I didn't know any better. They didn't have any how-to books out at that point, because we're talking about 1976 or so. So, when Lynn graduated, she went down to her home in Woodstock, New York, not far from where we live today, and I went down to mine in Long Island, and prepared to go in to the various companies with my portfolio. I think it was the summer of '77. And I did.

The result was *not* a resounding success. By and large, I didn't actually get to see anybody. I left my portfolio at Marvel and came back the next day to get it. I also left it at Continuity and a few other places. I did get to actually have an honest to

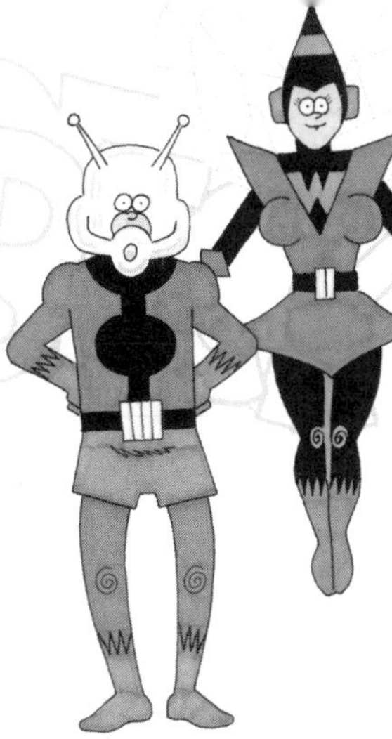

Above: *This spot illustration and assorted others in this feature are by Hembeck.*
Below: *Fred contributed many, many centerspread strips to* Marvel Age, *the House of Ideas promotional comic, throughout the mid- to late '80s. From* MA *#31 [Oct. '85)] Ant-Man and The Wasp TM & ©2021 Marvel Characters, Inc.*

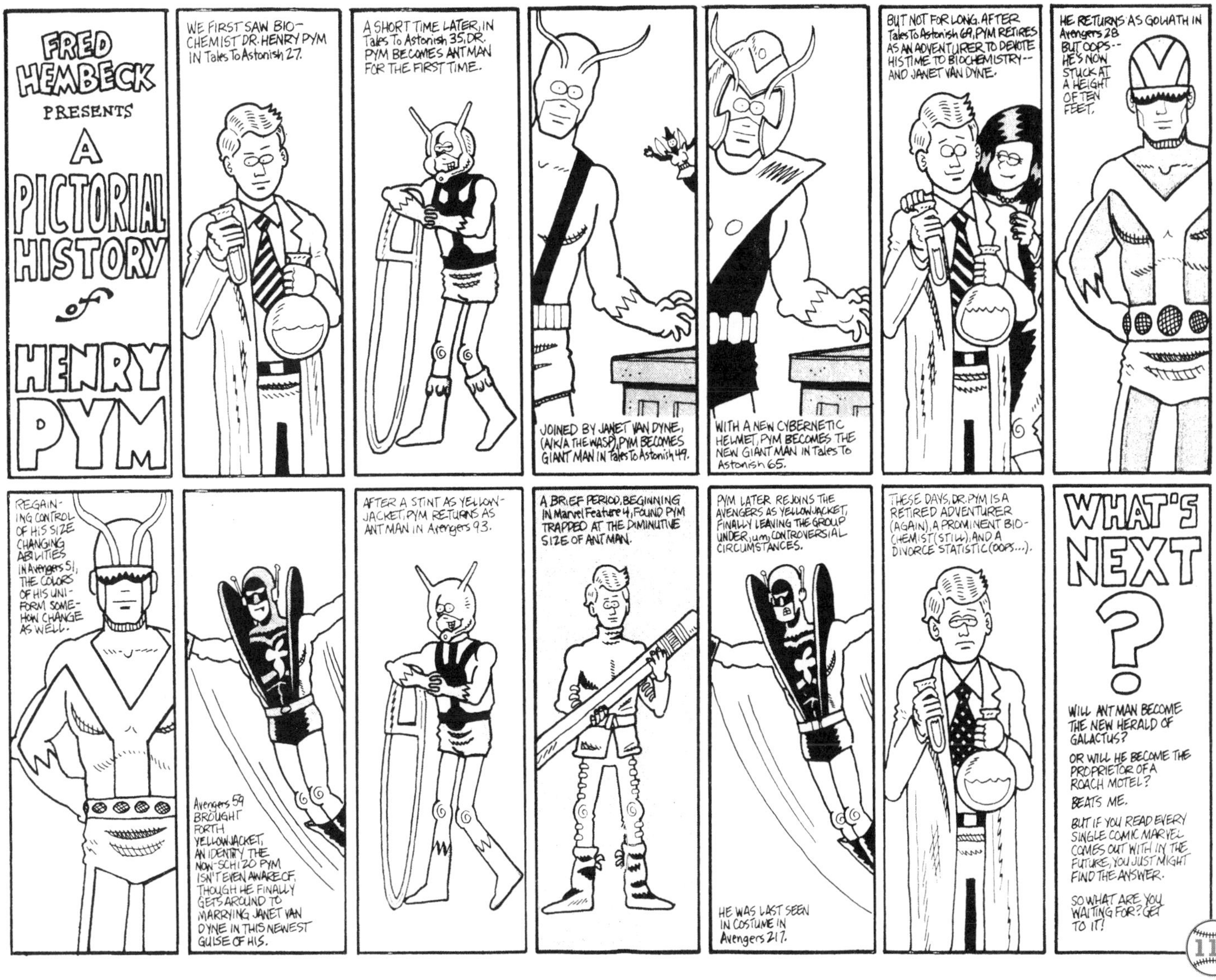

FRED HEMBECK PRESENTS A PICTORIAL HISTORY of HENRY PYM
WE FIRST SAW BIO-CHEMIST DR. HENRY PYM IN Tales To Astonish 27.
A SHORT TIME LATER, IN Tales To Astonish 35, DR. PYM BECOMES ANT MAN FOR THE FIRST TIME.
JOINED BY JANET VAN DYNE, (A/K/A THE WASP), PYM BECOMES GIANT MAN IN Tales To Astonish 49.
WITH A NEW CYBERNETIC HELMET, PYM BECOMES THE NEW GIANT MAN IN Tales To Astonish 65.
BUT NOT FOR LONG. AFTER Tales To Astonish 69, PYM RETIRES AS AN ADVENTURER TO DEVOTE HIS TIME TO BIOCHEMISTRY-- AND JANET VAN DYNE.
HE RETURNS AS GOLIATH IN Avengers 28 BUT OOPS-- HE'S NOW STUCK AT A HEIGHT OF TEN FEET.
REGAINING CONTROL OF HIS SIZE CHANGING ABILITIES IN Avengers 51, THE COLORS OF HIS UNIFORM SOMEHOW CHANGE AS WELL.
Avengers 59 BROUGHT FORTH YELLOWJACKET, AN IDENTITY THE NON-SCHIZO PYM ISN'T EVEN AWARE OF, THOUGH HE FINALLY GETS AROUND TO MARRYING JANET VAN DYNE IN THIS NEWEST GUISE OF HIS.
AFTER A STINT AS YELLOWJACKET, PYM RETURNS AS ANT MAN IN Avengers 93.
A BRIEF PERIOD, BEGINNING IN Marvel Feature 4, FOUND PYM TRAPPED AT THE DIMINUTIVE SIZE OF ANT MAN.
PYM LATER REJOINS THE AVENGERS AS YELLOWJACKET, FINALLY LEAVING THE GROUP UNDER, um, CONTROVERSIAL CIRCUMSTANCES.
HE WAS LAST SEEN IN COSTUME IN Avengers 217.
THESE DAYS, DR. PYM IS A RETIRED ADVENTURER (AGAIN), A PROMINENT BIO-CHEMIST (STILL), AND A DIVORCE STATISTIC (OOPS...).
WHAT'S NEXT ?
WILL ANT MAN BECOME THE NEW HERALD OF GALACTUS?
OR WILL HE BECOME THE PROPRIETOR OF A ROACH MOTEL?
BEATS ME.
BUT IF YOU READ EVERY SINGLE COMIC MARVEL COMES OUT WITH IN THE FUTURE, YOU JUST MIGHT FIND THE ANSWER.
SO WHAT ARE YOU WAITING FOR? GET TO IT!

anatomy. As the interview drew to a close, he said, "Well, kid, I don't think ya got it. I could tell you [that] you could get into comics, but I don't want to jerk ya off." So I said, "Oh, okay." He said, "See you later, thanks a lot." Then he smiled, turned to Julie Schwartz (who had just come in), and just like that, I'm out the door. Off to home I went.

Bullpen: *Were you devastated?*

Fred: I was pretty upset, but then I realized, "Come on, Fred! This is Vinnie Colletta judging your work!" If it was somebody I had respected, maybe I would have been more upset. On the other hand, if someone I *didn't* respect thought it was that bad… you could look at it either way, right? So I'm going to look at it the way I want, to make me myself feel better about it. So I went home on the train, got in the car, and almost pulled out in front of another car driving out of the parking lot. [*laughs*] So now I'm living on borrowed time, y'know. I'm like the fifth Challenger. [*Jon laughs*] So I went home and read the "Starlord" black-&-white comic by Chris Claremont, John Byrne, and Terry Austin [*Marvel Preview* #11, Oct. '77]. I really liked it, and said, "Wow! I still like comics!" Because I had been thinking to myself, "Can I read a comic and still like it after that experience?" But that comic — this was before they did *The X-Men*—made me realize, "Yes, I can read a comic and enjoy it!" Next thing you know, I pledged to keep drawing and keep working and trying to get into comics, but of course that's when I made the right turn without realizing it. [*pause*] Go ahead, you can ask me what that means.

Bullpen: [*Laughs*] *What does "made the right turn" mean?*

Fred: Well, that means that I became a cartoony cartoonist without quite realizing it was happening. I had just left college, as I told you, but still had a number of good friends there, and I wanted to keep in touch with them, so I would draw these illustrated letters to send to them. That's how the little character of Fred came about, because they obviously knew who I was and what I looked like, with the hair parted in the middle and the little beard and everything. I sent them all a couple of letters like that. Now, I'd had letters printed in comic books, and in fact, a couple of years earlier, I had had a *lot* of letters printed in comics. I thought, "Well, people who get their letters printed in comics get into comics!" But, of course, most of those guys were writers, as opposed to artists. But I had a lot of letters in *Deadly Hands of Kung Fu*, mainly because there was a lot of tiny type in there and they had two pages to fill. It was easier to get in that magazine, compared to a small page in *Fantastic Four*, for instance. So I would send several of these illustrated letters off to various writers, and one of them was Bill Mantlo, and it was ultimately a letter of comment about an issue of *Iron Man* that did it. He wrote back saying, "Wow, I really liked that letter! But because you used different color inks" — again, I was showing off with the colors, you'd think I'd learn — "we can't print it, but if you can redraw it, we'll print it." I go, "Really?" So I did it 10" x 15", and they printed it as a special letters page, and paid me $35 for it. It was in *Iron Man* #112 [July '78, page 27]. Around the very same time, I decided to send something off to *The Comics Buyer's Guide*, which was that first strip which was me interviewing Spider-Man. I sent in that strip as well as a cover and, on the cover were 50 or so characters stacked up, sitting for a group portrait, drawn in that little style I had just come up with. This was a style I had never really drawn before until maybe a month prior to leav-

This spread: *Here is Fred Hembeck's "switcheroo" alternative universe covers for Marvel and DC's respective early-'60s diminutive heroes, The Atom and Ant-Man. Above is a take on (inset right)* Tales To Astonish #40 *[Feb. '63]. Art ©2021 Fred Hembeck. The Atom TM & ©2021 DC Comics. Cover design, Ant-Man and* TTA *TM & ©2021 Marvel Characters, Inc.*

gosh interview at DC. Now, stupid me, I didn't realize stop and consider exactly who would be looking at my stuff. Of course, that's going to be the art director, and, of course, I read the indicia and should have known who that would be, but I was still shocked when I realized my stuff was going to be judged by Mr. Vincent Colletta. Now, I'm a big-hearted guy and I like almost everybody's artwork, but there was one guy whose stuff I couldn't stand. You know who that could have been? That's right: Mr. Vincent Colletta. I went, "Oh, no." So there he was, looking at my portfolio. A friend of mine had made some stats of my stuff, which I had in turn colored. I'm going all out, I'm coloring them, inking them, the whole nine yards. Vinnie says, "Why'd ya color 'em? Why'd ya ink 'em?" I say, "Uh, gee, I don't know." Then he pulls out some pages that were lying around to show me how to do it the right way, some Rich Buckler pages, some other stuff, and he told me to go home and get a copy of Andrew Loomis's book to learn how to do some better ing college, because a friend had asked me to do up a little flyer for his keg party that his fellow engineers were having. He was one of my roommates. So I knew it wasn't going to work if I did a Neal Adams-like drawing, so I scrawled up these little cartoony things and thought, "This is okay!" That's how that style pretty much came out of nowhere. It wasn't anything I'd ever developed. At the same time that I was swiping Neal Adams when I was a kid, I was swiping Mort Walker *Beetle Bailey* drawings, just for my own amusement, because it was my favorite humor strip. So that sorta feel was in there, that's where that came from. So I sent the cover and drawing in to [*CBG* editor/ publisher] Alan Light and he wound up printing the drawing. He said, "Send some more." Then I did one with The Flash, and next thing you know, he was actually paying me $15. So, all of a sudden, people were interested in my work.

So I never really went back to the straight style. This stuff happened almost right after the whole Vinnie Colletta meltdown story, but it was just a matter of me trying to keep drawing, so I didn't lose my momentum. I did buy the Loomis book, I still have it. It didn't help me with this stuff, but I still have it, so I took some of Vinnie's advice.

Bullpen: *What was it you were doing for* The Buyer's Guide? *Were they full-page strips?*

Fred: Right. Full-page strips. The first couple had nine panels, me interviewing the characters. I had a lot of opinions, read all the comics, and would just throw some corny jokes into the mix, and it seemed to come out okay. I did that with Spider-Man, because the title was getting a new artist and he was complaining about it in my strip. I also did one with The Flash complaining about being stuck in a Hostess Twinkie ad. Then I did a Marvel Comics Captain Marvel one where he was splitting his body into pieces, like that other [Myron Fass] Captain Marvel character did. It was all just silly stuff I could come up with, based on the knowledge of all the comics I had been reading for years by then. It seemed to go over pretty well. Next thing you know, the people from DC were contacting me to do those little comic strips for *The Daily Planet* promo pages. That was probably the next big thing I did after that Marvel letter page for Bill Mantlo.

Bullpen: *Did Alan Light pretty much buy anything you did or were there rejections?*

Fred: Only once did he ever reject something, and it was based upon the fact there was once a fanzine called *AFTA*. There was this fellow, Bill-Dale Marcinko, who put together this strange comic fanzine which was a couple hundred pages long. He started a hoax that he had gotten killed, but he really hadn't. That got him noticed, and somehow spurred sales. So I did this strip that was promoting it, and Alan said, "This is really just an advertisement, Fred. I can't really run this." So he didn't buy it, but that was the only one. I don't know whatever happened to that guy. He put out three issues of that *AFTA*, and it was amazing at the time.

Bullpen: *So this was in the mid-'70s?*

Fred: This would have to be '79 or '80, because my first stuff getting published was probably around late '77.

Bullpen: *So that must have been cool, right? I mean, this is a pretty quick ascension…*

Fred: It *was* cool.

Bullpen: *You were spotlighted right off, but you were a complete novice, and yet anyone who was of your age or a peer would take a relatively long time to get noticed.*

Fred: Yeah, I know! But I had done some stuff in fanzines years earlier that nobody really noticed, years earlier, just regular stuff.

The other thing was that I put my address on the bottom of the page. "Write to me if you want to…" I got all kinds of mail for a while. I even still have it packed away downstairs somewhere. I actually got some letters from the Hernandez Brothers. I didn't know who they were at the time, but I was found it while going through the box when we moved a couple of years ago. I also got a letter from Chris Ware.

Bullpen: *[Laughs] Dude!*

Fred: Yeah, I know! That was amazing. Chris doesn't return my calls now. *[laughter]* Some of the material I received was weird, though. One guy wrote and said, "Do you like the superheroines when their costumes are torn?" He went on for about two pages. I didn't write back to him. *[Jon laughs]* I imagine he runs a website now. It was very ego gratifying there for a while.

Bullpen: *Was there any money in it?*

Above and inset left:
Hembeck's "switcheroo" version of Showcase #36 [Oct. '61], swapping Marvel's Hank Pym for DC's Ray Palmer. Courtesy of and art ©2021 Fred Hembeck. Ant-Man TM & ©2021 Marvel Characters, Inc. Cover design, The Atom, Showcase TM & ©2021 DC.

Center insets for both pages:
One of Hembeck's extremely rare "straight" art jobs was his "Brother Voodoo" story in Marvel Super-Heroes Spring Special #1 (1990). To Fred's dismay, the unidentified Filipino inker completely obliterated the pencils, as we can see in these before-&-after examples. (By the way, Fred has a long, strange history with Marvel's infrequently-used '70s zombie super-hero, much discussed on the inside back cover of Fred Hembeck $ells the Marvel Universe.) Courtesy of F.H. Brother Voodoo vignette at far right is detail from the cover of Fred Hembeck $ells the Marvel Universe #1 [1990]. TM & ©2021 Marvel Characters, Inc.

Below: Hembeck emits a deep affection for the very weird 'n' wonky characters populating comics. One of the more bizarre was Brother Power, The Geek, an oddball concept devised by Joe Simon—co-creator of Captain America and longtime partner of Jack "The King" Kirby—in the late 1960s. Here's Fred's version. Art courtesy of and ©2021 Fred Hembeck. Characters TM & ©2021 DC Comics.

Fred: Not tremendously, but at that point, those *shekels* went a little farther than they do nowadays. Next thing you know I'm doing a regular thing for *The Comic Reader.*

Bullpen: *What was that?*

Fred: Just like a half-page. I did a back cover and a couple of covers, odds and ends here and there. I even did a cover or two for *The Comics Journal,* a Jim Shooter cover [#60, Nov. '80]. I was all over the place at one point.

Bullpen: *What were you doing for a "real job"?*

Fred: I didn't have one. We just managed to eke out a living, between *The Buyer's Guide* stuff and my wife's salary. Then we managed to get the people at Eclipse interested… actually, Richard Bruning came to me — he was a friend of [Eclipse co-publisher] Dean Mullaney — and they wanted to collect my strips into a book. It was actually the second publication Eclipse ever published, right after the *Sabre* graphic novel by McGregor and Paul Gulacy. So *Hembeck's Best of Dateline* was my first collection that came out, and I got a couple of bucks from that.

Oh, actually, I *did* have a job, you're right. What am I thinking? I had my job at a gas station, just sitting in the booth taking money.

Bullpen: *Could you literally draw while you were working?*

Fred: Yes, I did, in fact, which leads to an odd story: I was doing a little cartoon for *The Comic Reader* one night at the job, and a woman comes up to the window and says, "Oh, you're doing comics! My husband draws comics!" I say, "Really?" She says, "My husband is Bob Layton!" I say, "Really! Okay." She goes, "Do you live around here?" I say, "Yeah, I do!" Then she asks for my phone number, but I was flustered, and we had just moved, so I gave her the old phone number for the *last* house we'd lived in by mistake without realizing it. So I don't hear from Bob for months. One day it's really hot, I'm in the house, just in my shorts (not underwear shorts, but shorts), and there's a knock at the door. It's Bob Layton and his wife! "Yeah, Fred, we couldn't find ya, but we tracked you down!" I say, "Oh,

come on in, Bob!" So Bob comes in, and he was a very excitable guy, so he's telling me all sorts of stuff. Next thing you know, he's hiring me to be his background artist, and I actually did three pages of backgrounds for Bob, two pages of "Ant-Man" over John Byrne in *Marvel Premiere* [#47 or 48, April or June '78], and a page of John Romita, Jr., in *Iron Man* [#117, Dec. '78, page 5].

Bullpen: *Could you identify them today?*

Fred: One panel had a piece of paper, so I wrote people's names on it. Then old Bob took off and left town. This was right after the DC "Implosion," because I remember him calling up and telling me about it. Then Bob just went off, and I didn't hear from him until years and years later, so I lost out on my one chance to become a background artist or even to work my way up to being a regular inker.

Bullpen: *But you got paid for the work you did?*

Fred: Oh, yes, but I was bummed when he went away.

Bullpen: *You were doing work for DC prior to their "Implosion," right?*

Fred: Yes, I was working on that little comic strip for the promotional house text page, *The Daily Planet,* which they decided to call *Hembeck.* I was suggesting it be called *Dateline* but they said other people wouldn't know what that meant. So they plastered my name on it. That's why Dean Mullaney wanted the books to be called *Hembeck,* because of the strips in the DC comics.

Bullpen: *Did you like having a relatively unusual name like that?*

Fred: I didn't as a kid, but later I did.

Bullpen: *When you could brand yourself.* [laughs]

Fred: Yes, definitely! I've never been that crazy about "Fred," but what are you gonna do? The Hembeck thing is working well for me now. Nobody *else* has got it!

Bullpen: *[Laughs] Just one other person in the U.S., you say?*

Fred: Right.

Bullpen: *You had been doing material for* The Comic Reader *and* The Comics Buyer's Guide. *So, it was in the late '70s when the Eclipse book came out?*

Fred: Yes, because the very next book was called *Hembeck 1980.*

Bullpen: *Was this a perfect-bound, graphic novel-sized publication?*

Fred: Nope, it was magazine size, but not perfect-bound. Forty-eight pages, 8½" x 11", saddle-stitched, like the old *CBA*.

Bullpen: *Was there any money in it?*

Fred: Yes. It wasn't big money, but at the time it seemed pretty good. I was just starting out and we were living in a small little room on top of this older couple's house, a separate apartment, so it was fine at the time (before we started "moving on up," as they used to say on *The Jeffersons*). Then Dean was really dragging his butt on getting the second book out. We had moved up from the Kingston area to the Troy area, because at that point Lynn was going to RPI, which was a college of some sort. I can't think of what it stands for. [*laughs*]

Rensselaer Polytechnic Institute… I became friendly with the people at a comics shop in Albany, the city next to Troy, a place called Fantaco Enterprises. These guys were *not* Fantagraphic Books. To this day, people think that I had these books published by Fantagraphics.

Bullpen: Fantaco was run by Tom Skulan. They did [the horror magazine/comic] Gore Shriek, *right?*

Fred: Right. Tom was more of a monster guy than a comics

guy, but he had a comics shop, and he had this really talented cartoonist named Raoul Vezina.

Bullpen: *Right! Raoul's work was excellent! Whatever happened to him?*

Fred: He died. It was a sad thing. It happened in the mid-'80s, when Raoul's asthma got out of control, from what I heard. He was a really nice guy, too, well liked by everyone.

Bullpen: *He was pretty young.*

Fred: Yes, he was. Raoul was about the same age as I was. He might have been a year or two older, but not much.

So Raoul was working there behind the counter and was always a cartoonist. Fantaco wound up putting one of his books together. But I had this other book all ready to go, the

second collection, some of which was new material. I got sick of waiting for Dean, and he was being a pain in the butt about it, so I asked, "If you guys aren't gonna publish it, do you mind if these other people do it?" So he said okay. He was not a bad sport about it, but from that point on I worked for Fantaco, putting out books of either new or old material, or half-and-half. I did seven books total for them, including a reprint of the Eclipse book. I also helped with their *Smilin' Ed* book, which was

Below: Though his DC assignments were less frequent than those offered by Marvel, Fred still occasionally found employment with the comic book folks at Time-Warner. Here's a rarely-seen Christmas Party invite drawn up by Hembeck. Courtesy of the artist. TM & ©2021 DC Comics.

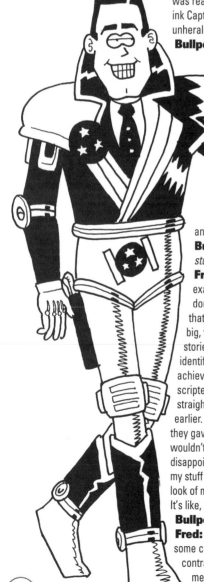

basically meant doing some back-up strips. That was Raoul's magazine.

Bullpen: *You also contributed to their* Chronicle *books.*

Fred: And the *Chronicle*s, yup. So I did those. That was during the period when we lived up there in the area.

Bullpen: *How was it working at Fantaco?*

Fred: It was okay for a while. It certainly seemed okay. But… I don't know. Things just got kind of strained between the artists and the owner, and, although I can't remember the exact reason *why* everyone was upset, it all just kind of dissolved by the time we finished up there, not just for myself, but for the other people, too.

Bullpen: *Now, Fantaco was Tom alone?*

Fred: Yes, it was pretty much Tom alone. He was *the* publisher, but he did have some people working at the shop who were advisors. He also put on several comic conventions, too, the Fantacons.

Bullpen: *Were they held up there?*

Fred: Yes, they were in Albany, in The Egg, this odd-looking structure, shaped like—you guessed it—like a round egg.

Bullpen: *How was the comics community around there?*

Fred: Pretty good! John Caldwell was up there, who now does cartoons for *MAD* magazine, *Playboy*, and all the big ones. I actually gave Bill Anderson his first assignment—Bill's an inker—and when I met him, he was about 16 years old, and he was really good. When I did *The Fantastic Four Roast*, I let him ink Captain America's shield on one panel, which was his unheralded debut.

Bullpen: *Oh, you generous man, you!*

Fred: I'm such a sweet guy, aren't I? [*laughter*]

Bullpen: *Have you always inked your own stuff?*

Fred: Pretty much, but there have been times when Marvel or DC has had other people ink me. Dave Hunt inked two pages of my stuff, and Joe Albelo inked several of my *Spider-Ham* stories, but by and large it's been just me.

Bullpen: *Has anyone imposed their own style on your stuff, just for kicks?*

Fred: Yeah, I guess so. This doesn't exactly pertain to the exact spirit of your question, but I once did a straight story, done as a challenge. It was when Marvel came out with that book called *Marvel Super-Heroes* [*Spring Special* #1], a big, thick comic, in 1990 or so, which had a lot of eight-page stories in it there. At that point, I had somehow become identified with Brother Voodoo. So Scott Lobdell (before he achieved noticeable fame for all the *X-Men* books he wrote) scripted a "Brother Voodoo" story and I penciled it in a straight style, the kind Vinnie liked so much several years earlier. So I did a decent job, I thought, I turned it in, and they gave it to one of the guys from the Philippines. Man, you wouldn't have known I drew it! It was *totally* changed. It was a disappointment to me, because while I certainly wanted to see my stuff made to look better, but I still wanted it to retain the look of my stuff, but this guy even changed some of the layouts. It's like, "*Come on*, buddy!"

Bullpen: [*Laughs*] *Did you get the original art back?*

Fred: Some pages I did get back. I think I actually have some copies of the pencils, so I can actually compare and contrast. That *would* be fun, hours and hours of entertainment, woo-hoo!

Bullpen: *Have you ever done anything straight since?*

Fred: No, except for one panel in the last Marvel book I did, which was *Fred Hembeck $ells the Marvel Universe*, number one-and-only [Oct.'90], a mostly-reprint collection of my *Marvel Age* strips. I've had no real desire. It's too hard and, besides, people seem to draw much better now than they did in 1977.

If I'd started out as a regular comic book artist back in 1977, I probably could have worked my way up to being mediocre, but nowadays! *Geesh!* You look in *Diamond Previews* and see all this incredible art, and you wonder, "God, how can these guys draw so good?"

Bullpen: *But this focus on intense realism has probably worked for your benefit at times, right? You were obviously a throwback, in a way, to Mort Walker, applying that style to fannish things, and that made you immediately noticed.*

Fred: Yes, that's true. People have told me, "At least your stuff looks like *your* stuff. No one really gets it mixed up with anybody else's, so you have *that* working for ya!"

Bullpen: *Do you agree with that assessment?*

Fred: Yes, I do. For better or worse. I'm not saying it's better than other stuff, but it does look pretty much like its own deal.

Bullpen: *Do you like your work?*

Fred: When I get it right, yes. I can look through some stuff and go, "Wow, that looks pretty good!" Then other times I go, "Geez, that doesn't look so good at all. In fact, it looks pretty awful!" I was looking through my old artwork not long ago, as I was preparing to post some of it on the website, *www.hembeck. com*. It's funny, because some of the earlier stuff is really pretty good, although there's a couple of technical glitches here and there. But then there was a period in the early '80s, when I got stupidly cocky, like, "Hey, I'm pretty darn good! I don't really have to try that hard!" And I wasn't really trying as hard as I should have. I mean, I thought I was, at the time, but I look back and go, "Geez, the quality sure went down." Then, come the '90s, I was really making a concerted effort to improve, trying hard again. So, y'know, it comes and goes. You have good days and bad. Decades too, apparently.

Bullpen: *Did you ever try to develop your own strip for the mainstream, for a syndicated strip?*

Fred: Never a syndicated strip, because I never was able to think in three-panel terms. The DC thing forced me to do it in *The Daily Planet* pages, but I'm just not that concise. That's my big problem, I tend to ramble.

Bullpen: *Oh, you think you can be wordy, eh?* [*laughs*]

Fred: Yeah! It's been known to happen, even to this day.

Bullpen: *Were you always a character in your strips, from the word go?*

Fred: Yes, from that first *Dateline* strip. I didn't plan it that way. It was an outgrowth of writing letters to my friends, which were these little cartoon letters starring me, telling them what was new.

Bullpen: *Is there anything that separates the Hembeck character from you? Obviously, you've done autobiographical stories…*

Fred: Yes, I've done some stories loosely based on reality, that's true. Obviously, you're going to exaggerate things to try and make it funnier. My big comedy idol was Jack Benny, so I have this self-deprecating sense of humor, where you use yourself as the butt of the joke, and that works for me. I use that, but it just wasn't really a conscious decision at the time. It wasn't until I stumbled across *The Jack Benny Show* reruns [originally aired between 1950 and '65] in the mid-'80s I went, "Oh my god, *now* I see what I'm doing!" Because I watched them as a kid, but they weren't available to me for a long while.

Bullpen: *What, that self-deprecation?*

Fred: Well, you know, Jack Benny always made himself the butt of jokes. I mean, his persona always had a big ego, but no one in the cast of characters around him took him very seriously, and more often than not, *they* would have the big laugh lines, because they were playing off of his excesses. I didn't exactly do that, but I always did try to act pompous, but at the same time, get the comeuppance whenever necessary (which is generally all of the time, when you act like that!).

Bullpen: *That's an aspect of Benny's endearing qualities, right?*

Fred: Yes, exactly. Jack Benny was the best.

Bullpen: *There's two kinds of humor, right? There's a mean kind of humor, where you're laughing at the expense of someone else, and there's a kinder type of humor, where you laugh at yourself, often revealing greater truths.*

Fred: Right. I try to do the mean kind of humor in as nice a way as possible. I try to insult people in such a way that it all comes out as a real happy joke for them.

Bullpen: *Did you ever do a strip on Vinnie?*

Fred: No. Do you know what happened with Vinnie? He wound up inking a book of mine at Marvel, *Fred Hembeck Destroys the Marvel Universe* [one-shot, July '89]! [*laughter*] "Not Vinnie! Chic Stone! Heck, anybody! But not Vinnie!"

Bullpen: *Vinnie is a* horrible *choice for your kind of line! Chic Stone would have been* perfect!

Fred: He *would* have been perfect!

Bullpen: *With his big, fat line.*

Fred: I know! The editor at the time, Larry Hama, was using a lot of the older artists. I'm going, "Not Vinnie! How about Chic Stone?" But no. They sent me the pages back to check, before being published, and there were panels where Vinnie didn't even ink the eyes! There are no dots! Come on! You know what my eyes look like, the drawings! How can you forget the dot?

Bullpen: *How much work does a dot take?*

Fred: Oh, lordy! So the book got delayed and delayed, and when it eventually did come out, Vinnie was already dead. I think it was one of the last two things ever published that had his name on it (the other was an *Inhumans Special* [April '90] Richard Howell penciled). He probably had absolutely no idea of the back story of the artist he was inking. "I'm tellin' you, kid, you're not gonna make it." Well, he was right, sorta, because I clearly didn't make it the way I was expecting.

Bullpen: *How would you describe your personality? You were shy in high school. Did college make you more outgoing?*

Fred: Yes, though not to any overwhelming extent, but I gained more self-confidence. I'm always pretty good around people who I know and like, but with strangers, I get a little bit reticent. I'm not going to walk into a room with full of people I don't know and light up the that room. I'm pretty much just going to be quiet until I'm comfortable. But if I'm with people I like, I'm usually pretty peppy.

Bullpen: *You were also in an interesting position, working within mainstream comics to a degree, and yet still on the periphery.*

Fred: Right.

Bullpen: *Seeing how creatives are treated within the business, did that give you any insight?* [long pause] *You were there, you had some looking at what was going on with Marvel under Jim Shooter, for instance. Did you walk away with any insight?*

Fred: Well, Shooter always treated me really well, but then, I never really dealt with Shooter after *Secret Wars*, which is when everybody seems to think he got weird. I always dealt

with the good Shooter, the pre-*Secret Wars* Shooter. He liked my stuff, luckily for me, but we only did those two big projects and one issue of *Spectacular Spider-Man*, which was during Assistant Editors' Month. But I never had any problems with them at that point.

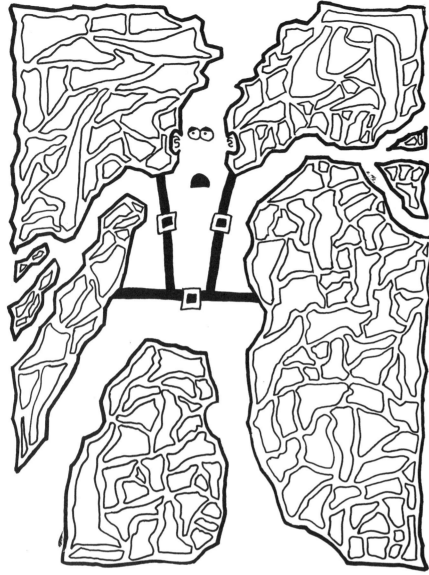

Bullpen: *Were you making a lot of money from mainstream comics?*

Fred: Not a lot but, pooling our resources here at the house, I managed to make enough. Actually, *The Fantastic Four Roast* [May '82] helped pay for the house, so that was good. "Hey, Lynn, it paid for the first house!" What're ya gonna do?

Bullpen: *When did you get your big break, actually doing a mainstream comic book?*

Fred: That would probably be *The Fantastic Four Roast*. That came about… It just evolved. I had done the Fantaco things, which were selling fairly well and making a fair amount of bucks, pumping a few of those out each year. One day, I was at a comic convention—I always remember this vividly—and Shooter was there as well, just walking around. This was when Shooter had just become the big editor. So I went up and introduced myself, and he went, "Oh, yeah, I know who you are. I really like your stuff." That came as a complete surprise, but a pleasant one. A bunch of fans started gathering around and listening to Shooter talk. He was saying, "Yeah, we're going to have some great deals for creators at Marvel soon. Say we want to do a Fred Hembeck comic. We can do that, yeah, and we'll give *you* the copyright!" I'm thinking to myself, "Yeah, like *that's* ever gonna happen!" But then, amazingly, it did! One day, a year or two later (because he apparently wasn't in any real rush to do it), Shooter calls me up and says he wants to celebrate *The Fantastic Four's* 20th anniversary by publishing a roast comic book. Whoever they originally had scheduled to do it

didn't feel comfortable with the concept, and so Shooter thought of me. So I wound up writing it, and doing the layouts and putting my character in as well. That was really good experience, and it sold reasonably well.

Bullpen: *This was a retrospective of the entire run of* Fantastic Four?

Fred: Well, it had no ads and it ran 32 pages. Every Marvel character that had its own book was appearing in it, and we divided it up so that each page was drawn by the artist who at that time was peniler of that particular book. So the Daredevil page was drawn by Frank Miller. (*I* did layouts for Frank Miller! I'm probably the only guy in comics who can say that.) Sal Buscema did the Hulk page. John Byrne did a couple of Fantastic Four pages. Mike Golden did a page. Mike Zeck did Captain America. I drew the wraparound cover, which Terry Austin inked. Otherwise I just drew my little character on the inside cover, but it was put together in an odd way where I'd send the artists the layouts, but I didn't really have the dialogue figured out yet. So the pages would come in not in sequential order, and I would have to write the dialogue in after the pages were completely inked. But it all managed to work out, strangely enough.

Bullpen: *Have you sat down recently and read it?*

Fred: I've read it several times. Not recently, but I've always thought that book really worked well. I mean, at least compared to some of the other stuff.

Bullpen: *Now, did you get some of the pages because you had done some of the layouts on them?*

Fred: Well, that was entirely up to the artist. Two of them actually gave me their pages: John Byrne and Frank Miller, so I have those pages. On the other hand, I was sitting next to one guy at a convention who was selling pages he did in my book. [*laughter*] But that's okay. That *was* his page to sell, I believe. So that was really cool.

Bullpen: *Mike Golden, Frank Miller, and John Byrne? Not too shabby, Fred!*

Fred: Yeah! The Golden page was one where I had all the characters streaming in, so he had panels of, like, 15 characters per, so it was very crowd-intensive. Michael did a really good job, obviously.

Bullpen: *Who did the X-Men pages?*

Fred: See, that was the thing: I thought it was going to be Dave Cockrum, but it turned out to be Denys Cowan, and I'm not sure why. I think at the last minute they couldn't get Dave to do it.

Bullpen: *What was the climax of the comic?*

Fred: Well, the whole thing was an actual roast, where people would go up to the podium and say some humorous comments about the Fantastic Four, who was were sitting there at the head table, but there was a mysterious package that was going to blow up. It turned out to have been really delivered by Willie Lumpkin, but he was being hypnotized… I forget the exact ending, but it was a big shock. A big shock to us all!

Bullpen: *Did you read* Ultimate Fantastic Four?

Fred: No, I've never read an *Ultimate* comic. I've read the *original* comics. Why?

Bullpen: *Oh, they inserted the name "Lumpkin," and I was curious where that's going to go, if anywhere. So that was the first mainstream book?*

Fred: I would say so. Then we did the issue of *Spectacular Spider-Man* [#86] that came out during "Assistant Editors' Month" [Jan. '84], written by Bill Mantlo (I still had the Mantlo connection going). Bill and I did a story we were trying to sell to Epic, but that never did get sold, so I wound up publishing it in one of my Fantaco books. It was a 10-page story called "Erosion," which was wordless, a story of how one little pebble turns into the Grand Canyon in 10 pages, with all kinds of crazy things happening in between. [*"Erosion" was eventually*

published in The Hembeck File (Hembeck Series #5), Feb. 1981.]
So I worked with Bill for a while. Bill was calling me on the phone in those days, back and forth.

Bullpen: *What was Bill like?*

Fred: He was very enthusiastic and he was very much into my stuff. I mean, how can you not like a guy like that? One time he told me, "Oh, your stuff reminds me of Alex Niño!" Of course, I thought he was crazy, but I think it was because, superficially, we both use the same little dots in the way we ink. Otherwise, I just don't see it. Because Niño is really a genius and I'm just this guy, but I always remember Bill saying that! No one else has mentioned it since. Another thing Bill called up and said was, "I'm working with this new guy on *Spectacular Spider-Man*, who is *really* good. This guy is one of the best I've ever met doing comics." He was talking about the two issues Frank Miller did [#27–28, Feb. & Mar. '79]. He may've been off the beam with me and Alex, but he sure got that one right!

So when we collaborated on that special issue of *Spectacular Spider-Man* [#86, Jan. '84], Bill sends me a plot that's very short, maybe a couple of paragraphs, and a substantial portion of the book is described basically as, "And then they fight," but I had never done any fight scenes before, right? So I turn in these five or six pages, but Marvel doesn't like them, quite correctly, so they make Bill rewrite it with specifics as to what was going on. Bill calls me up and doesn't seem to be all too happy with the situation, telling me I let him down. And I'm saying, "Well gee, you could have given me more description." [*grumbling sound*] After that, I never spoke to the guy again, we just kind of drifted apart. It wasn't a falling-out, per se, but I always felt kind of bad, and then, of course, what happened to the guy… it's a shame. [*Bill was was struck by a car in the early '90s and suffered irreparable brain trauma.* — **Ed.**].

Then, of course, I think to myself, "Well, at least Bill thought up that great idea about the Hulk." [*Jon laughs*] But I get your magazine [*CBA* V2, #1], and you've ruined my dreams! You ruined it for me, Jon! [*laughter*]

Bullpen: *How is that my fault?* [laughs] *So where does it go from there?*

Fred: From there, I wind up working on *Marvel Age* with [editor] Jim Salicrup [#14–21, 23–140, 1984–94]. We had some other stuff going on regularly, we'd still do the fan magazines at times, going in and out of that stuff.

Bullpen: *How was the* Marvel Age *stuff?*

Fred: It was pretty good. Jim is a really good guy, and he's always been very encouraging, always very hands-off. He liked my stuff and pretty much let me do what I wanted. Sometimes that wasn't good, because I look back at some of those and think, "Y'know, this could have been a little bit better," but more often than not—especially later in the run—the stuff looks pretty good to me. Then I did stuff for *What The—?*, which Jim also edited [#2-4, Sept.-Nov. '88].

Bullpen: *For* Marvel Age, *what specifically were you doing?*

Fred: There was a regular strip in there every month, a centerfold that ran across in any configuration I felt. The only criterion was it had to pretty much focus on something that they were pushing that month. Generally I got away with doing that without being too crass. Although, occasionally what I did was.

Bullpen: *Did you get paid for pencils, inks, and writing?*

Fred: And lettering.

Bullpen: *How'd you learn to letter?*

Fred: I've always had decent handwriting, so it all just kind of fell into place. In the early days, I didn't even line the stuff. I still don't. Now I letter it in pencil, then I go back and put the ruling lines in afterwards, just to make sure it's straight. Because I tried putting the lines in first, and it just seems to work for me, even though I'm doing it backwards.

Bullpen: *I don't see too many corrections on your stuff, right?*

Fred: No. I've gotten better at doing the lettering with the lines in the last couple of years, no doubt.

Bullpen: *Were the* Marvel Age *strips sequential or were they full-page?*

Fred: Two pages, across the centerfold. I did it for 120 issues. I missed the first couple. Jim left the company after about #70, and the next couple of people just kept it going. Then Steve Saffel came in, and he seemed to be a nice guy. He called me up, very enthusiastic, told me how much he loved my stuff, told me how he was going to be the new editor for *Marvel Age* and how it's going to be great for me, and then said, "Oh, yeah, I'm gonna cut it to one page." Oh, *that's* nice. Then he kept futzing

with it! "Oh, you've gotta redraw it, I don't get this joke." After years of Jim just taking what I'd send it, it was a change.

Bullpen: *A real* hands-on *editor?*

Fred: Oh, yeah. I did a Ross Perot joke, like, six months after Perot was a [1992] Presidential candidate. He said, "Oh, people aren't going to remember who he is!" But they did. Later on he said, "You were right, Fred, people remembered him." *Now* they might not, but six months after the election, they did. We ended up doing one-pagers. But some of them, he actually made them better, so I can't blame Steve. But it was just kind of funny where it was one of those deals where they tell you how much they love you and then they cut the stuff.

Bullpen: [Laughs] *But you lasted for, what, 50 more issues?*

Fred: Yeah, probably, until the thing ended. Even after the

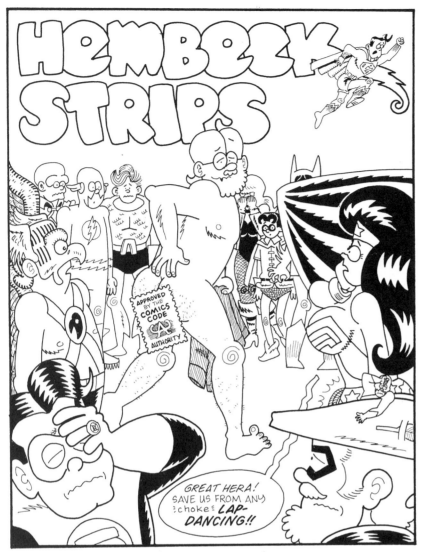

GREAT HERA! SAVE US FROM ANY ≈choke≈ **LAP-DANCING!!**

APPROVED BY THE COMICS CODE AUTHORITY

Above: *We're not sure if compiler R. Gary Land has any more copies of his limited edition collection of strips Fred drew for DC Comics between 1978 and '81, but* Hembeck Strips *is worth tracking down… Included is an auto-biographical essay by F.H. and comprehensive checklist of that* Daily Planet *feature. Characters TM & ©2021 DC Comics. Art ©2021 Fred Hembeck.*
Below: *Cover detail of* Comics Interview *#22 [1985]. ©2021 F.H.*

assignment ended, they did these *Marvel Age* special editions, like, *Captain America* and *X-Men*, instead of the regular *Marvel Age*. I was in those, too, and those ended in the mid-'90s.
Bullpen: *I recall you did a* DC Sampler *cover.*
Fred: Yeah, I did that *DC Sampler,* plus a couple of pages… Actually, I was supposed to have some pages in *Amazing World of DC Comics,* but that got cancelled, and those two pages wound up on the inside covers of *Flash #300.* So that was a good place to be. Carmine and Hembeck together. Oh, I also did the back-ups in *'Mazing Man,* "Zoot Sputnik." [#7–10, July-Oct. '86] I was working from Bob Rozakis's scripts, so that wasn't all my own.
Bullpen: *What was "Zoot Sputnik"?*
Fred: It was a core group of four or five characters. The handsome guy, the gal, the older man, the young boy. One issue there'd be a war story, the next there'd be a cowboy story, next there was a science-fiction story, going from genre to genre, all with the same characters. It's hard to explain.
Bullpen: *Did you have your own fans, people who would write you?*
Fred: Yes, I did. I had a young guy who ran the Fred Hembeck fan club, Philippe DeJean, who would send me odd items. It ran for a couple years. I think it was just him and his friend in a neighborhood of New York.
Bullpen: *Was it a fanzine?*
Fred: Yes, but I think there were probably only three copies of each issue printed.
Bullpen: *Did he interview you for it?*
Fred: We corresponded back and forth. He was a teenager.

Bullpen: *Is there a checklist of Hembeck stuff?*
Fred: Yes. It was in *The Comics Buyer's Guide* in 1998 or so [#1249, Oct. 24, '97]. When I came back to *CBG,* they ran a big article about me and put together a checklist. I've been meaning to put it up at my Web site, but I still haven't done it, because getting together all that information kind of bores me. I should just copy what they did and not worry about any stuff that's so obscure, I can't even remember it myself. That's what I'm planning to do.
Bullpen: *How long had you been in* The Buyer's Guide*? Pretty much always?*
Fred: No, not always. I was there from, like, 1977 until '81 or so, then wandered off [between #209, Nov. 18, '77, and #571, Oct. 26, '84]. I came back in the mid-'80s. I remember specifically it was after my mom died, but my dad was still around. I did some strips, but just wasn't really into it then, and went instead to Marvel and other odds-'n'-ends — First Comics [*E-Man* #6, Sept. '83; *Grimjack* #29, Dec. '86], Blackthorne [*Laffin' Gas,* #2, '86], *Comicscene* magazine — and then I came back to CBG in 1996, '97 [#1249, Oct. 24, '97], somewhere around there, with a renewed enthusiasm… and no fans. [*laughs*] I was doing better stuff than I had done in a long, long time, and you know, they had those annual *Buyer's Guide* polls, remember? Y'know, you vote on for your favorites each year? Because years earlier, they'd have these awards for "Favorite Fan Cartoonist." I won it several years in a row, and so they got rid of the category. I guess it was like, "We know who's going to win it, so why bother running the category again?" So, years later, I come back, and I say think to myself, "Well, let's see how I do on the this thing, here. I'll probably come in after Mark Evanier's column, because Mark's really good, and he's been there for years, so that'd be okay." Turns out I place fifth or something. The next year I'm ninth. The year after that I'm like staggering in at 15th. I think the last time I slipped in was just ahead of *"Manga* News." [*laughter*] "Least Favorite: *Manga* News and Hembeck." [*laughter*] "But I'm doing my best stuff here, what's going on?" I think the audience had changed and they didn't know who the hell this guy was with the cleft in his head. [*Jon laughs*] So it was disappointing. *The Buyer's Guide* people were really good to me for a while. Then, of course, their magazine shrunk to virtually nothing, and they couldn't afford me. After all, with eBay and the Internet, a comics fan really doesn't need *The Buyer's Guide,* for news *or* for selling comics, unfortunately.
Bullpen: *So it's a disappointment?*
Fred: Yes, because I sent in 25 strips and they *still* haven't printed them all, but they say they will eventually. So it was a disappointment. You know, I had this big summer a couple of years ago, when I all of a sudden had everything lined up. It was the summer of 2000. This one fellow called up, said he wanted me to work on his new version of *The Comic Reader,* and I came up with this "Little Freddy" concept for it, a truly autobiographical strip that mixed in elements of the *Dateline* stuff (which I wound up doing some of it for your magazine). *TCR* was going to be monthly, in color. Then, shortly afterwards, Jim Salicrup calls up and wants me to work for Stan Lee Media on the Internet, and that's going to be weekly and big money, and it *was*. I wound up doing nine strips for them, but no one ever saw it, because we all pretty much know how that story ended. Then, of course, I had a page in Jon B. Cooke's *Comic Book Artist.* Well, guess which one's the only one still running my stuff now? Jon B. Cooke's *Comic Book Artist!* The Stan Lee thing went belly up (I dragged that sucker down). *The Comic Reader* never got off the ground, and *The Buyer's Guide* went away. One minute you're up; one minute you're down. It's the old Frank Sinatra song: "Flying high in April, shot down in May."
Bullpen: *How many* Little Freddy *strips did you do?*
Fred: I did four strips for a total of 10 pages, not counting the

ones that ran in your magazine.

Bullpen: *They were two pages a shot?*

Fred: Well, the first one was four pages, because it was the introductory one. Then after that they were two pages a shot. They can be seen at my website, which, by the way, tells an illustrated story, in illustrated fashion, pretty much the story about me getting the magical box of comics and all that good stuff I told you earlier. I just use the same stories over and over again in different media.

Bullpen: *So you had your ups and downs. You even had your name in the title of a comic book, didn't you? How did that come about? You did some destroyin', baby! [laughs]*

Fred: Yes, I did, yes, I did. Shooter called up, saying, "Let's do another comic book." *The Fantastic Four Roast* did pretty well. This a really long and involved story, which I really hate to keep repeating, but it's written up in extensive detail at the old Web site [*and in CBA V.2 #4, in the "Backstory" section* — **Ed.**]. [*CBG* columnist] cat yronwode broke the news that Jim Shooter was going to destroy Asgard, change Iron Man, and do horrible things to all of our beloved Marvel characters. The rumor came from [Marvel writer] Doug Moench, who apparently was upset at Shooter and had left to go to DC. So we decided to spoof that situation. It was a big 48-page comic, with a 24-page framing story, which took place in the Marvel offices, starring Shooter and three fictitious assistants by the name of Bruce, Clark, and Diana. That was fun to write, but the part where I had to depict all the characters getting killed wasn't so much fun. That wasn't really my forte. So I had to struggle through it, but during the time when this happened, my mom died—people I cared about were dying—and I'm thinking, "This is not good!"

Bullpen: *Too much death?*

Fred: Exactly! So that's one of the reasons for its protracted genesis. Then, when it was just about to actually come out, it was shifted away from Shooter and over to another editor who didn't want to deal with it, and pretended he didn't have it. There were all kinds of crazy stories going on. When it was finally ready to come out, there was that whole big thing between Marvel and DC about the aborted *JLA/Avengers* book, and because I'd made some winking references to this whole thing being a plot by Shooter (who was acting as a sleeper agent programmed by Mort Weisinger) [*Jon laughs*], they didn't much like that. I didn't use any names, please understand, but you could figure it all out if you knew a little bit about recent comics history. Like I said, the original title was supposed to be *Jim Shooter Destroys the Marvel Universe.* But when Shooter called back the second time, he said, "Well, you know, I'm an editorial person here. The executives here don't want to have my name in the title." I said, "Oh, okay." He said, "So how about we use *your* name?" I said, "Oh, okay, if we must." But actually, Jim is much more of a character in the story than I. I'm just his hired dupe.

When the book finally *did* come out, years later, they just printed the middle section. Because they're not going to be printing 20 pages of Jim Shooter while he was running Valiant Comics at that point, or some such. But because we had some extra pages to fill, I wound up doing a new framing sequence that went over the past framing sequence to make it a bit more understandable. I got my friend Joe Staton, who lived in the town where we lived at the time, to ink it. Vinnie was no longer with us, but I wasn't inclined to be calling him anyway. [*Jon laughs*] But I always thought that the best part of that book was the stuff that was never actually published. The mid-section I really felt was iffy. There were a couple of pages I really liked, such as a Daredevil page with a little Mel Blanc-like character from the old *Jack Benny Show*, with the scythe, which, of course, played into the whole thing with Elektra and the *sai*. "Si, sai, sue," that bit. So that's why that worked and I always liked

that page. But some of them were really stretching it.

Bullpen: *What was it about the framing sequence that you enjoyed so much?*

Fred: Well, it was just like a wacky sitcom. You had Shooter as the straight man, with three assistants who provided the comedy. He was also the one plotting to destroy the Marvel Universe, but was doing it without really knowing it consciously. He's, like, hypnotized. It's like something triggers this in him, but he doesn't realize it's happening. This all comes out in the end framing sequence. So that was a lot more fun to write. Then I had to justify it by killing off all the characters in the middle. Then, years later, I see the Sergio Aragonés books with Mark Evanier, the ones where he destroys DC and Marvel, and I remember that when I first got those, I was afraid to read them for a long time, because I thought, "Geez, if I read these and they're what I did, only *better*, that'll bum me out big time." But I finally did read them, and they *were* better, but they weren't the way I would have done them, even at my best, so I didn't feel so bad. But they s*laughtered* the heroes in a much better way. They just went, "Whoop, kill 'em all," all at once. Not page-by-page, trying to come up with specific ways… They came up with an easier way of doing it. Mark and Sergio are not exactly known for

IBID presents

FORGOTTEN MOMENTS IN DC COMICS HISTORY

1960: Famed TV Detective, ROY RAYMOND, applies for membership in the recently formed JUSTICE LEAGUE of AMERICA...

no Go, Kal—keep trying.

...@?☆!!...

We're sorry, Roy, but no matter how often Superman adjusts the antenna, we just can't seem to get proper reception here in this cave!!...

...unsuccessfully...

...um, and would you mind ditching that pipe?...

FRED HEMBECK 2003

for GARY !!

Above: Fred drew up this cute JLA cartoon for uber comics fan Gary Brown, as this IBID fanzine cover illo attests. Characters TM & ©2021 DC Comics. Art ©2021 F.H.

Below: Comics Interview #22 ['85] featured this cover art changed before publication. TM & © Marvel Characters, Inc.

being bloodthirsty, after all.

Bullpen: *Did you do a comparable thing at DC?*

Fred: No, I never did. I've done some bits and pieces at DC, but I don't think I ever did a full book at DC. I did a *Who's Who: [The Definitive Directory of the DC Universe]* page, though, for "Zoot Sputnik" [#26, April '87].

Bullpen: *Did you create Zoot?*

Fred: No, Bob and Stephen DiStefano did, I believe.

Bullpen: *Obviously you are the most identifiable character within your own strips.*

Fred: For better or worse.

Bullpen: *Did you think about creating your own properties?*

Fred: Oh, I did that a couple of times, but it they never really went over real big.

Bullpen: *What were they?*

Fred: Well, I did this kids strip, which still hasn't been published, except some of it is at the Web site. It was called *KIDZ*, about a group of kids who take over a cable TV station, and KIDZ are the call letters. There was a crazy clown involved, a decapitated dummy, and all kinds of crazy stuff. It was my version of a comic aimed towards — and based on —kids.

While I can't say I actually created it, but I did come up with a thing at Marvel called "Petey" [*Web of Spider-Man Annual* #5 ['89]; *Spectacular Spider-Man Annual* #9 ['89]; *Marvel Tales* #235 [Mar. '90], #248 [April '91], #251 [July '91], #252 [Aug. '91]; *Untold Tales of Spider-Man* #23–24 [Aug., Sept. '97]; which

was my version of Peter Parker as a kid, only done in a *Dennis the Menace* type story. That was my own idea, but obviously I'm working off of the Lee and Ditko stuff. So when I did the KIDZ, that was me trying to do the same thing, only with my own characters. I wanted to do that for Tundra, but kept working on it, working on it, working on it. I figured, "Wow, I'll finish the layouts and I'll give it to 'em, and then they'll want to publish it." But I never did finish the layouts, and next thing you know, they're gone.

Bullpen: *Did you work it out with [Tundra publisher] Kevin Eastman?*

Fred: He never knew about it! Y'see, I'd planned to tell Tundra about it only after all the preliminary work was done. Smart guy, huh? I had met them years earlier and actually did a *Teenage Mutant Ninja Turtles* story [#2, second edition, Jan. '85], and [*TMNT* creators] Kevin and Peter Laird were really nice guys, and pretty rich then. This was well before the toys and movie, but even after just the initial excitement, they were rich for comic book guys at that particular point, as opposed to being rich for regular people like later on. So I did a *Turtles* story, and it appeared in a reprint issue. It's a five-page story, and it appears in one of those reprints that has, like, a Richard Corben cover on it.

Bullpen: *Did you write it?*

Fred: Yes, I wrote it. It's got some allusions to *Daredevil* in it or something, I forget what it was, but it was one of my wacky little takes on things.

Bullpen: *Were you involved in the genesis of "Spider-Ham"?*

Fred: No, "Spider-Ham" started without me. That was another artist, actually, Mark Armstrong. He did the original book. I wound up doing a fill-in issue [#4, Nov. '85]. They were placating me after we had an argument over the whole *Destruction of the Marvel Universe* getting cancelled over and over. I worked off of Steve Skeates' script on that one and Joe Albelo inked it. But years later, I wound up doing back-ups of "Spider-Ham" in *Marvel Tales,* which I wrote and drew [#216–17, Oct., Nov. '88; #224–26, June, July, Aug. '89], and Joe Albelo inked (although I inked the last one or two [#226]). Then I said to Salicrup, who was the editor, "Can we do 'Petey' instead?" He said, "Sure." So out with the ham and in with the kid.

Bullpen: *How many strips of that did you do?*

Fred: I must have done seven or eight and half-a-dozen of the "Ham" as well.

Bullpen: *Are you proud of "Petey"?*

Fred: Yeah. As I always say to Lynn, I'm most proud of my little "Petey." [*laughter*] She'd say, "I know, I know! I'm tired of that joke, I've been hearing it for years!"

Bullpen: *Were there allusions to the good kid strips you liked? Did he even have enough pages to get into adventures?*

Fred: Yes. The first one was heavy on the Al Wiseman swipes, I'm a little embarrassed to say.

Bullpen: *A little too much Dennis there?*

Fred: A little bit too much *Dennis* there. Well, actually, at one point where there's a person who's screaming, it looks like the old head sticking up and the big smile where you can see the tonsils. [*Jon laughs*] After the first one or so, I pretty much said, "No, I've gotta do this on my own." But I continued to swipe the guy's lettering style.

Bullpen: *What about plot-wise? The adventure aspects?*

Fred: No, there weren't enough pages, although I did do an eight-pager at one point. They were drawn like *Dennis* and written like *Little Lulu.* I also had one that had just a little touch of sentimentality to it, like *Little Archie.* But there weren't any adventurous episodes like some *Little Archie* stories, if you know what I'm saying. It was more farcical humor.

Bullpen: *How much did you get completed of KIDZ?*

Fred: Well, I have 301 pages of layouts, which I now fully realize is insane. Last year, when I wanted to do the Web site, I managed to put up 68 finished pages, but I just ran out of steam on that idea soon after. See, the odd thing was, the way I structured the story was that after page 31, everything happens in a steady flow, so there's no places to break. Which is kind of dumb, but… y'know, someday.

Bullpen: *So it's a 300-page graphic novel, so far?*

Fred: So far, yes. [*laughter*] I've forgotten how it ends! But it doesn't have *scope* in terms of time and place; it all takes place in this one building. But we keep switching back and forth from one character to another, and there's a lot of crazy wild things going on. I always tell people it really gets good around page 150. [*laughter*] But no one's seen it besides me! I've very proud of a lot of it, but what are you gonna do?

Bullpen: *What are you going to do?*

Fred: Right now I'm trying to come up with something more concise that I can merchandise on coffee cups and things along those lines, put on T-shirts. Something I can put out a strip every three days, say. I haven't done it yet, but that's my plan for the near future.

Bullpen: *Now, this has nothing to do with Hembeck, per se?*

Fred: Right, this is totally different, and I don't know what it is yet. I've had some ideas, but I haven't really nailed it down.

Bullpen: *There had to be, obviously, some disappointment with this CBG popularity poll.*

Fred: I gotta admit, it was a little discouraging! [*laughs*]

Bullpen: *But you obviously still have a love for comics, right? Do you see a parting of the ways, that you would be out of it completely?*

Fred: No, I love comics—I love *old* comics—I have to admit that in the last couple of years, I haven't read many new ones. Up through the '90s, I was on the comp list for DC and Marvel, but ever since mid-decade, I got bumped off and have been having to pay my own way ever since. I used to read them compulsively, all of them, and then we had our daughter—Julie's 14

now—and it took away some of my time. A lot of my time, actually, but I'm not complaining, because she's such a great kid. In recent years, I've still been buying a bunch, but each month I decide, "Well, I think I can live without *that*," and cut another title off the must-buy list. I'm all filled up. I'm actually thinking of selling some on eBay, just to make some room.

Bullpen: *How many comics do you have?*

Fred: When we moved here from Kingston six years ago, I had 125 long boxes full.

Bullpen: *That's 125 times 300?*

Fred: Something like that, yeah. We probably have enough to fill another 25 boxes or so. Yikes.

Bullpen: *Is that like half-a-million comics?* [Obviously, your editor can't multiply without a calculator — **Ed.**]

Fred: Maybe closer to a zillion. [*laughter*]

Bullpen: *Well, my math was never any good.* [laughs]

Fred: So, I've lost my taste for reading, but I've still been buying Frank Miller and Alan Moore, the higher echelon stuff. I haven't had a chance to read 'em, but someday I'm going to want to. That's why I'm thinking, "Well, *Ultimates?* Nah, I don't think I need no stinkin' *Ultimates!*" Let's not even broach that

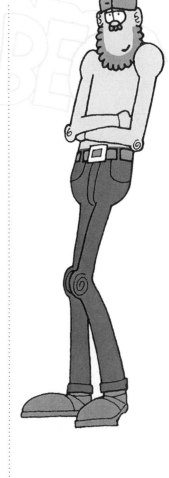

This page: *You can find out more about Fred's zillion-page graphic novel, KIDZ, at his website, www.hembeck.com. Courtesy of and ©2021 F.H.*

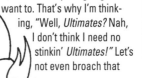

KIDZ by FRED HEMBECK 1993

them, I tended to go back and read the actual comics, and I said, "Y'know, maybe I should read the old comics. I don't really need to read the new ones." So, that's why I've lost interest in new comics. I still collect some but…

You know the funny thing I've discovered over the years? People who work in comics don't really *read* that many comics. Many've read them when they were kids, but once they get into the business, they usually don't read them, and most don't even keep them. They'd get the comp copies and then just give the comics away. In this area, there are a lot of people who work in comics—the Hudson Valley area—and that's generally true. [Inker] Terry Austin is one of the few guys who actually reads comics (not that he reads them all!). He tends to read a lot of the ones I don't, and back when I was still keeping up, it was pretty much *vice versa*. I think the last comic book Bernie Wrightson read was an EC, to tell you the truth. And I mean, off the rack! So I'm a late guy for burning out on them, as far as somebody who's actually been in the comics biz.

Bullpen: *Is it tied to a lack of work found within the business?*

Fred: No. It's tied to the lack of *time*, the feeling I've been here before, the feeling that, y'know, do the characters really have to be this nasty? The last really wonderful comic I read was *Preacher.* I didn't read that whole sprawling saga until it was almost over, and then I read it in big chunks. I thought that was one of the best things I'd ever read in comics. But, if that very same story had been tied to *The Flash,* for instance, it would have been really annoying to me. If you want to do this kind of gritty approach, do it like Garth Ennis: Make up your own characters, people. But when they take these grand old iconic characters and make them into really slimy weasels, what's the sense in that? Do they really need to do this? It just can be so disconcerting. I'm not really upset, like some people tend to get, but it's just like, why even bother? You get older and start thinking, well, maybe I should read the old ones instead of the new ones. Contrary to that little mini-rant, though, I'm certainly not bitter. I've had a good life, everything is just fine for me.

Bullpen: *You have a daughter?*

Fred: Yes, I do.

Bullpen: *One child?*

Fred: Right. One child.

Bullpen: *Does she like comics?*

Fred: No. When she was younger, I would read the *Little Lulu* volumes to her, which she loved. That's the only time she really was interested in them. She's never read them since. She was still letting me read them to her when she was 10—she could read at that age, of course—but she liked the idea of me reading to her. Kids come over here—there's comics all over the house—but none of them actually would think to pick one up and read it. Of course, they're all girls, right? One time, a neighbor girl actually came up to me and started asking me stuff about the *Justice League* characters. I said, "Oh, that's interesting, want to read a comic?" She said, "No, no. I just saw this cartoon show the other night, and I wanted to know more about them."

Bullpen: *Right. Those are the only conversations I have with my kids about comics: if they involve cartoon shows.* [laughs] *About*

Above: *Hembeck the Hyborian! This illo graced the inside front cover of* Hembeck Series #7 — *"Dial H For Hembeck" — and is obviously a pastiche of the legendary Frank Frazetta painting, "The Barbarian," which originally appeared as cover for the Lancer paperback,* Conan the Adventurer *[1966]. All courtesy of and ©2021 Fred Hembeck.*

Right inset: *Hembeck apparently digs wonky cartoon shows, as seen in this pic courtesy of Our Man Fred.*

Opposite page insets: *Top is Fred's lovely spouse, Lynn, and below that is a not-so-recent photo of their daughter, Julie.* **Opposite page right:** *DC's odd '60s "mystery" character, Eclipso, bids adieu. Originally published as the inside back cover send-off in* Hembeck Series #2 *[Feb. '80]. Eclipso TM & ©2021 DC Comics.*

subject, because I didn't quite understand the point of the whole concept to begin with. Why are we doing these? Why do we need several different versions of the same characters? But I don't necessarily mean them any ill will. I guess it's the old books that mostly keep me interested these days.

I do a lot of cover reproductions of old comics, where I do them up in my goofy style. A couple of years ago I discovered that, over at Staples, you can actually reduce pages and get real crisp copies. You reduce them, then paste them onto a page, then write something on them, and *voila!* You've got yourself a strip for *The Buyer's Guide!* So I'd make four covers, then eventually put those covers on eBay and sell them. That worked out good for a while there. Then, when I started with the website, I decided I'd put those up and write something about them, something clever, hopefully. When I wrote about the Web site: do you have any idea what kind of traffic you're getting?

Fred: We're getting decent traffic. It could always be better. I've gotten a couple of plugs from some of the bigger news sites. I'm linked to Mark Evanier's site, which gets a lot of traffic. I don't have a message board, so I don't get a lot of people writing to me like they do to Peter David. I'm not spouting off about a lot of the new stuff that's going on in comics, mainly because I'm just not following it. But I have found that I really like writing, something I never knew before, because I've previously only written strips. I never learned how to type properly, but I've taught myself somewhat in the last year. Just recently I learned how to color using Photoshop. So we have a lot of new stuff on the site — artwork, a lot of covers, a lot of old stuff, stuff for people who like comics — and we're trying to put up some stuff for normal people, too. We also recently added a separate section focusing entirely on the Beatles, spurred on by the 40th anniversary of that *Sullivan Show* gig.

Bullpen: *Is there any way to make money by doing this?*

Fred: Just hopefully by selling some of the originals or doing commissions. I hope to start a strip that could catch on in such a way that you one could put together some books. You see, my brother-in-law is not into comics, but he's into computers, and there's this one strip he goes to that's about computers, and it's really not drawn all that well, but the strip's creator has got all these books out, he's got cups and T-shirts… I'm going, "Geesh! I could draw

better than *that* guy! Why aren't I making a mint like him?" (Of course, I don't really know if the guy's making a mint, but you know what I'm saying.)

Bullpen: *You're actively developing characters?*

Fred: That's what I'm hoping to do, yes. I'm working on that. See, envy is a good way to keep one working harder. Once you get envy, you get the bitterness and the bile builds at the bottom of your stomach, and that drives you to work harder on stuff. And, by the way, I'm saying this in a light-hearted manner, of course. [*laughter*]

I've had so much stuff that didn't get published for the longest time, but on the internet, you can put it out there the next day. So all those pages I was telling you about—from the *Destruction of the Marvel Universe* to *KIDZ*—they're all on there. Take a look at it.

The website has been taking up my time for the last year, trying to make that a going concern, trying to come up with new stuff as often as I can manage over there. And trying to get all the people who are reading this right now to check it out.

Collection Editor's Note: *Fred Hembeck's* Dateline: @?*! *strip appears in every issue of* Comic Book Creator *magazine. Please see next page for other life developments for Hembeck.*

THE END

VISIT HEMBECK.COM

JOIN FRED AND FRIENDS AT HIS OWN BRAND-SPANKING-NEW OFFICIAL WEBSITE FOR…

☆ NEW AND ONGOING COMIC STRIPS!

☆ RARELY SEEN GEMS RESCUED FROM THE ARCHIVES!

☆ BEHIND THE SCENES GLIMPSES INTO THE COMICS BIZ!

☆ FRED'S PERSONAL COMMENTARIES REGARDING A WIDE VARIETY OF SUBJECTS!

☆ AND, OF COURSE, FUN, FUN, FUN!! (…TIL YOUR DADDY TAKES YOUR MODEM AWAY!..)

DESIGNED TO APPEAL TO LONG-TIME COMICS FANS AND THE GENERAL PUBLIC ALIKE!

established January 1, 2003
©2004 FRED HEMBECK

http://www.hembeck.com

COMIC BOOK ARTIST
ALL★STARS

FRED HEMBECK

INDEPENDENT CARTOONIST

FRED HEMBECK

005-6
FRED HEMBECK
CARTOONIST
BORN: 1/30/53 BIRTHPLACE: MANHATTAN, NY
SCHOOL: STATE UNIVERSITY OF N.Y., BUFFALO
1st "REAL" PUBBED: IRON MAN #112, 7/78

F.H. WORKED AS BACKGROUND ARTIST FOR BOB LAYTON IN THE LATE '70s ON SUCH COMICS AS IRON MAN & "ANT-MAN"!

MEMORABLE WORK:

"DATELINE: @?#?!"

PROFESSIONAL COMIC BOOK/STRIP ART HIGHLIGHTS

DATE	PUBLISHER	FEATURES/GENRES
'60s-'70s	VARIOUS	"Crude" straight drawings published in various fanzines (Fred's description, not ours!)
1976	ALAN LIGHT	1st work in Comics Buyer's Guide (then The Buyer's Guide For Comic Fandom), #140 cover, 7/23/76,
1977-81	ALAN LIGHT	also draws covers of #213, 252, 267, 293, 312, and 364
1978	MARVEL	"Dateline: @?#?!" begins in CBG (#209, 11/18/77), runs in nearly every issue 'til the early 1980s
1978-81	DC COMICS	1st widely-seen work, illustrated letter of comment in Iron Man #112 (7/78)
1979	ALAN LIGHT	"Hembeck" strips run bi-weekly in "The Daily Planet" house hype page
1980	FANTACO ENTPR.	"What's Up: Doc" strip runs in The Comics Buyers Guide, begins 11/9/79
1982	MARVEL COMICS	Hembeck: The Best of Dateline: @?#?! published. By 1983, six more Hembeck magazines published
1984-94	MARVEL COMICS	Fred produces Fantastic Four Roast #1 (5/82), writing and drawing layouts for many collaborators, including Frank Miller and John Byrne
1983-84	KRAUSE PUBS	Produces strip for virtually every issue of Marvel Age between #14-140, including many centerspreads
1989	MARVEL COMICS	"Dateline: @?#?!" strip returns to Comics Buyer's Guide, #482 (2/11/83), runs until #571 (10/26/84)
1990	MARVEL COMICS	Writes and draws Fred Hembeck Destroys the Marvel Universe (7/89)
1997-2000	KRAUSE PUBS	Draws "Brother Voodoo" strip in Marvel Super-Heroes Spring Special #1 in a straight style; also writes and draws Fred Hembeck Sells the Marvel Universe (11/90)
2003-Pres.	SELF-PUBLISHED	"Dateline: @?#?!" revived in the Comics Buyer's Guide (starting with #1249, 10/24/97) www.hembeck.com Web site launched

Hembeck ©2004 Fred Hembeck

Collect 'em All!
Trading card data compiled with information supplied by Fred Hembeck.

COMIC BOOK ARTIST™ BULLPEN was published between 2003–04 by RetroHouse Press, C/o Jon B. Cooke, P.O. Box 601, West Kingston, R.I. 02892 USA. Jon B. Cooke, Editor. Vol. 1, #5/6. All characters © their respective copyright holders. All material © their creators unless otherwise noted. ©2021 Jon B. Cooke. Cover art ©2021 Fred Hembeck. All characters ©2021 their respective copyright holders.

Fred sez:

Fred Hembeck remains ensconced in New York's Duchess County with wife Lynn. Since the publication of the *CBA Bullpen* interview, several compilations of Fred's work have been published: Image Comics 2008 massive, near 1,000-page *The Nearly Complete Essential Hembeck Archives Omnibus*; and a pair from Marvel—2015's *House of Hem* and 2016's trade paperback, *The Marvel Universe According To Hembeck*. You can regularly find Fred's full-color covers on six seasonal and special issues of the weekly *Comic Shop News*, and his *Dateline: @#$!* strip is in every issue of Jon B. Cooke's *Comic Book Creator*.

Additionally, there's the occasional job for one of the big two, most recently the "Where's Stripesy?" feature in DC's *Stargirl Spring Break Special*. Sketch cards featuring literally hundreds of different characters drawn in the quirky Hembeck style can always be found on eBay, or—if you're just looking, not buying—on Fred's Facebook page. Commissions also help Fred keep food on the table (email *fred@hembeck.com* for details). Having survived the pandemic (with barely a change in lifestyle; such is the life of a cartoonist), Fred still finds time to read the occasional comic book, and looks forward to soon spending more time with his first grandchild, Hannah, when daughter Julie and partner Dave move a wee bit closer and masks can come off for good.

WELL, THAT'S ALL FOR NOW!! AU REVOIR!!

STEVE TREVOR WAS *NEVER* LIKE THIS!

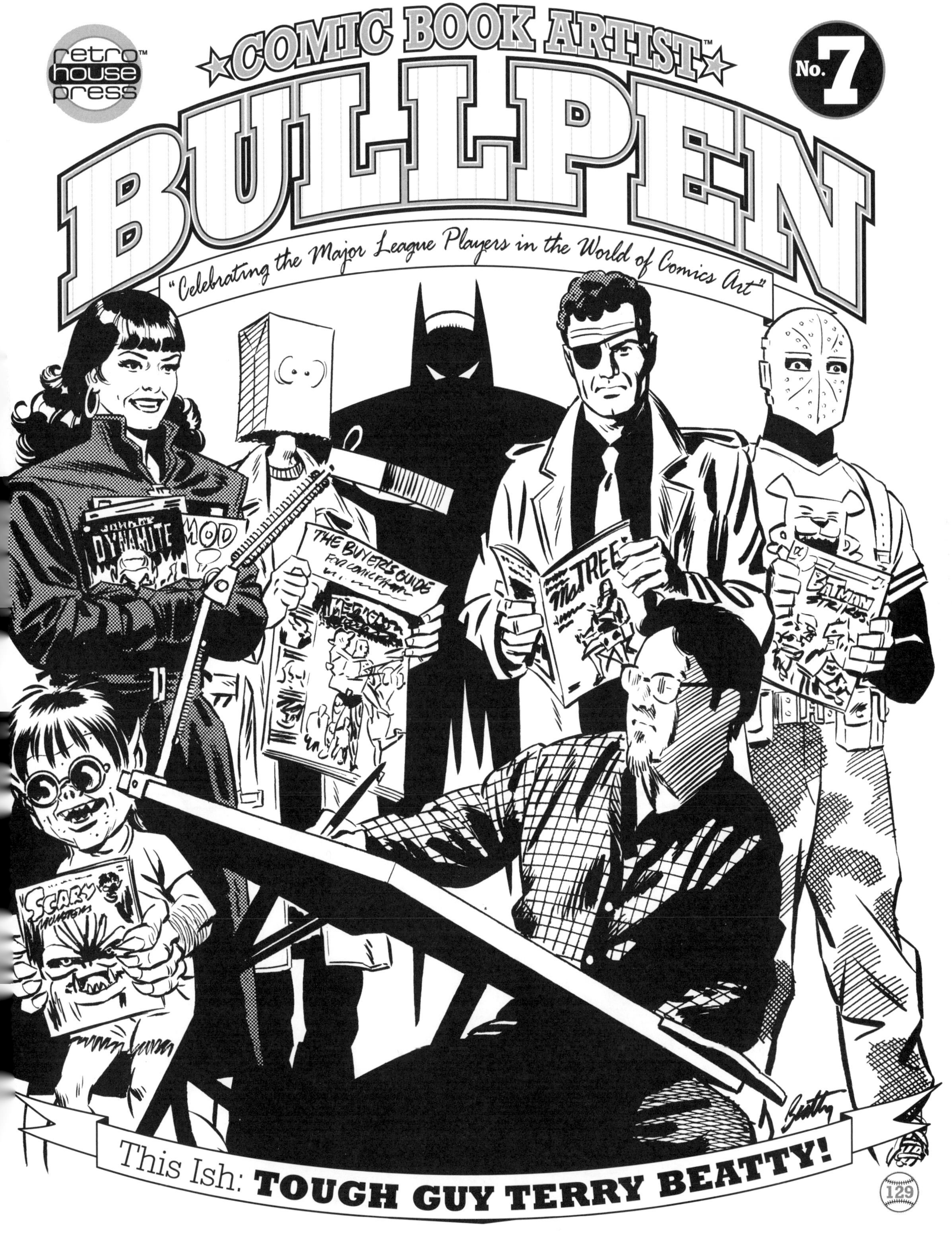
retro house press
COMIC BOOK ARTIST
BULLPEN
No. 7
"Celebrating the Major League Players in the World of Comics Art"
DYNAMITE
MOD
THE BUYER'S GUIDE FOR COMIC FANDOM
Ms. TREE
BATMAN STRIKES
SCARY
Beatty
This Ish: TOUGH GUY TERRY BEATTY!

DOCTOR DOOM, THING, HULK, CAPTAIN AMERICA and WASP TM and © MARVEL COMICS
BATMAN, SUPERMAN, PLASTIC MAN, CAPT. MARVEL, BIG BARDA and METAMORPHO TM and © DC COMICS

This page: *Previously unpublished Ms. Tree illustration by Terry Beatty. Courtesy of the artist. Ms. Tree ©2021 Max Allan Collins & Terry Beatty.*

a life in crime

Terry Beatty

Whether as penciler or inker, painter or sculptor, comic book artist or book illustrator, Terry Beatty is one remarkably accomplished craftsman, a man who rose in the ranks from fan cartoonist for The Buyer's Guide to artist co-creator of long-running independent comics series Ms. Tree to his current stint as inker on

CBA Bullpen: *Where are you originally from, Terry?*

Terry Beatty: I was born where I'm sitting right now: Muscatine, Iowa, a little town on the Mississippi River.

Bullpen: *Have you always lived there?*

Terry: Yeah, until the fifth of November, when I'm packing up my last truck to go to Minneapolis.

Bullpen: *Why Minneapolis?*

Terry: For one, my wife got a job there. For another, the art scene up there is just terrific, and the music and movie scenes are just amazing.

Bullpen: *"Cull-cha!"*

Terry: Right. And after 45 years in this little town, I think I've gotten everything out of this place that I'm gonna get, and frankly, everything I love about it are aspects that don't exist anymore. People say, "What do you love about Muscatine?" I say, "Well, I love our wonderful old Art Deco movie theater that's now a parking lot, and the old news-stand that isn't there anymore…" So the best aspects are gone anyway. I may as well move on to someplace different.

Bullpen: *Have you been to Minneapolis with any frequency?*

Terry: Oh, yes. It's my wife's hometown and I've spent quite a bit of time there. I like Minneapolis. They have some great comic book shops and a real good twice-a-year convention run by the local comics club. Those folks couldn't be nicer. It's a great place to be.

Bullpen: *When were you born?*

Terry: 1958.

Bullpen: *So you pretty much grew up with the Marvel age of heroes, right?*

Terry: I have three older brothers, and when I was a little grade school kid, they were bring-ing home comic books from 1963 on. There was a certain amount of DC stuff, but mostly the Marvel books. Of course there were—what?—*eight* Marvel books at the time? And that probably in-cluded *Millie the Model*. [*laughs*] I really got hooked on comic books quite early.

Bullpen: *Did you go through a funny-animal phase?*

Terry: No, I went straight to super-heroes. I was reading the Superman family titles. I have a real nostalgia for [artists] Curt Swan and George Klein, that era of Superman. The *Jimmy Olsen* books, especially. Then there was all the Jack Kirby and Steve Ditko stuff at Marvel. I never had a period where I was reading the Archies or any of the stuff aimed at younger kids. I was five and was reading *Fantastic Four*. It did wonders for my vocabulary and reading ability.

Bullpen: *What did your parents do?*

Terry: My father was a schoolteacher who taught English at the local junior high and then ultimately at the high school. My mom was a housewife, but she always had an interest in art, and there were always books on artists and illustrated books around the house.

Bullpen: *Fine art?*

Terry: Yes, but a lot of illustration work, as well. I vividly re-member the Rockwell Kent version of *Moby Dick* and then all those classics with the Frank Godwin illustrations. I recall a few things by Charles Dana Gibson, a portfolio of prints of Gibson girls. I remember being just fascinated by the line-work in that. And she also is responsible for putting the first pencils and crayons in my hands. The story is that when I was a toddler and she was teaching a Red Cross First Aid class, she'd put me in a playpen in the back of the room with paper and crayons, and the people taking the class didn't know I was there. Before I could walk or anything, I was absorbed in making marks on paper. So I guess I haven't advanced any, really. [*laughs*] That's what I still do.

Bullpen: *So you have three older brothers?*

Terry: Yeah.

Bullpen: *How much older are they?*

Terry: Six, 11, and 12 years older.

Bullpen: *Did you have any sisters?*

Terry: No. The three older brothers technically are half-brothers, from my mother's first marriage. She was widowed and then remarried.

Bullpen: *So were you "kind-of" an only child?*

Above: Early Ms. Tree character pose. Pencils and inks by Terry Beatty. Ms. Tree ©2021 Max Allan Collins & Terry Beatty.
Center inset: *Artist's self-caricature. Courtesy of and ©2021 Terry Beatty.*

Interview by Jon B. Cooke

A Life in Crime

DC's "animated-style" <u>Batman</u> titles (and perennial <u>Scary Monsters</u> cover painter). Terry is also a smart and insightful interview subject, as found in this chat (conducted by phone on Oct. 25, 2003, and subsequently copyedited by T.B.).

Terry: Yes, I'm this weird combination, because up until I was 12 or so, there always were a couple of the older brothers in the house, and I very much had that experience of being part of the larger family. My mother had the unerring ability to cook, say, one more piece of chicken than there were people at the table, so we had the brothers racing to finish the food, to grab the last piece. [*laughter*] I had an almost *Leave It to Beaver* upbringing. But I was Beav and there were three Wallys in the house. But then, when I was a teenager, they were out and gone to college or married or whatever, and then I had that experience of being the only child. And I *am* my father's only child.

Bullpen: *Were any of your brothers creative?*

Terry: A little bit. They were mostly jocks but they all had some interest in art or music or some combination of the above. Like I said, they were the ones who brought home the comic books.

Bullpen: *Were they pretty much just readers?*

Terry: Yes. Well, my brother Lynn drew a little bit, but he never really followed up on it much.

Bullpen: *All of your comics were hand-me-downs?*

Terry: No, I started buying my own pretty early. That's where the allowance money went, and even through high school, I would skip lunch and spend my lunch money on comics (which, I've heard, is actually something of a common experience among comic book geeks).

Bullpen: *You mentioned that you had exposure to a number of comic strips as well. Did you have a well-stocked newspaper?*

Terry: The local paper here ran a number of story strips. They ran *Steve Canyon* from day one (though, of course, I wasn't around when that started, but that's just a fact I know). *Buz Sawyer* was in the local paper. We got a number of different newspapers. The *Des Moines Register* ran *Li'l Abner* and a few other cool story strips. But I was always begging my parents to get the Davenport, Iowa, paper that had all the King Features stuff, and then eventually had *Dick Tracy*, as well. We'd go to some friend's house and I'd get to see *The Phantom, Flash Gordon, Prince Valiant,* and *Johnny Hazard.* They gave in and subscribed by the time I was about 12, so I would get my weekly Sunday hit of Frank Robbins and Hal Foster.

Bullpen: *Did you feel a particular kinship toward the adventure stuff?*

Terry: Well, I always loved the adventure strips, but I have to say, there was this period where I was very much into the humor work as well. Along with the comic books, my brothers were bringing home those paperback collections of *MAD* that reprinted the Harvey Kurtzman/ Will Elder-period comic book stuff. Far more so than the then-current version of *MAD* magazine, those paperbacks were a major influence on me as a kid. Then that led me into being interested in underground comix, and then looking into the vintage newspaper strips, and when there started to be some books being published on comics history, getting very, very interested in the newspaper strips of the '30s.

Also, I was a kid who grew up on old cartoons every afternoon on TV. So there was *Popeye* every afternoon, and then I discovered the reprints of E.C. Segar's *Popeye* comic strips. There was this part of me that wanted to do funny humor stuff, as well. So I was very torn in the early years of wanting to be a cartoonist but wondering which road I was going to choose to travel. It was just a coincidence that I ended up doing adventure stuff. When I was about 18, I really thought I was going to be a humor cartoonist.

Bullpen: *I've been interviewing a number of underground comix artists, and the influence of MAD*

Above: *Previously unpublished Archon gaming illustration (Noir) by Terry Beatty. Courtesy of the artist. ©2021 the respective copyright holder.*

comics is just incalculable.

Terry: Yes, I don't think you can underestimate the influence of Kurtzman, not just on cartoonists, but on pop culture and the world as well. I think there's a whole generation that learned to distrust authority from Harvey Kurtzman. [*laughter*] I think for the whole rock 'n' roll generation, it's not just the Beatles who influenced us— it's Harvey, too.

Bullpen: *I've been talking a lot to Jay Lynch, and he brought up something I never thought about before, which was the relationship between* MAD *comics and the Tijuana bibles. These little pornographic comic book pamphlets would take recognizable, known, licensed characters like Popeye and put them through provocative situations. Minus the sex, that's what* MAD *comics did. Jay said there's a subconscious taboo element that really enhances the subversiveness of it. I thought, "You know, that makes a lot of sense!" [laughs]*

Terry: Yes, I think he's right on that one.

Bullpen: *Do you remember where you were when you saw Kurtzman?*
Terry: When I first saw the work?
Bullpen: *Yes.*
Terry: Because I'll tell you where I was when I actually first saw the man Harvey Kurtzman! I was standing at the urinal next to him in a men's room at a comic book convention. I thought, "Now is not the time to introduce myself." [*laughter*] I first saw Harvey's work probably sitting in my bedroom at my parents' house just flipping through one of the little paperbacks—*MAD* or *Son of MAD* or whichever— and I have a very vivid memory of "The Heap" satire. That might have been the first thing I read.

Bullpen: *Did you have friends who were also into comics?*
Terry: A few. I had a very good friend in grade school named Kerry Grady, now a graphic artist and the co-owner of a design firm in Chicago, and he's very successful. We did a lot of drawing together, cartooning and such. Then I had a good buddy named Dave Askam, who I met in high school, who is now VP of

an ad agency. He never drew, but he wrote and had a very serious interest in comics, as well. There was a small group of us.
Bullpen: *Were you known as an artist in grade school?*
Terry: Yes. In grade school, Kerry and I were the "artist guys." We were always in a friendly competition that I think was good for both of us. It made us work harder at trying to be the best.
Bullpen: *Did you contribute to school newspapers or the yearbook?*
Terry: I did a little bit of that, but actually we had a more subversive thing going on. There were some upperclassmen a year or two ahead of us that started an underground humor newspaper, and my little group eventually took that over. It was called *The Schagnogleeack Times,* named after this little cartoon character, Sam Schagnogleeack, who was a nebbishy guy with a bag on his head. He was the mascot of the publication.
Bullpen: *Who invented him?*
Terry: Well, it was the upperclassmen, really. I was the first one to come along and flesh him out and make him a character. We did two issues of a comic book, as well, with stories. So that was my first published work, I suppose you could say, although it was just printed and hand-stapled and sold around the school.
Bullpen: *Was this pre-Xerox? Was it mimeographed?*
Terry: Well, the newspaper was mimeographed. This thing we actually sent to the local printer.
Bullpen: *Offset?*
Terry: Yes, it was offset printing, but on separate sheets. We had to collate every issue and staple it.
Bullpen: *Did you like that? Did you get into publication there, the tactile nature of it?*
Terry: Oh, very much, yes. I liked having a certain amount of control over that, putting the newspaper or comic book together. There's a certain sense of accomplishment, of being in charge.
Bullpen: *Do you still have copies of* The Schagnogleeack Times?
Terry: Yes, packed away somewhere.
Bullpen: *What was the effect of seeing your work in print? Was it a profound moment?*
Terry: Gosh, I don't remember the first time, really... I guess the one thing I learned from the comic book was just what's going to work for reproduction and what won't. I learned to draw bigger and bolder and not be so detailed with the pen-work. Which, I guess, is a lesson every cartoonist learns the first time they see print.
Bullpen: *Did you have a favorite artist that particularly influenced you early on?*
Terry: There's such a long list, so it's hard to play favorites, and I've gotten to know so many of the great cartoonists over the years, thanks to attending conventions, that my personal feelings toward a lot of them have colored my opinion of them and their work as well. I suppose, if I had to press, that I'd say Kirby. That influence was so strong. And Jack was such a nice guy, too. Such a sweetheart.
Bullpen: *How about Toth?*
Terry: You know, I've always admired Toth. I don't think I can list him as a major influence. I've discussed this with other cartoonists. There's a technical brilliance to his work, and again, I admire it to the high heavens. But there's also a certain coldness to it that it just doesn't draw me in the way Kirby or Ditko does. Or even somebody like [*Batman* artist] Dick Sprang, or [*Dick Tracy* cartoonist] Chester Gould, where there's more liveliness to the characters on the page.

Bullpen: *Are you any relation to [Marvel artist] John Beatty?*

Terry: John and I have discussed this, but we can't quite figure out any real connection, although I believe his family is mostly from Pennsylvania. I do know that my family had some ancestors that came from Pennsylvania, so there's probably some connection way, way back there.

Bullpen: *But you two are friends?*

Terry: We've met a couple of times, talked to each other on the Internet. I think we have a bit of a mutual admiration society going on as far as each other's inks are concerned. We're not really cousins. [*laughs*] Although I do have a cousin who's a former comic book inker, and that's Barb Kaalberg.

Bullpen: *What has your cousin done?*

Terry: She inked tons of stuff during the boom years, 10 years ago or so. She started out at Malibu and ended up doing a lot of work at DC, but she got out of the business and hasn't done anything in comics for quite a while.

Bullpen: *What were your aspirations in junior high and going into high school?*

Terry: Well, I was convinced from age five I was going to draw comic books, and that's all I wanted to do. Silly me.

Bullpen: *Do you still have comic books that you had when you were five?*

Terry: No. I have repurchased some of them. I would always go through my collection and sell stuff to buy new stuff, so most of my original comics are long gone.

Bullpen: *Do you think it was an advantage, in a way, being born in '58? There was something really golden that took place in the early '70s, in that you had all this retro stuff being reprinted, Nostalgia Press doing these beautiful volumes, all these reprinted comic strips. Plus, all this incredible contemporary work coming out of the mainstream, with Bernie Wrightson and Michael Kaluta, and people like that. Plus Kirby was reaching his peak, and the undergrounds were in full swing on top of that.*

Terry: Yes, I think you're absolutely right. I think it was a wonderful time, growing up in the '60s and '70s, an absolutely wonderful time, not just for comics but for pop culture in general. You turned on the TV and the late movie was a Universal monster film, or some crime movie from the '30s. On the radio you had rock 'n' roll from the '60s and '70s. It was just great stuff. Of course, now you turn on the late show and you get a made-for-TV movie from the 1980s, y'know? There's just not a lot of comparison there. So yeah, I'm very grateful I grew up when I did.

Bullpen: *I'm just wondering if our generation may have been too appreciative in the sense that maybe a lot of us didn't go off to do like work? I'm just wondering sometimes, because you look at The Studio guys, and you look at the guys who came out from San Francisco, and you just look at this incredible explosion of creativity. And by the time we came of age in the late '70s, it was pretty… dry.*

Terry: [*Laughs*] I'm a complete pop culture fan. I'm a total fanboy geek about a million things. And you can get so caught up in all of this pop culture and art, that your art then somehow becomes about *that*, rather than being about life. And there's only so much you can say about, "Hey, this is a great old movie," before it doesn't have much meaning to it. It's the difference between, say, a Quentin Tarantino film that's just entirely full of references to other movies and a John Ford film, which is about life.

Bullpen: *Were the Universal monster movies important to you?*

Terry: Oh, absolutely. We had *Chiller Theater* here on Friday or Saturday nights. There I was, a five-, six-, seven-year-old kid trying to stay up until midnight to watch the movie on the weekend. My parents would let me do so, but I was asleep probably halfway through most of them. The show was hosted by a character named Doctor Igor, who I discovered later played by a guy named Gene King. He also was Jungle Jay on weekday afternoons, showing *Tarzan* and *Bomba* movies. I just absolutely loved that stuff. I still do.

Bullpen: *Were you a sociable kid? Were you athletic?*

Terry: No. I was the tubby kid with glasses who hid in his room, who drew and read comics.

Bullpen: *When did your mom remarry?*

Terry: 1957, a year before I was born.

Bullpen: *My older brothers were musicians, so I felt like I was co-opted out of that. Was that the same with you regarding athletics?*

Terry: I don't know. I was just naturally inclined to be a kid with books and art. That was my thing. The older brothers were jocks, and they were really good at it. That was their natural inclination. But if you threw a ball at me, it would hit me in the head. [*laughter*] Which partially was because I needed glasses and we didn't know it until I was in fifth grade. You have no point of comparison. If you're a kid and you're nearsighted, you don't know

NUMBER ONE

SCHAGNOGLEEACK COMICS AND GOOFIES...

The ORIGINAL PAPER-BAG BOY!

AND BARF the WONDER DOG!

The FIRST COMIC BOOK COLLECTION of The Adventures of--- SAM SCHAGNOGLEEACK (AND HIS FRIENDS!)

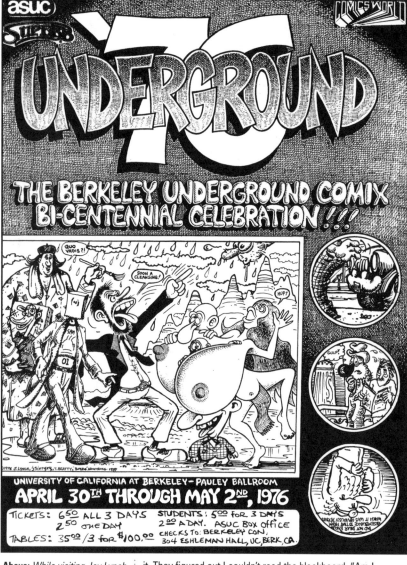

Terry: I think so. My father didn't want to be caught being too emotional about anything or saying too much.

Bullpen: *Did you have any dreams of getting away from the Midwest and going either West or East?*

Terry: No, that didn't interest me that much. It really was just about wanting to have a career in cartooning, and at one point I thought it was going to be newspaper strips. Ultimately I took stabs at making that happen, but that's an awfully tough market to break into.

Bullpen: *When did you encounter your first comic book professional?*

Terry: I knew Max Collins from the time I was in high school, but he hadn't written any comics yet; he wrote crime novels. The *Dick Tracy* gig didn't come along until later. But I became friends with Max. I also visited an older cartoonist named Jo Fischer, who did a strip called *Nine-To-Five*, and it was mostly girly cartoons about secretaries and such. He was 80-years-old or something. Quite a character.

Bullpen: *How'd you meet him?*

Terry: Through Collins. Max was always searching to see if there were any other cartoonists or comic artists in the area.

Bullpen: *How'd you meet Max?*

Terry: He had been one of my father's students in junior high school.

Bullpen: *Max is from the same town?*

Terry: Yes, from the same town, though he is 10 years older than me. He had a letter published in one of the Neal Adams and Denny O'Neil issues of *Green Lantern* (though it was signed as Al Collins because his dad was Max… he's Max Allan Collins, Jr.). I pointed that letter out to my dad, and he said, "Oh, Al was one of my students." I remember my dad giving him a call: "Oh, I saw your letter in a comic book." Then, mid-'70s, he published his first crime novels, *Bait Money* and *Blood Money*, the "Nolan and Jon" books. Nolan is a retired thief and Jon is an aspiring cartoonist and comic book collector. And all of the Jon stuff really hit home with me, and I thought, what, was Max spying on me? [*laughter*] I think one of the books talks about Jon keeping his comic books in his dresser and his clothes in a cardboard box, which at the time I was doing. [*Jon laughs*] What the heck! I didn't realize this stuff was not unusual for comic fans. So I got to know Max after those books were published and I was just this geeky kid who introduced himself as his former teacher's son. Not long after that, I took a class taught by Max at the local junior college. He taught a class in film. So we started getting to be friends through that, and I kept showing him my artwork as it progressed. He always said, "It'd be cool to work on something together at some point." He kept waiting for me to get good enough. After he got the *Dick Tracy* gig, he got wind that the Tribune Syndicate was looking to revive *Little Orphan Annie*. So we put together samples for that, and he had a meeting in Chicago with them about *Tracy*, and he brought me and the *Annie* samples in afterward, and they were quite interested. We actually thought we had the gig for a couple of weeks. Then they got Leonard Starr's samples, and that was the end of that! So then we went on to do a few other sample projects, a few small things, and it ultimately led to *Ms. Tree*. So that's okay.

Bullpen: *What was the genesis of Ms. Tree?*

Terry: Max and I had done, for about a year, a project we called *The*

it. They figured out I couldn't read the blackboard. "Am I supposed to be able to?" You get the glasses and you walk outside at the optometrist's and say, "You mean I'm really *supposed* to be able to read that sign three blocks away?" [*Jon laughs*] I didn't know.

Bullpen: *Were your parents always encouraging about art?*

Terry: Yes, they were very supportive, my mother especially. My father put up with it. He never said much. In fact, once I was in my mid-20s, I finally said to him, "Dad, I always show you my work. Why don't you ever say anything about it?" He said, "Well, you know what you're doing." Oh, okay. Well, I guess I'll just take that.

Bullpen: *[Laughs] Is that his Iowa stoicness?*

Comics Page. It was a self-syndicated, weekly tabloid page of comics for small town weekly newspapers, or shoppers. We never had quite enough clients to make it a success, but one of our clients was *The Chicago Reader,* which is a free arts and entertainment newspaper in the city. They only ran one strip from this page. It was six comic strips, all humor strips, except for the minute mystery. It was the *Mike Mist Minute Mist-ery.* That ran in *The Reader.* Dean Mullaney was at the Chicago Comicon and saw this thing, and he was a big *Tracy* fan and thought Collins was great. He said, "This is neat, this little *Mike Mist* strip, and by the way, I'm starting Eclipse, a comic book company." He asked Collins if we had enough of these to do a comic book compilation. Well, we *did,* because we had about a year's worth. So we did that. We were supposed to get royalty payments on that, and I've never seen a dime, by the way. Eclipse never did pay me a single penny on that thing. [*laughs*] But then, after that came out, Dean had called Max on the phone one day and said, "I'm starting *Eclipse* magazine, and it's going to be a black-&-white anthology, and we'd like to have a detective feature in there. Can you and Terry come up with something?" So Max pretty much invented *Ms. Tree* on the phone with Dean, and called me and said, "Do you want to draw a comic book?" [*laughs*] And I came up with the visuals. Suddenly I was an adventure strip cartoonist!

Bullpen: *How was your experience?*

Terry: Producing the work was good. Working for the independent comics press was always kind of interesting. People who are just buying and reading the comics have no idea what's going on behind the scenes, of having to make phone calls to the East Coast to try to get your paycheck, and all the b.s. that goes on behind it all. But we did one story for *Eclipse* magazine, and then we got spun off into our own color comic book for nine issues. So it was a nifty deal. And then went on to other publishers and kept going for 50-some issues.

Bullpen: *Fifty-some issues?*

Terry: Yes, we did up to 50 issues… Our last Renegade Press issue was #50, and then we did, I think, 10 more at DC, but they were those big, fat quarterlies, so they had a good deal more content than did the AV and the Renegade Press issues.

Bullpen: *Have there ever been nibbles for the character in other media?*

Terry: Oh, yes. We've had movie and TV options all along, but nothing ever quite came of it. At one point ABC was very interested. There was a script for a TV movie that was done. Then USA Network was going to put it on their schedule. They actually had a casting call out. Then they got a new president. [*laughs*] You can finish *that* story.

Bullpen: *But there's still life in her, right?*

Terry: Oh, yes. It's still being talked about by some people in Hollywood, and there's talk about a series of trade paperback reprints of the original stories, so who knows.

Bullpen: *How would you characterize Ms. Tree?*

Terry: Well, she's a pretty screwed-up human being, actually. She's this revenge-happy, trigger-happy lunatic, basically. [*laughter*] In real life, she would have been dead a long time ago. I don't know how she survived all the stuff she went through. She is a pretty dark character. I have to say, at the end of our DC run, as much as I loved working on that series, it was a relief to be able to walk away from her, because she was in such a dark place. When I'm drawing characters, especially if it's a feature that I co-own or co-created, as the artist, I have to be the actors on the page. So I realized I was going along with all of her dark neuroses all of these years. [*laughs*] "I need to get out of that point of view for a little while! It'd be healthy to take a break." Although at this point, I think both Max and I would love the chance to do another *Ms. Tree* story.

Bullpen: *Have you done graphic novels? I guess the quarterlies were pretty fat, right?*

Terry: Yes, they were 48 pages apiece, those stories. In some instances, those would count as graphic novels. There were some continued storylines, and I think if you were to take them all together, they'd add up to one. Of course, the *Johnny Dynamite* series Max and I did has just been reprinted in graphic novel format. Although it was drawn as four issues of a comic book, so depending on your definition of "graphic novel," it either is or isn't.

Bullpen: *When did you encounter fandom for the first time?*

Above: *MOD #1 [June '81] is a definite curiosity of Terry Beatty's career. Published by Kitchen Sink and containing contributions from Bob Burden and Bill Griffith (among others), this one-shot represents what might very well be Terry's singular effort as an editor and it also contains rare examples of scripting by the guy.*

Inset left: *Revealing an interest in the cartoons of Max Fleischer, Terry wrote and drew this Mr. Bug Goes To Town pastiche entitled "Mr. Bugg Goes To Hell" for MOD #1. Courtesy of Bob Burden & ©2021 Terry Beatty.*

THE PHONY PAGES

This page: *In the early '80s, Terry Beatty was a very frequent contributor to Alan Light's* The Buyer's Guide for Comic Fandom, *drawing covers, contributing articles, writing the regular column "Sideways," and producing the frequent "Phony Pages" features (which later were compiled into Renegade Press collections). The Steranko parody at right included a header which (for reasons forgotten by T.B.) did not appear in the printed TBG: "Reproduced is the cover art for issue number four of* Brooke Shields Agent of F.U.R.Y. *(Fightin' Union of Rebellious Youngsters). Shields was the first 'designer' comic book (hence the steep cover price). The art and stories were provided by Jean Designeranko, a fashion designer with a bent towards psychedelic and 'pop' imagery. Despite carrying the Calvin Klein seal of approval, the series folded after half a dozen issues." Below is a curious melding of a popular TV sitcom and a Western comics mainstay. All courtesy of and ©2021 Terry Beatty.*

Terry: Well, it probably would have been through *The Buyer's Guide For Comic Fandom* produced by Alan Light in East Moline, Illinois, which is about a half-hour's drive upriver from here. Max knew Alan. At one point, Alan was collecting original comic art, and I think Max and Alan did some art deals together. I got to know him through Collins. I know it would have been about '77 or so. He'd gone weekly with *The Buyer's Guide* and was having a little trouble getting new art for the covers every week. So I became the semi-regular *Buyer's Guide* cover artist, and was also doing columns and cartoons for the magazine. As far as I know I was the only person who got paid for doing *Buyer's Guide* covers. It wasn't a high-paying job, but it still made it professional work in my eyes, as opposed to fan work.

Bullpen: *What was Alan Light like?*

Terry: Well, he was very quiet, a very nice guy. He was very interested in comics at the time, but I understand now, since he sold the publication off to Krause Publications years and years ago, that he has no interest at all, that he doesn't follow it anymore. I haven't seen him for years, so I have no idea what he's up to.

Bullpen: *I guess he was a controversial personality for a little while, right? Or was that just in relation to* The Comics Journal.

Terry: Oh, yes, probably. You don't even want to go there.

Bullpen: *[Laughs] Were you able to emulate other artists' styles on the covers you drew?*

Terry: Yes, that's mostly what I did: I would do tribute covers to other artists. Alan gave me free rein, so it wasn't like I had to do Jack Kirby every month. I mean, I was doing Everett Raymond Kinstler and Zack Mosley. [*laughs*] I was getting pretty obscure there, at some point. We did some experimentation. We did the 3-D cover, the whole red-&-green 3-D process. Did quite a few two-color covers. Did one in three-color. Also did a cover for, I believe it was the 400th issue, in which I drew 400 characters. [*laughs*] I broke up the cover into grids and drew these tiny little heads of all these characters. Again, that was basically swipes of other artists' work, but it was fun to do. The telling thing is that the ones that I felt that I didn't get, the ones that were

the hardest and that I thought I'd failed on? Anybody who ever tells me that the *Peanuts* characters and Nancy and Sluggo would have been easy to draw, or that those guys really weren't very good artists, I always tell them this story. Four hundred comic book characters, copying dozens of artists, every one of them was easy except for those.

Bullpen: *Was that pretty much your professional gig, there? Could it pay well enough?*

Terry: Oh, no, that was just a little thing on the side. That wasn't anything to earn a living on, no.

Bullpen: *Did you go to college?*

Terry: Nope. Just worked toward doing commercial art and being a cartoonist.

Bullpen: *Your father was a teacher. Was he bothered that you didn't go to college?*

Terry: Not terribly so. Of the four of us brothers, two of us went, one of us finished. [*laughter*] But we all had things we went on to do that were good, solid, professional things, so he wasn't bothered by it at all. He knew that I was doing what I wanted to do. At the time there wasn't really any school with any solid cartooning course going on. The Kubert School didn't exist yet. I'm sure there were places I could have gone to learn commercial art, but I just went to the school of hard knocks and learned it on my own.

Bullpen: *In retrospect, how do you look at that? Would you have done it again the same way?*

Terry: I might have wanted to go to art school, but someplace where I was actually going to learn technique as opposed to the current "fine art" philosophy of the day.

Bullpen: *Did you have a regular day job?*

Terry: I was a disc jockey from 1975 to '77. I was still in high school when I started.

Bullpen: *A full-time job?*

Terry: Yes. During my last year of high school, I was working full-time at the local radio station. Had no social life. [*laughs*] I was either at school or working. You would have thought being the disc jockey at the local radio station would have made you hot stuff in high school, but it didn't help or do anything, actually.

Bullpen: *What was the station?*

Terry: Well, there actually were two. I worked weekdays at an AM country-&-Western station, and this was before country was big. This was when it was just, y'know, farmers listening, playing the tunes and hearing what the weather was going to be, that's pretty much what that station was. But the other station, where I worked weekends, was an alternative rock station, a very early one. So we were playing album cuts, and the bands were not on Top 40 radio. We had a large audience among college students in Iowa City and the Quad Cities, but here in Muscatine, the high school kids didn't begin to know what to make of it. Because We weren't playing Kiss or Blue Oyster Cult, we were playing… man, what *were* we playing? [*laughter*] I'm trying to even remember, in those early days… David Bowie and Iggy Pop…

Bullpen: *The advent of punk?*

Terry: Yes.

Bullpen: *Is music important to you?*

Terry: Oh, absolutely. It's a big thing for me. It's one of the things that convinced me to make this move to Minneapolis, because the last time I was up there, within the space of two weeks I saw four musical acts that I've been wanting to see for *years*, that would never have come around here.

Bullpen: *Do you have an eclectic taste in music?*

Terry: Yes, it runs the gamut from Cab Calloway to Rob Zombie.

Bullpen: *There wasn't that much freelance mainstream comics work being done through the mail, right? You pretty much had to be in New York to work in comics, right?*

Terry: Well, I never encountered that. I think that ended by the time I was really getting in. The independent comic field didn't have that connection at all, because, geez, Eclipse was in California someplace… their business offices were in New York, supposedly, but that was just where brother Jan [Mullaney] was cutting the paychecks (when he'd get around to it).

Bullpen: *Was it always a struggle to get paid?*

Terry: It was always interesting, let's just say that. But it's water under the bridge, so at this point it doesn't really matter. When I started doing stuff for DC, FedEx was picking up the packages and sending the pages out. It didn't seem to be any big deal.

Bullpen: *Were you at Aardvark-Vanaheim for a period?*

Terry: Yes. *Ms. Tree* went from Eclipse to AV, which at the time was being run by Dave *and* Deni Sim. Then, when their marriage broke up, Deni took the titles that weren't *Cerebus* with her and formed Renegade Press, and Max and I went with her and did *Ms. Tree* up to #50.

Bullpen: *How was your experience with Deni?*

Terry: It was quite good. Deni's very supportive and good-hearted, and she published some really good stuff. I think she maybe published a little too *much* stuff toward the end, when

the market was getting a little difficult. We were there before the black-&-white boom, and didn't benefit from it much, because we were already there. But we did get hurt by it when it went bust and that company eventually failed. But it was a good experience working with Deni. It was actually a really good experience working with Renegade Press's press liaison and sort of all-around assistant flunky. That was Wendi Lee, whom I married. [*laughs*] We'd met before Renegade Press, at the San Diego Con a number of years before.

Bullpen: *I assumed, because of Wendi being a mystery writer, that you met her through knowing Max.*

Terry: No, not at all. When we met, she was editing *The Telegraph Wire*, which was a comics fanzine being produced by Comics & Comix, the comic shop chain. Our first meeting was just, "Hi, nice to meet you." And it was my first San Diego Con, so I was like, "Yeah, *that's* a cute little blonde… but hey, look! There's Ray Bradbury!" [*laughter*] So I was off being a comic book idiot. And when we met again a couple of years later at a Chicago con, I said, "Hey, wait a minute. Have I met this girl before?" Then we would bump into each other at conventions.

This page: *According to Russ Maheras's wonderful TBG #1-400 index in his indispensible* Maelstrom #8 [July '02], *Terry Beatty contributed quite a few covers to Alan Light's adzine,* The Buyer's Guide for Comic Fandom, *in the late '70s and early '80s. Above is T.B.'s tribute to artist Ramona Fradon and her beloved co-creation,* Metamorpho *(a character Terry confesses that he'll trade his eye-teeth to draw). Left inset are two of T.B.'s Christmas illustrations used as* TBG *covers. All courtesy of and art ©2021 Terry Beatty. All characters ©2021 their respective copyright holders.*

So perhaps our story really begins during happier times — last month, at Warbucks Mansion...

Don't know 'bout you, Sandy, but I'm bored...

Beatty and Collins

Finally she ended up working at Renegade Press, so we were on the phone together a lot. Ultimately, when Renegade went the way of all flesh and Wendi was looking for what she was going to do next, I convinced her to come out to Iowa [*laughs*] and we got married.

Bullpen: *Was Wendi always an aspiring writer?*

Terry: Yes. When she got here, she was able to take the time (because I was pretty much supporting us through the comic book work) and to get her writing career in gear, and published quite a few Westerns and mysteries. Now that market has gotten so tough that she's taken a break from it and has gone back to the nine-to-five world for a while, but intends to come back to it at some point.

Bullpen: *Any books or any series of note that she did?*

Terry: The mystery novels are about a Boston-based female P.I. named Angela Matelli, she did about a half-dozen of those. Her Westerns are mysteries, too. They're about an ex-Texas Ranger named Jefferson Birch. And then she also did one big Western called *The Overland Trail*… not a mystery, a big, epic Western story.

Bullpen: *Is it compatible for an artist and writer to co-habitate, so to speak, in the freelance realm, when she was also working at home?*

Terry: It's great personally, because you each understand what the other's going through. It's not like some of the relationships I see where there's one person who really is just based in the nine-to-five world and doesn't understand this crazy person they're married to, who's working in the freelance world and has all of these oddball collecting interests. Wendi and I shared all these interests, but we also shared the difficulties of being freelancers and having some very tough times. We also had a lot of very solid times, but we had some lean times, too, as most freelancers will. Now that we've been parents for quite a while, and we have a 17-year-old daughter—Elizabeth—we're looking at college for her not too long from now… well, let's get something a little more solid going on here. So she has put the writing on the back-burner for a little bit and gone into the real world for a spell.

Bullpen: *You have one child?*

Terry: Yes, we adopted her at age 10. She was our foster child, and then we adopted her.

Bullpen: *So the black-&-white bust severely disabled* Ms. Tree?

Terry: Well, it pretty much did Renegade Press in. There was that period there where it was a little similar to the boom in comics a number of years ago, where there were all the al-

ternate cover versions and people were buying boxes full of the next first issue, and then when that went bust, it just hurt the whole business. The same thing happened with the black-&-white boom, which I guess the [*Teenage Mutant*] Ninja Turtles precipitated. There were all these new black-&-white titles coming out, which the direct market supported. I mean, anybody and their dog could make their own comic book, and as long as you could get orders of about 5,000, the comic would get in the Diamond catalog, and there they were. But, at some point, all the kids who were buying multiple copies of those issues for investment realized that was stupid. [*laughs*] There wasn't going to be anybody who wanted to pay ten times cover price down the line. So it all went bust, and Renegade went with it. Thankfully, Max and I had Mike Gold in our corner, whom we knew from First Comics and the Chicago comics scene in general. Mike was then an editor at DC, and we had already done *Wild Dog* with Mike at DC, and he brought *Ms. Tree* there.

Bullpen: *Mike spearheaded* Action Comics Weekly, *right? Was that the entrée for you?*

Terry: No. Actually, my first gig at DC was a page for the DC *Who's Who*. I drew Hop Harrigan or something lame like that. But I had been doing *Ms. Tree* for quite a while, and was invited by Denny O'Neil to pencil a "Slam Bradley" chapter for a 50th anniversary issue of *Detective Comics, #572*, I think, which Mike Barr wrote and Dick Giordano inked, which was quite nice. It was a wonderful anniversary issue of *Detective*, with Carmine Infantino in it, and there was a Dick Sprang two-page spread, and there was me. "One of these things is not like the others." [*laughter*] But it was a nice little entry point. Then Max and I sold them *Wild Dog,* which we did as a four-issue mini-series. Mike got *Action Weekly* going, and we were given the option of either another mini-series or being in *Action Comics*. Well, I think both of us were comic geeks enough to say, "Geez, *Action Comics?* That's where Superman came from! We can be in *Action Comics!* Won't that be cool?" Of course, we didn't have the powers of precognition, so we didn't know that the weekly format just wasn't going to work. So *Wild Dog* spun out after that. We did do a one-shot special, and that's been the end of that character, although at every single convention appearance I do, people ask about it. It's been 10 years since I drew the character, maybe more.

Bullpen: *What was the premise of the character?*

Terry: First of all, he was a Midwesterner, set in the Quad Cities [Davenport and Bettendorf, Iowa, and Moline and Rock Island, Illinois], because every comic book character is in New York or some variation of New York. Well, we wanted to do something different, where we could tell a different kind of story. So we set him in our backyard, in a semi-rural area, and he was basically a blue-collar super-hero. He didn't have any super-powers, he just had weaponry and armor and gadgets that you could buy and put together yourself, and be the homemade super-hero. I think there was a lot of potential there that we just didn't have time to explore.

Bullpen: *What is the process of working with Max?*

Terry: He hands me a script and then I draw it. [*laughter*] If he puts too many actions in one panel, he's nice enough to let me break it up into two or three.

Bullpen: *Do you two see each other with any frequency?*

Terry: Not as much as we used to. When I was a kid and didn't have a family, and before his son was born, we had time to waste. He and I would go see the movies that his wife or my girlfriend didn't want to see, and go to the conventions together, and generally hang around. Once the pressures of a full-time career and family kick in, you just don't have as much time for that. Also, for a number of years, after being a disc jockey, and while trying to get my cartooning career together, ran sound for his rock 'n' roll band. So we spent a *lot* of time together. [*laughter*]

Bullpen: *What was the name of his band?*

Terry: Crusin'. It started out as a '50s/60s retro/nostalgia band, but ultimately turned into almost a '70s new wave band.

Bullpen: *What does Max play?*

Terry: Keyboards.

Bullpen: *Is Max a songwriter?*

Terry: Oh, yes! Actually, his earliest band in the '60s, The Daybreakers, had a single out on Atlantic Records (I can't tell you the date, exactly) that was recorded down in Nashville. It was called "Psychedelic Siren." It was something of a regional hit.

Bullpen: *Have you ever played an instrument?*

Terry: No, I'm not a musician myself, but I've always been very interested in music.

Bullpen: *Have you done radio work since?*

Terry: Nineteen seventy-seven was the end of my disc jockey days. Of course, being a cartoonist, I've done a lot of interviews and stuff, but as the subject rather than as the interviewer. Recently, I thought, moving to Minneapolis, maybe I might look into seeing if there are any studios up there that are looking for anybody to do voiceover work for commercials or whatever, see if that might be some little side project. But it's not anything that I'm dying to go do.

Bullpen: *Working with DC, was that a comfortable move for you?*

Terry: Well, yes. It was what I'd been working for, for a lot of years. When I started out, it was, "Gosh, I hope when I grow up I can draw comics for DC and/or Marvel." That independent-comics thing didn't exist when I was a little kid looking forward to a comic-book career. I'm glad it came along. I'm glad it's still there to some extent, because creator ownership of properties is a good thing. Having a regular comic book come out with that DC logo on it, the folks who brought us Batman and Superman all those years, was a pretty cool deal.

Bullpen: *Have you ever worked for Marvel?*

Terry: I've inked five pages for them. [*laughter*] I've been a comic book professional for over 20 years, and I've inked five pages for Marvel Comics.

Bullpen: *What five pages?*

Terry: It was for that *World's Greatest Comic Book* series that they did a couple of years ago, this faux Lee & Kirby *Fantastic Four* series, which pretty much just proved that none of us are Jack Kirby… although it was my job to be Joe Sinnott, technically. I think I got really close with one or two panels.

Bullpen: *Uh… Terry? Joe is still alive. You can't be him.* [*laughter*]

Terry: Yes, I know. [*laughs*] They should have just hired him to ink the whole darned thing because it would have been much more consistent.

Bullpen: *This is a real curiosity from the '70s: this Underground Jam. What was that?*

Terry: Oh, the advertisement, the Berkeley con thing? My buddy Dave, who I men-

tioned earlier, went with me to Chicago one day. We skipped school and drove to the city. We were going to see an Electric Light Orchestra concert. [*laughs*] Before the show, we went up to Jay Lynch's apartment to say hi and hang around, and Jay was there, and Robert Crumb and his band were there, because they were playing a gig as well (although they were playing at a bar, so we would have had to be 21 to get in, and we were 18, so that left that out). Jay was working on this ad for this Berkeley underground comix convention, and he just handed me a Rapidograph and said, "Here, draw something." And so I drew that Sam Schagnogleeack character, the character from our goofy high school underground newspaper, and it became my first *really* legitimate published piece—a jam with Jay Lynch and Bob Armstrong and an uncredited Robert Crumb (among others).

Bullpen: *The little head coming in from the upper right?*

Terry: Yes, that little head at the top is Crumb. Apparently, there was some thing, because Crumb had some legal issue going on, his agent or lawyers were not letting him draw at the time…

Bullpen: *Oh, Crumb's IRS problems?*

Terry: Right. Crumb was there hanging around. I got to flip through one of his sketchbooks. This was not one of those printed versions people have seen lately, but one of his sketchbooks, one of the real deals. Dave and I kept looking at each other, and I could tell we were both thinking about just grabbing it and hightailing it out of there. [*laughter*] But Jay knew where to find us, so… we didn't do it.

Bullpen: *Were you friends with Jay for a long time?*

Terry: I was friendly with Jay. I haven't been in touch with him a whole lot in recent years. I see him at the Chicago conventions and say hi and see how things are going. I mean, basically I was a little kid who admired what he did, more so than… being "friends" is pushing it a little.

Bullpen: *Did you do the little character underneath the breasts?*

Terry: It was the character in the long

MAX COLLINS and TERRY BEATTY'S Ms.TREE

"A Christmas Tree"

Above: This provocative "bondage" cover by Terry Beatty was one of the items seized in the notorious "Friendly Frank's" case of the late '80s. Courtesy of T.B. ©'21 M.C. & T.B.

coat with the bag on his head.

Bullpen: *How did MOD come about?*

Terry: Oh, *MOD.* Boy, I don't know, I guess Denis Kitchen had a lapse in taste when he told me he'd publish my book. [*laughs*]

That was something I pitched to Denis. I wanted to get together a bunch of new artists and do sort of a new wave underground, because there were a lot of people whose work I was seeing, who I thought were very good, but weren't being published much. Bob Burden was one of them. It's my understanding that it was Kitchen Sink's worst selling comic book ever, until Cat Yronwode's *Bop.*

Bullpen: *Must be those three letter titles. [laughs]*

Terry: I don't know. Well, actually, there is a reason for it, and it has to do with their sales outlet being the head shops, and that was sort of dying. And also, we were producing something that wasn't a hippie book. It was the next generation, and it was being sold in the wrong place.

Bullpen: *You edited it?*

Terry: Yeah, I edited it, wrote a certain amount of it, and drew a little bit of it.

Bullpen: *Do you like writing?*

Terry: Oh, yes. Don't do as much of it as I'd like, because, gosh, the cartooning just takes up so much time. Wendi and I have published somewhere between half-dozen and a dozen short story collaborations. And I've written a few comics for other people. Mike Gilbert and I collaborated on a *Mr. Monster* story. And some other things that just won't come to mind right now.

Bullpen: *What were the short stories? Were they mysteries?*

Terry: Some of them, but also other genre stuff. I know there is a vampire story and a werewolf story, and a story in one of the *Twilight Zone* anthologies.

Bullpen: *Were they small press or were they printed in anthologies?*

Terry: No, actual legitimate, real books. [*laughs*] Little paperback things you find in the racks at all the stores.

Bullpen: *Obviously, short story anthologies, right?*

Terry: Right.

Bullpen: *You worked with Max on some projects that you co-created. Did you want to strike out on your own at all? Have you attempted?*

Terry: Yes, I've pitched a few things, but nothing's really taken off. Max and I did *Ms. Tree* for 12 years, and that kept me a little busy. [*laughs*] Then I had several years there where I was inking various and sundry other comic books, some of the *Elfquest* titles, and just keeping busy putting ink on paper and bringing in a paycheck. Then the *Batman* animated comics came along, and that's kept me very busy since.

Bullpen: *How'd you get that job?*

Terry: Here's how that happened: I was looking to line-up a little more work, and I had heard through the grapevine that the licensing department at DC was always looking for talent to produce the art for T-shirts and lunchboxes, etc.—and especially was looking for people who could do the animated style. So I threw some samples together, sent them off to the licensing guys, and thought, "Just for the heck of it, I'm going to send copies of these to the editors of the *Batman Adventures* comic book." Now, I knew Rick Burchett had that inking job, and I figured Rick was going to have the assignment as long as he wanted it, and there wasn't much chance of me wresting that away from him (which I

wouldn't want to do anyway, because he's a friend of mine). But I also knew that once in a while, they'll do a fill-in, so why not send the samples? I never heard from the licensing guys, never heard a word back, but not long after sending the samples, I got a call from one of the editors at DC saying, "Rick's gonna take a break to work on *Superman Adventures,* so how would you like to ink *Batman Adventures* for six months?" I said yes pretty fast, and that six months has turned into, at this point, over seven years. I think that's something of an unheard-of run these days in comics, to be with one project that long. Although if you want to get technical, it's been a string of projects rather than just one long one, with the change in the title and the format and mixing it up a little. It's also not a completely unbroken run, because there are at least a half-dozen fill-ins by other inkers in there, but I'm the main guy, I guess.

Bullpen: *Is it penciling and inking?*

Terry: No, primarily inking. I penciled and inked one issue on my own, and then penciled and inked a segment of another issue, but I'm pretty much the inker. If it's a project that I'm not creator or co-creator of, I actually prefer that. And, again, I'm enough of a comics geek that I like working with all these different artists and seeing what the end result is. And then I end up with a pretty nice art collection, too. [*laughs*]

Bullpen: *Are you an art collector?*

Terry: Yes, although not as much as I used to be. I actually had a fairly impressive original art collection at one point that has been whittled away when the need to pay quarterly estimated tax payments has come up. I've just got a few nice pieces at this point, but nothing terribly major.

Bullpen: *What was the best thing you ever owned?*

Terry: Well, to name a couple things, I had an Enoch Bolles pin-up cover oil painting, a beautiful blonde in a swimsuit with fur wrapped around her, which was gorgeous. Then I had — and this was an odd original, because it was a partial — half the panels from a *Terry and the Pirates* Sunday page by Milt Caniff. Where the other panels had gone, who knows? It was hand-colored by Caniff with Terry kissing the Dragon Lady. I also had a Chester Gould *Tracy* Flattop daily.

Bullpen: *Do you troll eBay?*

Terry: Yes, I do look, but not as often as I used to, because I'm too tempted to want to bid and shouldn't be buying anything right now.

Bullpen: *I pulled out* MOD, *and you did a bit of writing in here. Who's George Kochell?*

Terry: George used to do cartoons for *Starlog* and fanzines. I've lost touch with him, haven't had any contact for years.

Bullpen: *"Mr. Bugg Goes to Hell": you've mentioned* Popeye *before, so you're a Fleischer cartoon fan?*

Terry: Oh, sure.

Bullpen: *This is cool stuff, this is different.*

Terry: Yes, well. Generally, I think it goes down in the books as a failure, but it was fun to do.

Bullpen: *You also have a Wally Wood pastiche, E.C. Comics… And these* Bill Griffith Observatory *strips are reprints?*

Terry: Yes, those are strip reprints. They go back to a point where we were doing *Ms. Tree* for Eclipse and were going to spin it off. We originally had talked about spinning it off into a crime comics magazine. It wouldn't have just been *Ms. Tree, Ms. Tree* would have been the lead feature, and there would have been other detective series. I really wanted to get Griffith to do *Detective Zippy*

for us. [*laughs*] I talked to him about that quite a bit but it just never happened. Still, it would have been nice.

Bullpen: *You always had an interest in undergrounds?*

Terry: Oh, absolutely. Again, that comes from my early exposure to Kurtzman and Elder, because the undergrounds grow right out of that. Crumb's the next step. So I loved that stuff, and was exposed to it a lot earlier than I was supposed to have been. [*laughs*] I think it's long enough now that I can probably tell this without getting anybody in trouble, but you know when you mail-order stuff? You have to send the

Above: *One of Terry Beatty's favorite* Ms. Tree *covers. Courtesy of the artist. ©2021 Max Collins & Terry Beatty.* **Inset left:** *The damsel detective swings an axe (à là* Elvis*) in a* Ms. Tree #50 *[July '89] piece on the "Theme from* Ms. Tree*" flexi-disc insert in that final Renegade issue. The song was performed by the Max Collins rock 'n' roll band, Cruisin'. Art by & courtesy of Terry Beatty.* Ms. Tree *©2021 Collins & Beatty.* **Opposite page bottom:** Ms. Tree *letters column logo by T.B. (SWAK: "Sealed With A Kiss") is a homage to Steve Ditko's* Amazing Spider-Man #8 *panel. Header ©2021 Collins & Beatty. Panel ©'21 Marvel Characters, Inc.*

⟨R⟩enegade Press

people a form that you sign which declares, "Yes, I'm over 21"? [*stage whisper*] I learned that you can get away with that even if you're only 15!

Bullpen: [*Incredulous*] No!

Terry: They *really* don't check! [*laughter*] So I probably have one of the best underground collections of anybody my age, because I was getting to buy them long before I was supposed to legally. There also were head shops in Iowa City, which is a college town, and at the time, I was a teenager, and my voice was this deep already, and my hair was down to my waist, so I'd walk into the head shops and they thought I was 18 years old. "Yeah, okay, I'll take that copy of *Slow Death* and that copy of *ZAP* and that *Yellow Dog* over there." So I had quite a nice underground collection.

Bullpen: *A lot of mainstream professionals, despite coming from fandom, don't look at that stuff. They just don't have an interest in that stuff.*

Terry: Well, I think that some of the time it's just that they weren't exposed to it.

Bullpen: *But despite the accolades they've heard, they won't catch up with it now?* [*laughs*] *What's up with that?*

Terry: Well, it's funny. You'll read interviews with cartoonists, sometimes very successful, very talented people, and some mention of some strip or cartoonist that you would think would have been an influence on them comes up, and they'll say, "Well, I don't know about that." That always surprises me because I've gone out of my way to educate myself about comics history, comics worldwide, so I was trying to scope out any and all European comics and Asian comics for years. Comics of *any* sort have always

been of interest to me.

Bullpen: *I've got these life drawings by you of a guy playing the guitar. Are you still taking classes?*

Terry: Yes. That comes from a local group of younger artists who invited me to join a once or twice a month group, where they just get together and everybody will take turns posing. Clothed, or sometimes in costume. It actually got kind of wacky, because the fellow who hosted it had a couple little kids, and oftentimes they would even pose for us. The little girl would come in with, like, a big Halloween witch mask on and strike a crazy pose. We had to draw her fast, get a quick gesture drawing, and then she'd be off running. [*laughter*] But there is a regular life drawing group that I go to when I'm in Minneapolis. It's a nice break from the more stylized cartooning work and helps me get my real drawing chops going again.

Bullpen: *Are you a sociable guy?*

Terry: Well, I think, like most artists, I tend to spend too much time by myself, and have that self-amused personality thing going on. [*laughs*] But I'm not such a hermit that I can't hang with other people and be in public. Doing the comic book conventions has been good for me in that sense, of just being out there and shaking hands and meeting people. I'm fairly comfortable with that, and am very comfortable speaking in front of people, too. I know some consider that one of their worst fears, to have to stand up in front of people and talk, but it's not a problem at all for me.

Bullpen: *What's your favorite work that you've done?*

Terry: I'm awfully fond of the *Johnny Dynamite* mini-series. Just in terms of subject matter, combining that retro-'50s private eye stuff with grade-B movie monster stuff, it was sort of a dream project. Yes, I think we'll go with *Johnny Dynamite.*

I remain very fond of *Ms. Tree*, and my experience on the *Batman* books has been very positive.

Bullpen: *What is it you like about Batman?*

Terry: Well, again, let's get back to the fact that I'm a pop culture and comic book fiend, again, it's *Batman*. I was a little kid reading those *80-Page Giants* full of Dick Sprang stories and watching the *Batman* TV show and eating it up with a spoon, and here I am, a 45-year-old adult, getting my paycheck from sitting around drawing Batman all day. How do you beat that? [*laughs*]

Bullpen: *Are you happy for Max's success with* Road to Perdition?

Terry: Oh, absolutely. He's one of my favorite writers, and I've thought for years that he's deserved more success with his work, and that there should have been some major movie of some of those books long

ago, and particularly the Heller books. I felt there should have been something on that before now. I was very happy to see Road to Perdition become the success that it is, particularly because it wasn't really that successful a graphic novel in its first printing. Now, my story on this is that I was originally pitched as the artist for that book. [laughs] But we had just come off our run on Ms. Tree at DC, which didn't exactly set the world on fire, and the editor at DC said, "Well, how about we team you up with somebody else?" I think I already had the Batman gig at that point, and I was busy, so it wasn't a problem for me. There is this little something that tugs at the back of my head that says, "You know, you could have drawn that. It would have been nice." [laughs]

Bullpen: Guy Gardner: *was that cool to do? Was there anything to that, or was it just a job?*

Terry: Well, getting to work with Joe Staton… Joe is one of my favorite cartoonists and favorite people, so any time they want me to ink Joe, that's fine by me. I'll be happy to do that no matter what the project is. *Green Lantern* was also a favorite comic book of mine as a kid. It was a panel in an issue of *GL* that opened my eyes to the fact that people *drew* comic books. So that was fun. Although the first six issues were more fun than the last, because I was pretty much getting to ink Joe however I wanted to ink Joe, and about halfway through the run, we were in the middle of the whole Image Comics boom, and we were pressured very much to make it look more "Image-y." We tried, but ultimately it was Joe and me, and neither of us is Todd McFarlane or Rob Liefeld, and it was just kind of silly. So I think by the time we were done with that book, we were ready to be done with it.

Bullpen: With the *Scary Monsters* covers, you've done some painting.

Terry: The painting came about because I saw this little monster fanzine called *Scary Monsters,* published by a guy named Dennis Druktenis, who lives near Chicago. I picked up the first couple issues, and it really was just a fanzine, and it was fun, and clearly came from the viewpoint of just guys who love monster movies. And they weren't being critical, they were just presenting it as, "Hey, ain't this cool? Isn't this fun? We love this stuff! Here it is." But it had the worst logo I ever saw on a magazine in my life. [laughter] So I sat down and drew a new logo. I'd never met Dennis, didn't know him from Adam, but I loved

his magazine. So I sent him this logo and said, "Please, for God's sake, use this, will ya?" [laughter] I got a call from him, or I think maybe I talked to him at the Chicago Con, and he asked me if I wanted to paint covers for the magazine. I said, "Well, I really don't know how to paint. I'm a cartoonist, but I've never really painted before." But he said, "I don't care." So I thought, "Well, okay. You're going to pay me to paint covers, and I'm going to learn how to paint." Now, it's a little dangerous, because I'm learning how to paint in public. But I'm something like 50 covers down the line, and I think I've learned a little bit about painting since the first ones.

There are some of them I just cringe at because they were produced too fast, on too tight a deadline, and there are some of them I just can't look at again. But I'm fairly proud of a handful of them.

Bullpen: *What was* Phony Pages?

Terry: That's something I did for *The Buyer's Guide,* for Alan Light. It was a spoof of comics history, and it was this very peculiar notion where I would take existing comic strips or comic books and combine them with other pop culture elements. So *Little Nemo in Slumberland* became "Little

Above: *Terry Beatty penciled and Dick Giordano inked this Wild Dog cover on Amazing Heroes #119 [6/15/87]. Wild Dog ©2021 DC Comics. A.H. ©2021 Fantagraphic Books.*

Insert left: *Wild Dog by Terry Beatty. From an issue of* Who's Who Update. *Courtesy of the artist. ©2021 DC Comics.*

Below: *Terry Beatty (left) and Max Allan Collins at a* Wild Dog *autograph signing at Tim's Corner in Rock Island, Illinois. Courtesy of T.B.*

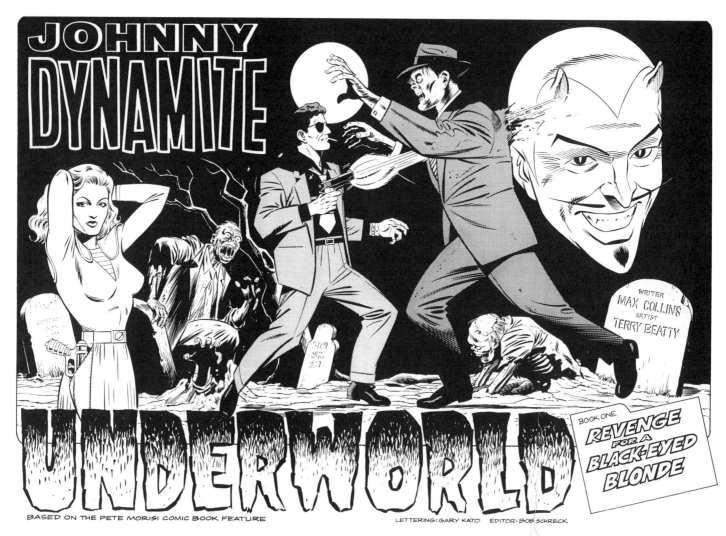

JOHNNY DYNAMITE

UNDERWORLD

BASED ON THE PETE MORISI COMIC BOOK FEATURE

LETTERING: GARY KATO   EDITOR: BOB SCHRECK

WRITER MAX COLLINS
ARTIST TERRY BEATTY

BOOK ONE
REVENGE FOR A BLACK-EYED BLONDE

Above: Killer double-page spread by Terry Beatty from the Dark Horse mini-series starring Pete Morisi's 1950s hardboiled detective Johnny Dynamite. This art is from #1 [Sept. '94]. Terry drew the four issues in collaboration with longtime creative partner, writer Max Allan Collins. **Inset right:** *Image from #1's splash page.* **Opposite page:** *Beatty painting promoting the series. The "Underworld" story arc is one of the artist's favorite jobs. All appear courtesy of Terry Beatty. Johnny Dynamite ©2021 the estate of Pete Morisi.*

Nimoy in Slumberland." [*Jon laughs*] But with this pompous, pretentious, kind of Maurice Horn-style comics history introduction to the examples of the feature being shown. Then at Renegade Press, Deni collected those into a two-issue mini-series. As we said, "Collect 'em both!" It was a very odd, very peculiar piece of work that only the most hardcore comics fans would even get.

Bullpen: *What was the job you did in* Mr. Monster's Triple Threat 3-D?

Terry: I think that was just a one-page pin-up, but Michael T. Gilbert and I did do a story together, one I wrote and then he sort of rewrote. Then he did roughs and I did the finished art. It turned out pretty nifty.

Bullpen: *What was the story?*

Terry: A little tribute to E.C. Comics. The premise was that there was an old man that was having these horrible nightmares and they were creating actual manifestations of creatures from his dreams. He hired Mr. Monster to come get rid of them, and then Mr. Monster realized that this guy is this old '50s horror cartoonist. So Mr. Monster tried to convince him that the monsters are manifestations of his guilt about having scared all these kids and that he actually did a good thing by drawing these horror comics,

because he's influenced all these other creators to do all these other horror films and books, etc., etc. Which of course, in the end, made the guy's nightmares even worse.

Bullpen: *You did a lot of work for* Elfquest?

Terry: Yes, both Wendi [Lee] and I worked for WaRP Graphics on the *Elfquest* titles for a little over a year. I inked something like two books a month for them for a while, which was a bit of a challenge, considering they were 24 pages apiece and it was fairly detailed art in most cases. Wendi did a little writing. Then she and I co-wrote a bunch of stories that my buddy Gary Kato drew and colored. Actually painted, it was fully painted art. Gary had worked with me on *Ms. Tree* as a letterer, background guy, and sometimes filling in on finishing my pencils. When I was working on *Wild Dog*, we relied on him a little more. Gary is a terrifically talented cartoonist, I think, who has never quite gotten his due in the business. We did this series of stories inspired by classic fairy tales that were then published as a hardcover book called *Elfquest Bedtime Stories.* The *Elfquest* fans either absolutely adored them, or thought they were heresy because we weren't following the *Elfquest* canon… we were messing with it just a little bit.

Bullpen: *What was* Mr. Hero?

Terry: A sci-fi series at Tekno. I did inks on a few fill-in issues.

Bullpen: *You obviously free-*

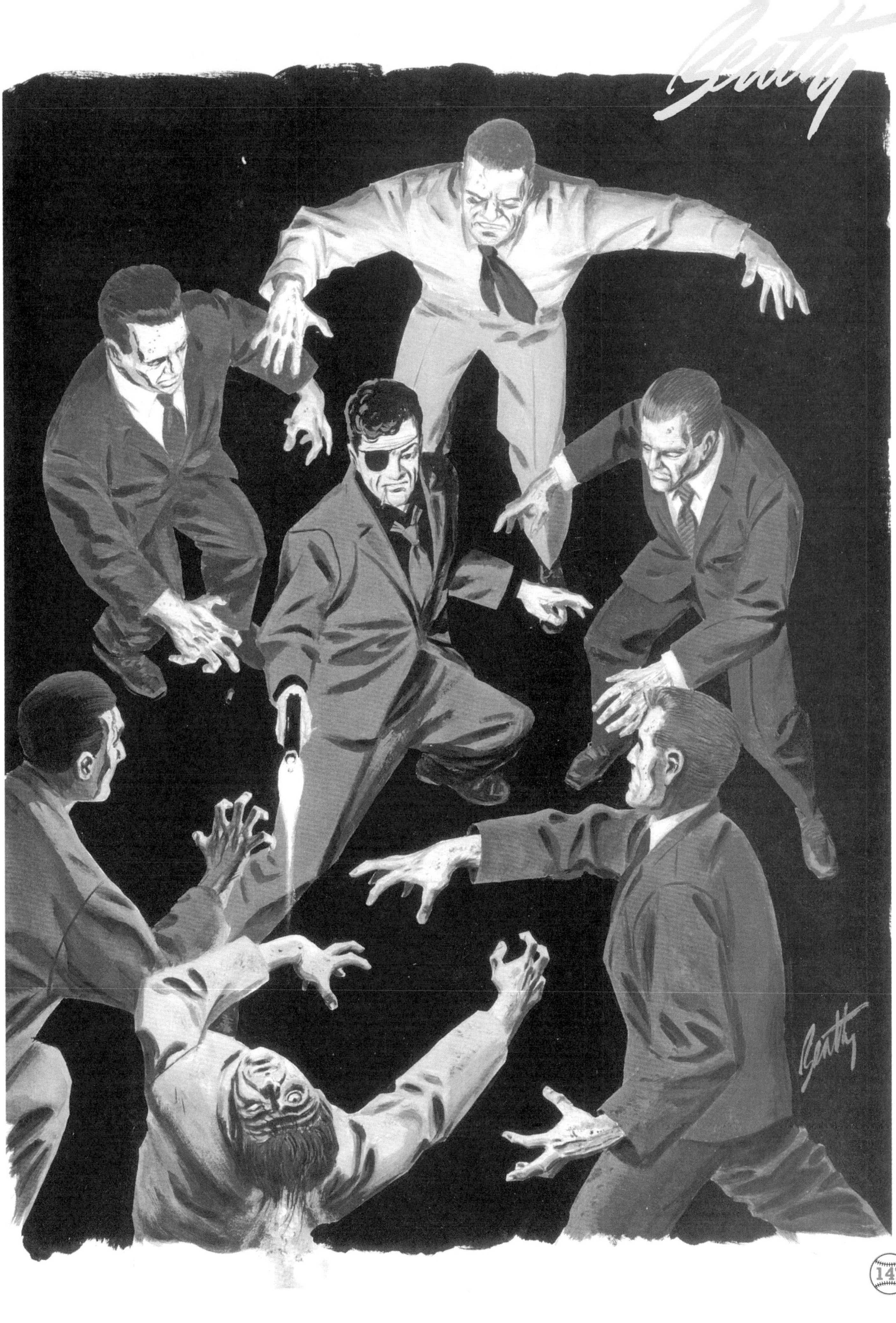
Beatty
Beatty

Above: *Husband and wife, artist Terry Beatty and mystery writer Wendi Lee, on the set of the Max Collins film* Mommy. *That's actor Jason (*The Exorcist*) Miller directly behind the couple. "We ended up on the cutting room floor," Terry says, "But, along with our daughter, Elizabeth (***inset right***), we did get a few seconds of screentime in the sequel." Courtesy of Terry Beatty.*

Above: *Terry Beatty cover painting for* Orchestrated Murder, *a multi-author mystery novel edited by Terry's spouse, writer Wendi Lee. Courtesy of and ©2021 Terry Beatty.*

lanced around. When you worked for WaRP, was that comparable pay as to working at DC?

Terry: Yeah. Later in the run, they were having some financial troubles and the pay rate got cut to the point where I couldn't hang around anymore. The same thing happened to Tekno Comix.

Bullpen: *Who was your connection at Tekno?*

Terry: Again, that was through Max Allan Collins. He was doing *Mike Danger* there, and Steve Leialoha had inked, I think, the first half-dozen issues or so and then had to leave, and they brought me in as inker. But, if memory serves, I had done a bunch of fill-in work there on various titles before that. Martin Powell was an editor there who had hired me to do a few things, and Chris Mills as well, who is a friend who had worked there for quite a bit.

Bullpen: *If you had a dream job, what would it be?*

Terry: Well, getting to work on *Batman* every month is pretty cool, and the *Scary Monsters* covers, as well. I had this wonderful moment a couple of years ago when I was preparing to do one of those covers: I was in my studio, sitting on the floor, sorting through issues of old monster magazines, trying to find the right reference. I just started laughing to myself and I said, "I'm sitting here doing for a living what I did for fun when I was seven." [*laughter*] On the other hand, I have been playing at sculpting quite a bit lately and I love doing that. But the comics work is really so demanding that it hasn't allowed me time to do any sculpting recently, and I would love to get back into that a little more and maybe explore that on a more professional level.

Bullpen: *Now and then, throughout your history, you have these homages and pastiches and this appreciation, from* The Phony Pages *to* MOD….

Terry: Because I'm a fanboy geek, Jon. [*laughter*]

Bullpen: *Given time and a comfortable schedule, would you like to do something like that again?*

Terry: No. At this point, really, I want to explore who *I* am as an artist. With *The Buyer's Guide* covers and *Phony Pages*, I tipped my hat to artists whose work I admire. Still it might be fun to do some sculpts based on, 3-D version of some of the 2-D pieces I like by some of my favorite artists. That's one area where I might still want to do that, but I am 45 years old and I want to explore who *I* am as an artist, at this point.

Bullpen: *Have syndicated strips ever beckoned?*

Terry: Like I said, Collins and I tried that version of *Annie*. We actually pitched a couple other things, too. We tried a sequel to *Harold Teen* that would have been about his daughter, Carol Teen. The kids were like little punk rockers. It probably would have been a lot like the TV show *Square Pegs* before that even existed. But the Tribune Syndicate didn't quite see eye-to-eye with us on that one. A newspaper strip is still an interesting notion. I would have loved to have done *Dick Tracy*, but unfortunately, rather than keeping Max on and hiring me to draw it, they got rid of Max. [*laughs*] They pulled in Michael Killian and Dick Locher, and they're doing their version, so there it is.

Selling an original concept for a strip is very tough, and even if you do get to the point where you sell something and try to syndicate it, having a success is even tougher, because for a new strip to come along and be successful, they've got to kill a bunch of old ones. Aunt Minnie down the street doesn't like it when they take *Henry* out of the comics page, and the last thing any newspaper editor ever wants to hear is any complaint about the strips, because they hate running the comics page anyway. It's just an annoyance to them.

Bullpen: *You've periodically gone out and tried new things: sculpting, painting. Is art continually a discovery process for you?*

Terry: Well, absolutely. It seems the more I'm at it, the more I realize I don't know and the more I have to learn. So I'm always working at it, always trying to learn new things.

POSTSCRIPT & UPDATE: This interview was conducted when I was 45. I'm 63 now. Lots of water under the bridge since then. I finally got to go to art school—not as a student, but as an instructor—teaching for several years in the comics program at the Minneapolis School of Art and Design. Wendi and I split and went our separate ways, and I got married again. My wife, Erika, and I had two children, Kirby and Lara, now 12 and 9. We left the Twin Cities ten years ago.

My *Batman* inking gig came to an end after an 11-year run, and I retired from creating the *Scary Monsters* magazine covers after its 100th issue. I drew the final graphic novel in Max Collins' "Perdition" series, and got to draw a *Tarzan* story and a *Popeye* one-shot—fulfilling a wish to draw some long-time favorite characters. *Ms. Tree* is being reprinted at long last, thanks to Hard Case Crime and Titan Books.

And I did finally get into the newspapers, drawing the Sunday

ONE LONELY KNIGHT

Mickey Spillane's Mike Hammer

Max Allan Collins and James L. Traylor

POPULAR PRESS

adventures of *The Phantom* for King Features for five years, and now writing and drawing King's *Rex Morgan M.D.* strip seven days a week. I have no plans to retire, and hope to keep writing and drawing as long as fate allows.

—**Terry Beatty, May 4, 2021**

Top inset: *Cover illo by Terry Beatty on a book about Mickey Spillane.* **Above:** *Terry cover painting for Spillane's novel,* Together We Kill. **Bottom:** *From far left is Alan Light's 1983 photo of Terry and Max; Lee Bermejo's cover art graces Max and Terry's graphic novel,* Return to Perdition *[2011]. Hard Case, an imprint of Titan Books, is currently reprinting Terry's signature series,* Ms. Tree, *in a series of collections.* One Mean Mother *cover art by Denys Cowan, and* Skeleton in the Closet *cover by George Pratt.* ©2021 the respective copyright holders.

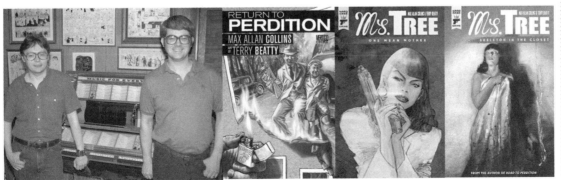

RETURN TO PERDITION — MAX ALLAN COLLINS AND TERRY BEATTY

Ms. TREE — ONE MEAN MOTHER

Ms. TREE — SKELETON IN THE CLOSET

Beatty At The Drawing Board

Beatty fan Jason Strangis, who was the first to suggest a *CBA* feature on T.B., conducted the following chat with the creator (done via e-mail, on Aug. 29, 2003), which explores Terry's day-to-day routine. This Q&A was copy-edited by Mr. Beatty.

Jason Strangis: *Is comics a tough business to break into, Terry?*

Terry Beatty: Sure seems to be… sometimes it's tough to break *out* of, too!

Jason: *Any advice for aspiring artists?*

Terry: Learn the new technology, but back it up by learning real skills. It doesn't matter how well you've mastered Photoshop if you can't actually draw and have no sense of design. Study the work of the great artists who trod this path long before you. Don't make the mistake of thinking that something must be new to have value. Beyond that, hang in there, follow your heart and head, and as Chet Gould told me: "Never give up." Oh, and subscribe to Mike Manley's *Draw!* magazine!

Jason: *What is a typical week like for you?*

Terry: This week? Work, work, work, work, go to a movie, work, work , work, go to a concert, work.

Jason: *What is an average drawing day like for you? When do you usually start and finish?*

Terry: I get up, have some breakfast and check my e-mail (and eBay auctions if I have any running). Then I put some tunes in the CD player (Legendary Shack Shakers, Los Straitjackets, Elvis Costello, etc.) or turn on the radio or TV as background noise (rockabilly tunes on Live 365 or an old movie on TCM), and then I get to inking. Take a break, play with the cats, read some more e-mail. Ink. Lunch. Ink. Good music or bad TV in the background. Ink. Take a break just to stretch. Ink. Supper/family time. Maybe I'll ink a little more if deadlines demand. Take a walk, watch a movie, read a book or magazine. Crash and start again the next day. Thrilling, huh? (On days I'm sculpting or painting, just substitute either one for inking.)

A couple times per month I'll take in a life drawing session — that tends to help "re-charge" my artistic batteries. For periods of "work avoidance," it's antique shops, used bookstores, thrift stores (just found the coolest rockabilly style jacket for only $2.50! Plus a "Harmonica Gang" album of Western songs for a buck… ahh, life is good!), record stores, live music and movies. Then there's my figural model kit obsession, which goes back to being a kid in the '60s buying all those Aurora monster models. Oh yeah, I read a comic book once in a great while.

Jason: *Sounds like you're a collector of all sorts of things.*

Terry: Yeah, I've got the collecting bug bad. Our move to Minneapolis necessitated me selling off large portions of my various collections, but I still have tons of "stuff," and keep adding on. In addition to the model kits, there's vintage pin-up items (calendars, matchbooks, etc.), 3-D stuff like old View-Master and Tru-Vue reels, comic strip collectibles—especially Al Capp, Milt Caniff and Hal Foster items, Big Little Books, Universal Monsters items, TV and movie cowboy stuff, old comedy star items (Eddie Cantor, Bergen and McCarthy, Jack Benny, Phil Silvers, etc.), not to mention scads of books, records and DVDs.

Jason: *How about deadlines? Do you ever find yourself "swamped" with too much to do?*

Terry: I'm a two-page-a-day inker, so I can ink two books a month if the schedules jibe. But far too often things get backed

Above: *Terry Beatty inking a page of* Batman Adventures. *Courtesy of the artist.*

Below: *From left to right, the stages of composing a Terry Beatty* Batman Adventures *page. First a preliminary page design, next the pencils, and finally the inked finished page. Courtesy of T. Beatty. Batman TM & ©2021 DC Comics.*

"…THE HALEY CIRCUS."
"MASTER BRUCE FINALLY LOCATED THEM IN A CITY IN THE MIDWEST."
"THE LOCAL MAFIA ASSUMED THAT AFTER THE INCIDENT IN GOTHAM, THE CIRCUS WOULD OFFER LITTLE RESISTANCE TO THEIR PROTECTION SCHEME."
"THEY DID NOT ANTICIPATE THE BATMAN'S ARRIVAL."
"OF COURSE, NO ONE EVER DOES."

up and you find yourself in a "crunch" with "dueling deadlines." I just finished a particularly difficult session—working through the weekend, late nights, with the flu, etc. It happens.

Jason: *In addition to your regular work, do you offer your services for commissioned artwork?*

Terry: When my schedule allows, yes, but lately I've been a little too busy. I've done a lot of convention sketch-style commissions in the past—but would prefer to move on to paintings and sculptures—something more challenging.

Jason: *I know that you are always busy at comic conventions drawing super-heroes for fans. Which characters do fans request the most?*

Terry: Well, since I've been the regular inker on the DC animated-style *Batman* comics, it has been, of course, the cast and crew of Batman… though I really enjoy drawing classic Marvel heroes as well…and *anything* Kirby!

Jason: *Do you have any favorites to draw?*

Terry: Harley Quinn is cute and sexy—a great design—and she's always fun to draw.

Jason: *You've been an inker on the animated-style* Batman *comics for quite a while. I assume you still enjoy the work?*

Terry: I did over seven years on the *Batman Adventures* titles. Though it's not an unbroken run. There were a few fill-in issues by others, and, of course, the book's title and direction changed a few times, but including *Batman Beyond* and *Annuals*, etc., I've inked a whole lot of "animated-style" *Batman*. And I'm pleased to continue my *Batman* run with the new *The Batman Strikes,* series, inking fellow Twin Cities artist Chris Jones.

I was part of the audience of little kids watching the *Batman* TV show when it first aired on ABC (in black-&-white at our house, as we didn't have a color set yet), and I grew up devouring those *80-Page Giant* issues I mentioned earlier. To work on a classic comic book character and be (a small) part of a history that includes Dick Sprang, Bill Finger, Charles Paris, Jerry Robinson, Shelly Moldoff, Frank Robbins, Jim Aparo, Frank Robbins, Neal Adams, Bruce Timm, etc., is a real treat and an honor for me. I've had the pleasure of working with some wonderful pencilers, writers and editors — a bunch of top-notch letterers, too—and the best colorists in the business. Add in that I have a couple Eisner Awards to hang on my wall thanks to my involvement on the series… what's not to enjoy?

Jason: *It must be selling pretty well for DC to continue this long.*

Terry: I know DC has taken some steps to get the book in front of more readers. They've done several digest-format collections and have sold them through school book clubs and such, with positive results. The whole "Johnny DC" promotion seems to have helped get the comic book into the hands of more kids, and we need that next generation of comics readers. The various *Batman Adventures* titles have had a lot of foreign editions in various formats. There are standard comic books, but also magazines and hardcover albums. I assume we'll see the same with *The Batman Strikes* when the overseas publishers run through the *Adventures* material.

Jason: *If you got to draw or ink any comic, what would it be?*

Terry: I like what I'm working on now, but it would be fun to do another *Ms. Tree* or *Johnny Dynamite* story with Collins, or something new and original I haven't even thought of yet. Some sort of one-shot featuring the Silver Age Marvel heroes would be fun. And I'd kill to do a *Metamorpho* comic—but only if I could do it Silver Age-style as well.

Jason: *Do you have a preference of penciling or inking?*

Terry: It's a whole lot easier for me to earn a living as an inker, but penciling… well, doing the *entire* art job is actually more satisfying, but far more challenging. I'd really like to be painting and sculpting more, and I'm planning to make time for both this year….

Jason: *Would you like to draw and write your own comic?*

Terry: I have done a certain amount of writing, and not just in comics. My wife (mystery author Wendi Lee) and I have had a good number of short stories published, mostly genre fiction. I'm not too interested in writing for any pre-existing company-owned comic characters any more, but would like to do something new and different and more personal. Someday.

Jason: *Anything else interesting on your drawing board?*

Terry: Well, I have been working on a set of trading cards for Monsterwax for some time. I have one more card to draw and then it'll be done. There are two sets, actually — though I understand they'l be sold together — both very EC-like horror material. Some of it is really grisly and creepy, far more so than what people are used to seeing from me. And I have to say, it's been a heck of a lot of fun to draw! I also have a series of figures I want to sculpt, but I don't want to say what the subject matter is until I have some of them produced and ready to show.

Jason: *Is drawing comics and magazine covers fun for you, or is it work?*

Terry: Okay, I get to draw *Batman* and paint pictures of Frankenstein and Dracula… and then I get *paid* for it! How the heck can that *not* be fun? Well, okay, there are days when it *is* work… when I'm down with a cold, but the deadline is looming, so I have to work anyway and *then* it's work. But other than that—well, even including that!—it sure beats diggin' ditches!

Above: One of T.B.'s favorite covers, from Batman Gotham Adventures. *Pencils by Bob Smith, inks by Terry Beatty. Courtesy of T.B. Batman ©2021 DC Comics.*

Left inset: Sam Scare, Scary Monsters *mascot, by Terry Beatty. Wish we had devoted more space to T.B.'s great SM work! But alas… Courtesy of Terry. ©2021 Druktenis Publishing.*

COMIC BOOK ARTIST
ALL★STARS

INDEPENDENT
PENCILER & INKER

Beatty

TERRY BEATTY

007

TERRY BEATTY
PENCILER • INKER
BORN: 1/11/58
BIRTHPLACE:
CURRENT RESIDENCE: MINNEAPOLIS, MINN.

T.B. JAMMED WITH ROBERT CRUMB & JAY LYNCH ON A 1976 BERKELEY COMIX CON PROMOTIONAL ILLUSTRATION!

MEMORABLE WORK:

MS. TREE
ECLIPSE / RENEGADE / DC

PROFESSIONAL COMIC BOOK/STRIP ART HIGHLIGHTS

YEARS	PUBLISHER	FEATURES
1976-77	SELF-PUBLISHED	Writes & draws comic strip, "The Adventures of Sam Schagnogleeack," for local underground
1979	SELF-PUBLISHED	newspaper, The Schagnogleeack Times, during senior year in high school
'79-'80s	ALAN LIGHT	Teams with writer Max Allan Collins to produce syndicated feature "The Comics Page"
		The Buyer's Guide for Comics Fandom contributor, including cover artist (numerous issues, starting with #328, 2/29/80), writer (numerous issues, starting with #299, 8/10/79), "Sideways" columnist (numerous issues, starting with #327, 2/22/80), "The Phony Pages" cartoonist (numerous issues, starting with #392, 5/22/81)
1981	KITCHEN SINK	Edits MOD #1 (6/81) and contributes as writer and artist to the one-shot underground comix book
1981	ECLIPSE COMICS	TCP strip "Mike Mist Minute Mist-Eries" collected (4/81); 1st "Ms. Tree" strip, Eclipse Magazine #1 (5/81)
1983-92	VARIOUS	Ms. Tree #1-9 (Eclipse), #10-18 (Aardvark-Vanaheim), #19-50, 3-D #1-2, Summer Special (Renegade), Best of Ms. Tree #1-4 (Pyramid), Ms. Tree Quarterly #1-10 (DC Comics). Co-creator. Artist on all issues
1987-89	DC COMICS	Wild Dog #1-4, Wild Dog Special #1, Action Comics Weekly #601-642. Co-creator. Artist on all issues
1990s	WaRP GRAPHICS	Cover artist and inker on various Elfquest titles
Mid-'90s	TEKNO COMICS	Inker on various titles, notably Mike Danger (written by Max Allan Collins)
1994	DARK HORSE	Johnny Dynamite #1-4 (written by Max Allan Collins). Artist on all issues
'90s-Pres.	DC COMICS	Inks innumerable comics, notably a regular assignment on the Batman "animated-style" titles
'90s-Pres.	DRUKTENIS PUB	Regular Scary Monsters cover painter (also designed current logo)

Ms. Tree ©2005 Max Allan Collins & Terry Beatty

Collect 'em All!

COMIC BOOK ARTIST™ BULLPEN was published between 2003–04 by RetroHouse Press, c/o Jon B. Cooke, P.O. Box 601, West Kingston, R.I. 02892 USA. Jon B. Cooke, Editor. Vol. 1, #7. This issue previously unpublished.

Major League Kirby!

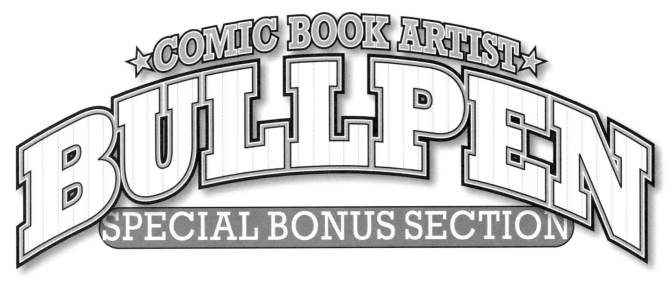

In the second half of the 1950s, comics great Jack Kirby was pinch-hitting wherever he could, to find work in the field he loved. Dr. Fredric Wertham, the U.S. Senate, and parents' groups had pushed the comics industry into self-inflicted censorship through the Comics Code Authority in 1954. Kirby's own company, Mainline Publications (in conjunction with longtime friend and teammate Joe Simon), was one of its victims, being counted out by the end of 1956, with its final stories being farmed over to low-paying Charlton Comics.

A string of 1950s newspaper strip and television pitches was the result of Kirby looking for a more lucrative outlet for his creative prowess, but none were successful. The closest he came to a hit during this era was in 1957, when he traded the final Simon & Kirby Mainline creation, *Challengers of the Unknown*, to DC Comics. Even more promising was an opportunity to produce a newspaper strip, *Sky Masters of the Space Force*, which came about thanks to a deal negotiated by *Challengers* editor Jack Schiff. But when Schiff demanded more of a finder's fee than Kirby felt it warranted, they wound up in court, and Kirby ended up being blackballed at DC until 1970.

A short stop at Archie Comics in 1959 resulted in a double play with old partner Joe Simon on *The Fly* and *Private Strong*, but it only lasted a couple of issues each. To make ends meet, Kirby had dug out a position at copycat publisher Atlas Comics (soon to be renamed Marvel), and produced a series of fantasy strips inspired by the success of the monster movies of that drive-in era. Then, in early 1960, Jack and wife Roz learned of the impending arrival of daughter Lisa (whom the future King of Comics dubbed "The Kid From Left Field" in his 1970 *Jimmy Olsen* #133 text page), and this surprise addition to the family added even more pressure to find any work possible   and thus, he turned to Topps, producer of an annual line of baseball cards.

Exactly how Kirby came to draw backs for the 1960 Topps card set, alongside veteran funnyman Jack Davis and others, isn't known. His earliest comic book depiction of "America's National Pastime" was in 1941's *Captain America Comics* #7, with the story "Death Loads the Bases." Having grown up on the Lower East Side of Manhattan, he couldn't help but be a baseball fan. For ten consecutive years, the World Series was played in New York City, with the Yankees winning five years in a row (1949–53). Jack's 1954 story "Bride of the Star" for *In Love* #1 was a product of that fervor and would've kept him warmed up for more trips around the bases. Though the 1957 move of both the Brooklyn Dodgers and New York Giants baseball teams to California left many New Yorkers sore, this new job would find Kirby chronicling nifty anecdotes about players from both the American and National Leagues.

As fast as Jack worked, it's a safe bet this wasn't the most challenging job of his 1960 output. These 60 illos—used on the statistics side of Topps major league baseball bubble gum cards—echo the "bigfoot" style he used for his '50s humor work for publications like Charlton's *From Here To Insanity*, in the wake of the popularity of *MAD* magazine and its many imitators. The inking on the cards is simple but effective, and may've been assisted by Kirby's wife, Roz, to maximize the family's income.

Contrary to a report in *The Jack Kirby Collector* #10, these illos were all done for the 1960 Topps card set, *not* 1961. There's no sign of Kirby art in the '61 releases—there simply wasn't time. Jack was already moving on to other work, winding up a very frustrating (and brief) 1961 tenure for *Classics Illustrated*, before finally hitting a home run with his co-creation of the Fantastic Four at Marvel Comics.

"And the crowd goes wild!"

— **John Morrow**

This page: *Splash pages from* Captain America Comics #7 *[Oct, 1941] and* Fantastic Four #54 *[Sept. 1966], and* Thing *pencil sketch by the King!*

1960 Topps Kirby Illos

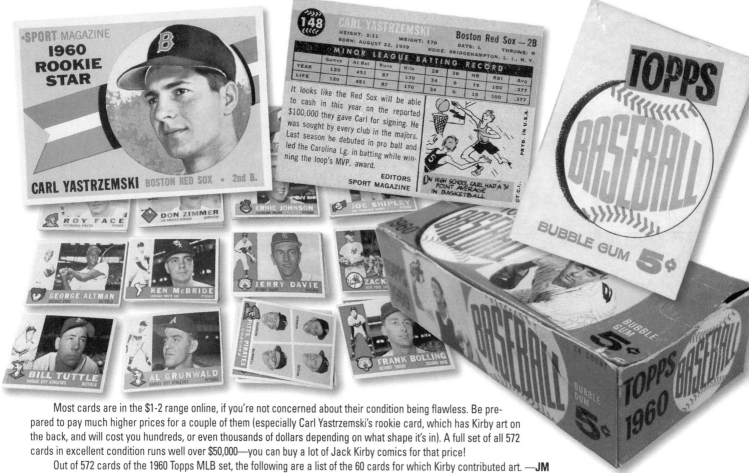

Most cards are in the $1-2 range online, if you're not concerned about their condition being flawless. Be prepared to pay much higher prices for a couple of them (especially Carl Yastrzemski's rookie card, which has Kirby art on the back, and will cost you hundreds, or even thousands of dollars depending on what shape it's in). A full set of all 572 cards in excellent condition runs well over $50,000—you can buy a lot of Jack Kirby comics for that price!

Out of 572 cards of the 1960 Topps MLB set, the following are a list of the 60 cards for which Kirby contributed art. —JM

111	Vic Wertz	Boston Red Sox	136	Jim Kaat	Washington Senators	177	Johnny Kucks	Kansas City Athletics
112	Jack Harshman	Cleveland Indians	137	Lou Klimchock	Kansas City Athletics	178	Woody Held	Cleveland Indians
117	Tom Borland	Boston Red Sox	138	Art Mahaffey	Philadelphia Phillies	180	Harry Simpson	Chicago White Sox
118	Bob Bruce	Detroit Tigers	139	Carl Mathias	Cleveland Indians	181	Billy Loes	San Francisco Giants
119	Chico Cardenas	Cincinnati Reds	140	Julio Navarro	San Francisco Giants	182	Glen Hobbie	Chicago Cubs
120	Duke Carmel	St. Louis Cardinals	141	Jim Proctor	Detroit Tigers	183	Eli Grba	New York Yankees
121	Camilo Carreon	Chicago White Sox	142	Bill Short	New York Yankees	185	Jim Owens	Philadelphia Phillies
122	Don Dillard	Cleveland Indians	143	Al Spangler	Milwaukee Braves	186	Dave Sisler	Detroit Tigers
123	Dan Dobbek	Washington Senators	144	Al Stieglitz	San Francisco Giants	187	Jay Hook	Cincinnati Reds
124	Jim Donohue	St. Louis Cardinals	145	Jim Umbricht	Pittsburgh Pirates	189	Don McMahon	Milwaukee Braves
125	Dick Ellsworth	Chicago Cubs	146	Ted Wieand	Cincinnati Reds	190	Gene Woodling	Baltimore Orioles
126	Chuck Estrada	Baltimore Orioles	147	Bob Will	Chicago Cubs	191	Johnny Klippstein	Los Angeles Dodgers
127	Ron Hansen	Baltimore Orioles	148	Carl Yastrzemski	Boston Red Sox	192	Danny O'Connell	San Francisco Giants
128	Bill Harris	Los Angeles Dodgers	154	Jim Davenport	San Francisco Giants	193	Dick Hyde	Washington Senators
129	Bob Hartman	Milwaukee Braves	163	Hector Lopez	New York Yankees	194	Bobby Gene Smith	Philadelphia Phillies
130	Frank Herrera	Philadelphia Phillies	165	Jack Sanford	San Francisco Giants	196	Andy Carey	New York Yankees
131	Ed Hobaugh	Chicago White Sox	168	Alex Grammas	St. Louis Cardinals	197	Ron Kline	St. Louis Cardinals
132	Frank Howard	Los Angeles Dodgers	169	Jake Striker	Chicago White Sox	198	Jerry Lynch	Cincinnati Reds
133	Manuel Javier	Pittsburgh Pirates	172	Willie Kirkland	San Francisco Giants			
134	Deron Johnson	New York Yankees	173	Billy Martin	Cincinnati Reds			
135	Ken Johnson	Kansas City Athletics	175	Pedro Ramos	Washington Senators			

Many thanks to relief pitcher John Morrow.

#111 Vic Wertz

#112 Jack Harshman

#117 Tom Borland

#118 Bob Bruce

#119 Chico Cardenas

#120 Duke Carmel

#121 Camilo Carreon

#122 Don Dillard

#123 Dan Dobbek

#124 Jim Donohue

#125 Dick Ellsworth

#126 Chuck Estrada

#127 Ron Hansen

#128 Bill Harris

#129 Bob Hartman

#130 Frank Herrera

#131 Ed Hobaugh

#132 Frank Howard

#133 Manuel Javier

#134 Deron Johnson

#135 Ken Johnson

#136 Jim Kaat

#137 Lou Kimchock

#138 Art Mahaffey

#139 Carl Mathias

#140 Julio Navarro

#141 Jim Proctor

#142 Bill Short

#143 Al Spangler

#144 Al Stieglitz

#145 Jim Umbricht

#146 Ted Wieand

#147 Bob Will

#148 Carl Yastrzemski

#154 Jim Davenport

#163 Hector Lopez

#165 Jack Sanford

#168 Alex Grammas

#169 Jake Striker

#172 Willie Kirkland

#173 Billy Martin

#175 Pedro Ramos

#177 Johnny Kucks

#178 Woody Held

#180 Harry Simpson

#181 Billy Loes

#182 Glen Hobbie

#183 Eli Grba

#185 Jim Owens

#186 Dave Sisler

#187 Jay Hook

#189 Don McMahon

#190 Gene Woodling

#191 Johnny Klippstein

#192 Danny O'Connell

#193 Dick Hyde

#194 Bobby Gene Smith

#196 Andy Carey

#197 Ron Kline

#198 Jerry Lynch

Special Thanks to All Who Supported *CBA Bullpen*

Adele Abel, Gary Abel, Ted Adams, Bill Alger, Terry B. Allen, Amazing Fantasy, Terry Austin, Bruce Ayres, Paul Bach, Tim Barnes, Vincent P. Bartilucci, Terry Beatty, Ric Best, Mitchell Biegay, Al Bigley, Frank Bolle, Jeff Bonivert, Gerald E. Botts, Craig S. Brown, Bud Plant Comic Art, Scott Burnley, Craig Byrne, Donald V. Calamia, Frank Campbell, Gabe Carras, Robert Cassell, John Castiglia, Kristine A. Cimmy, Ben P. Clift III, John D. Coates, Brian E. Cook, Andrew D. Cooke, Beth Cooke, Roger Craft, Randall Dahlk, Jim Dalton, Jose Delbo, David J. Dellario, Andrew Depoy, Eric Dinallo, Nik Dirga, Christopher Dosevski, Gary Dunaier, Ric Duran, Jaime Echevarria, Mike Egan, Mike Eiron, John Ellissech, Harry J. Feinzig, Manny Fiore, Joe Frank, Juan Gamazo, Tony Gambato, Greg Garlick, Kim Gibbs, Andrea Giberti, Paul Gravett, Steven Hager, James Hamilton, Thomas Hamilton, Donald Hawkins, Bryan W. Headley, Fred Hembeck, M. Thomas Inge, David Jeffrey, Charles J. Johnson, James Jones, Rob Kirby, Denis Kitchen, John Kloussis, Alan Kupperberg, Craig Ledbetter, Martin Lee, Paul Leiffer, Jim Lesher, Jim Lesniak, Bob Levin, Richard Limacher, Carl K. Lomax, Robert Loy, Jay Lynch, Albert Sjoerds Ma, Chris Ma, Michael J. Maginot, Russ Maheras, David Mandel, Patrick Markee, Patrick Mattauch, Robert Matteis, Kenneth McFarlane, Frank McGinn, James McPherson, Jeff Metzner, Gary Mills, Jack Morelli, Bill Morgan, John Morrow, Greg W. Myers, Darron Neale, Erik Nelson, Michael Netzer, Jon E. Nieman, Terrence J. O'Donnell, Brian O'Malley, Richard O'Neal, Ricahrd Onley, Perry Pandrea, Rick Parker, Mike Pascale, Mac Patterson, Xavier Pennway, Jay Scott Pike, Brian Postman, Jomo Powell, Sam Ray, Robert Rettinger, David A. Roach, John Roche, Richard Roder, Brian Ross, Benno Rothschild, Jeff Rougvie, Robert Rowe, Gary W. Runkel, Jason Sacks, Gary Sassaman, Michael Scanlon, Lew Sayre Schwartz, Stu Schwartzberg, Forrest Sellers, Daniel S. Serafin, Mike Sharp, Craig D. Smith, Luke Smith, Simeon Smith, Stephen Smith, Coleman Springer, Ross Sprout, Chris Staros, Paul Stines, Jason Strangis, Marc Svensson, Howard Taylor, Daniel Tesmoingt, Gregory Torres, Gene Turnbull, Mark Waid, Hames Ware, Robert Warner, Brett Warnock, Earl Wells, Bret Wesner, Jay Willson, Richard Younce, and all who participated in the Jack Abel tribute.

George Tuska

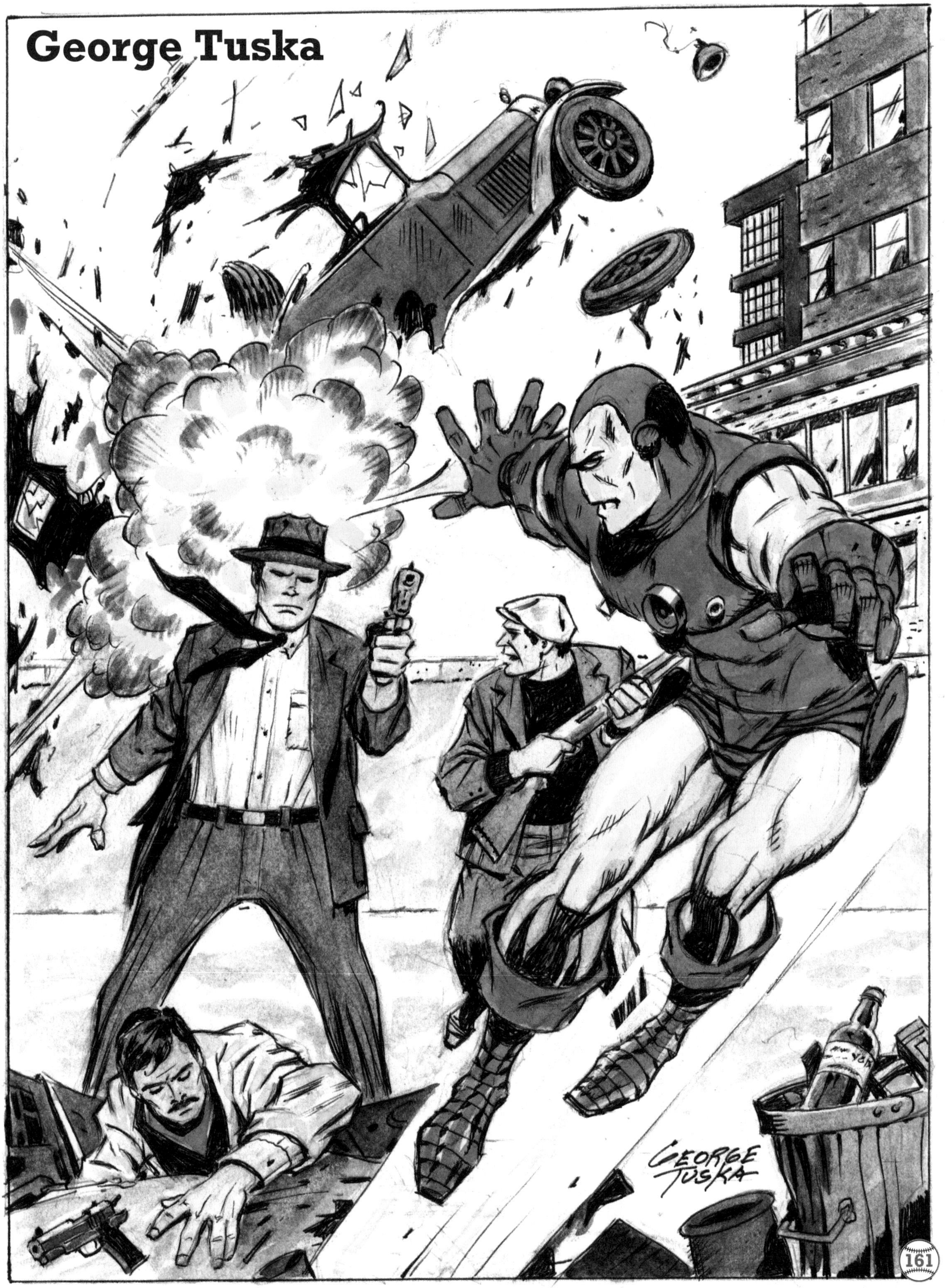
GEORGE TUSKA

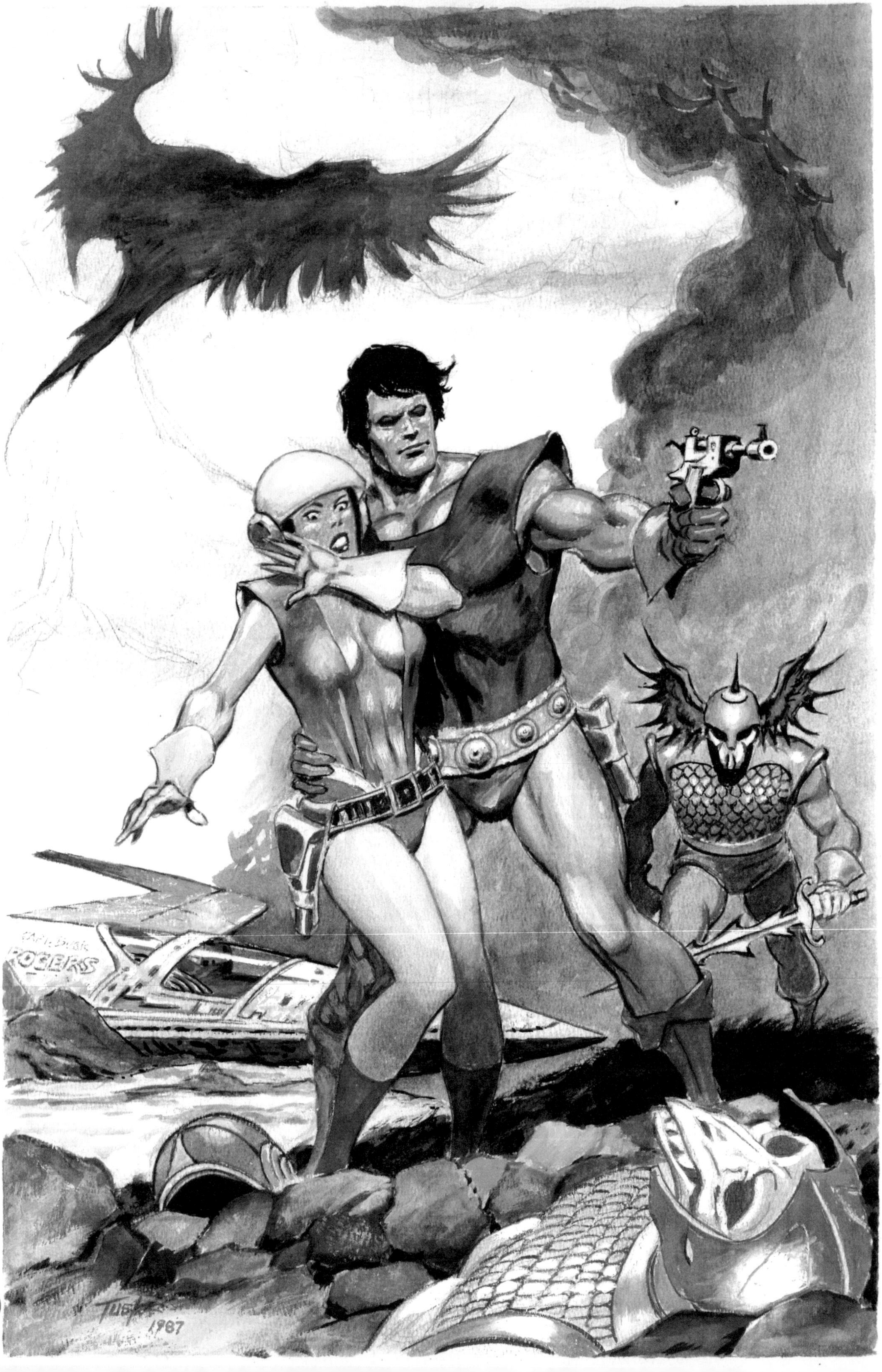
ROGERS
1987

SUPERGIRL-- THE MAID OF STEEL

HAWKMAN-- THE WINGED WONDER

THE ATOM-- WORLD'S SMALLEST SUPERHERO

GREEN LANTERN-- THE EMERALD CRUSADER

ELONGATED MAN-- THE STRETCHABLE SLEUTH

AQUAMAN-- KING OF THE SEVEN SEAS

THE FLASH-- FASTEST MAN ALIVE

GREEN ARROW-- THE AMAZING ARCHER

BLACK LIGHTNING-- THE LIVING DYNAMO

BLACK CANARY-- THE BLONDE BOMBSHELL

TAKE THE GREATEST SUPERHEROES ON EARTH-- EACH AN INVINCIBLE CHAMPION OF JUSTICE-- BAND THEM TOGETHER IN A COMMON CAUSE AGAINST CRIME AND EVIL--AND YOU HAVE THE...*JUSTICE LEAGUE*... AND ITS SUPER-ALLIES!

© DC COMICS INC. 1978 Distributed By C.T.N.Y.N.S

DAREDEVIL

GEORGE TUSKA

SUPERMAN

GEORGE TUSKA

Frank Bolle

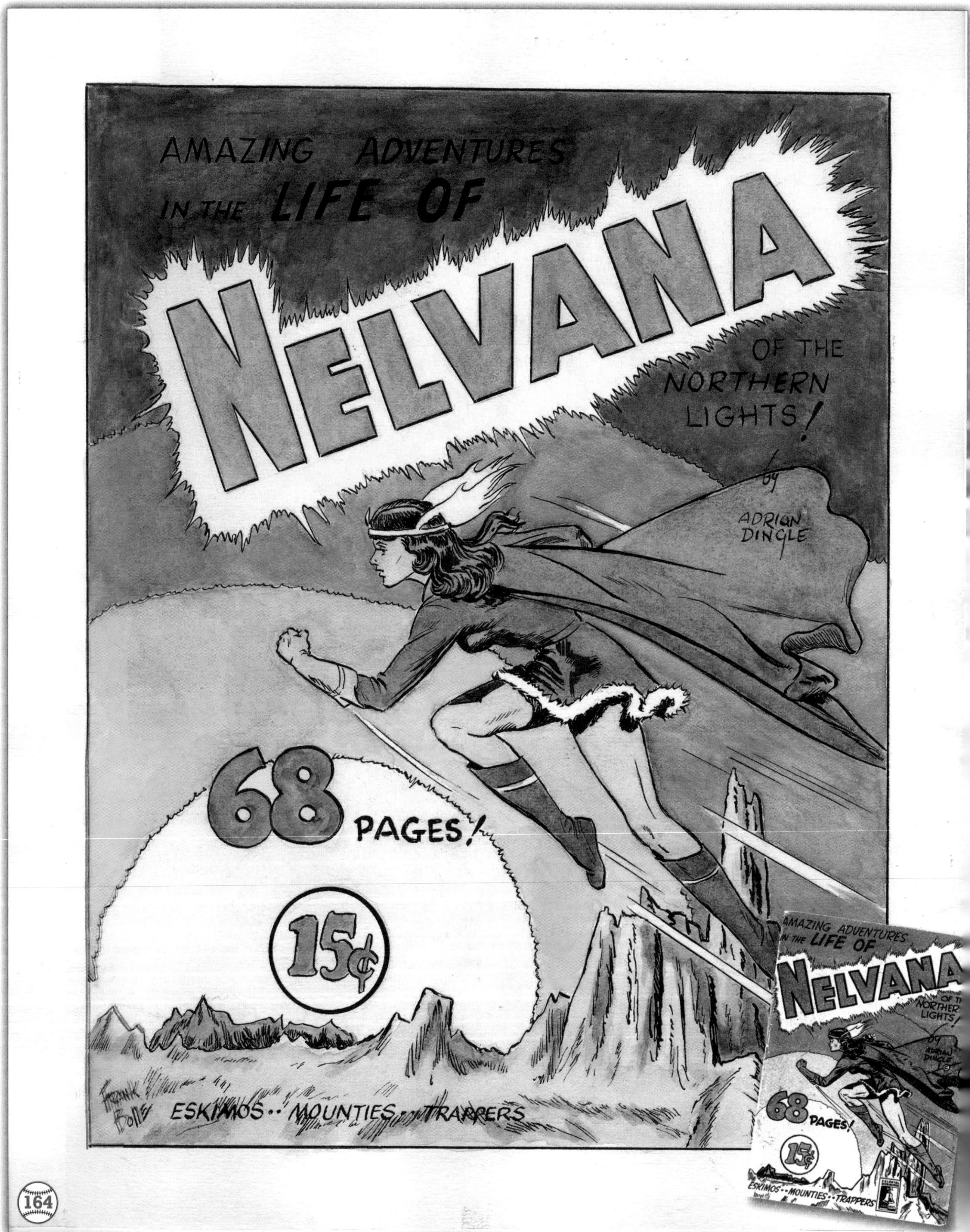
AMAZING ADVENTURES
IN THE LIFE OF
NELVANA
OF THE NORTHERN LIGHTS!
by ADRIAN DINGLE
68 PAGES!
15¢
FRANK BOLLE
ESKIMOS.. MOUNTIES.. TRAPPERS
AMAZING ADVENTURES
IN THE LIFE OF
NELVANA
68 PAGES!
15¢
ESKIMOS.. MOUNTIES.. TRAPPERS

Page 164: A Frank Bolle commission re-creating the cover of the famed Canadian super-hero, Nelvana of the Northern Lights's one-shot, published in 1945. At inset bottom is Adrian Dingle's original edition. **This page:** At top, hand-colored by the writer-artist and inscribed to 3-D comics legend Ray Zone, is the original art for the April 29, 1984, Winnie Winkle Sunday strip. Frank worked on the strip from 1980–1996. At left are two comics collaborations by penciler Frank Bolle and inker Leonard Starr, both appearing in Crown Comics #9 [May 1947]. **Pg. 166:** A fascinating artifact of the 1970s, two strips by Frank Bolle adapting the Clive Cussler thriller novel, Raise the Titanic, presented in the promotional "Best Seller Show Case." The daily and Sunday newspaper feature ran from Aug. 15 to Oct. 9, 1977. At top is the Aug. 21th strip, and below is the Oct. 9th strip, representing both the first and final Sunday funnies editions:

165

ON APRIL 15, 1912, THE UNTHINKABLE HAPPENED – THE 'UNSINKABLE' TITANIC, PLUNGED 2½ MILES TO AN ICY GRAVE, IN ITS HOLD AN INCREDIBLY RARE SUBSTANCE – BYZANIUM – THAT COULD INSURE AMERICA'S SECURITY FROM FOREIGN ATTACK!

IT ALL STARTED IN A MINING TOWN IN COLORADO IN 1911.

THE FRENCH GOVERNMENT WANTS TO HIRE YOU MINERS FOR A SECRET MISSION. THE PAY WILL BE GOOD, I ASSURE YOU.

THE ISLAND OF NOVAYA ZEMLYA 50 MILES OFF THE RUSSIAN MAINLAND...

WE'RE HERE, GENTLEMEN.

FOR 3 MONTHS THE COLORADO MINERS UNDER THE LEADERSHIP OF JOSHUA BREWSTER DUG FOR THE RARE BYZANIUM....

WE'VE GOT ALL THERE IS. ONLY WE DON'T HAND IT OVER TO THE FRENCH GOVERNMENT – WE KEEP IT FOR OURSELVES!

THE AGENTS OF THE FRENCH PURSUED THE FLEEING MINERS RELENTLESSLY – UNTIL ALL WERE DEAD SAVE JOSHUA BREWSTER.

BREWSTER – AND THE PRECIOUS BYZANIUM – ESCAPE, AND BOARD THE 'TITANIC' ON ITS DOOMED MAIDEN VOYAGE....

75 YEARS LATER.... IN JULY OF 1987.

SINCE WE NEED BYZANIUM FOR OUR VITAL MISSILE DEFENSE SYSTEM, THERE'S ONLY ONE THING TO DO— RAISE THE TITANIC!

TO BE CONTINUED

THE CLIMAX OF AN INCREDIBLE AND DARING EXPEDITION — THE TITANIC AFLOAT IN NEW YORK HARBOR! FINALLY THE VAULT CONTAINING THE VITAL BYZANIUM IS ABOUT TO BE OPENED...

...AND WHEN OPENED REVEALS...

THERE'S NO BYZANIUM HERE... ONLY THE CORPSE OF JOSHUA BREWSTER!

I DON'T UNDERSTAND— WHAT HAPPENED TO THE BYZANIUM THAT WAS SUPPOSE TO BE IN THE TITANIC'S VAULT, MR. PITT!

I'VE GOT A HUNCH THAT IT WAS NEVER ON BOARD IN THE FIRST PLACE!

WE'RE HEADING FOR THE VILLAGE OF SOUTHBY– AND FOR THE GRAVE MARKED "JAMES THORNTON"...

©1977 Universal Press Syndicate

I THINK WE'VE HIT SOMETHING!

IT LOOKS LIKE THE BYZANIUM, MR. PITT!

HOW DID YOU KNOW THE BYZANIUM WOULD BE HERE, MR. PITT?

I REMEMBERED THE DEAD MINER'S DIARY WE FOUND ON THAT RUSSIAN ISLAND...

"WE ALL ASSUMED THE "T" STOOD FOR TITANIC. IT REALLY STOOD FOR JAMES THORNTON, THE MINER WHOSE BODY WE FOUND ON THAT ISLAND!"

March 12, 1912.... Soon we leave for home on the Titanic. The precious ore we so desperately labored to rape from the bowels of that cursed mountain will lie safely in T's vault in Southby.

LATER...

SO YOU SEE, MR. PRESIDENT, BREWSTER BURIED THE BYZANIUM "IN SOUTHBY" BECAUSE HE FEARED FOR HIS LIFE. HE MARKED THE FALSE GRAVE WITH THORNTON'S NAME HOPING THAT AMERICANS WOULD FIND THE DIARY AND DECODE ITS MEANING.

AND THANKS TO YOU, DIRK, WE DID– THAT'S WHY WE'RE NOW BUILDING OUR FOOL PROOF BYZANIUM DEFENSE MISSILE SYSTEM!

THE END

Jack Abel

"While most colleagues preferred other inkers on my Legion stories, Jack's embellishment always looked good to me and lent a professional stability to the art. Being in his company was one of the more edifying and pleasant ways to spend one's time at Continuity. It's a privilege to have known and worked with this precious man. R.I.P., dear Jack."

— **Michael Netzer**

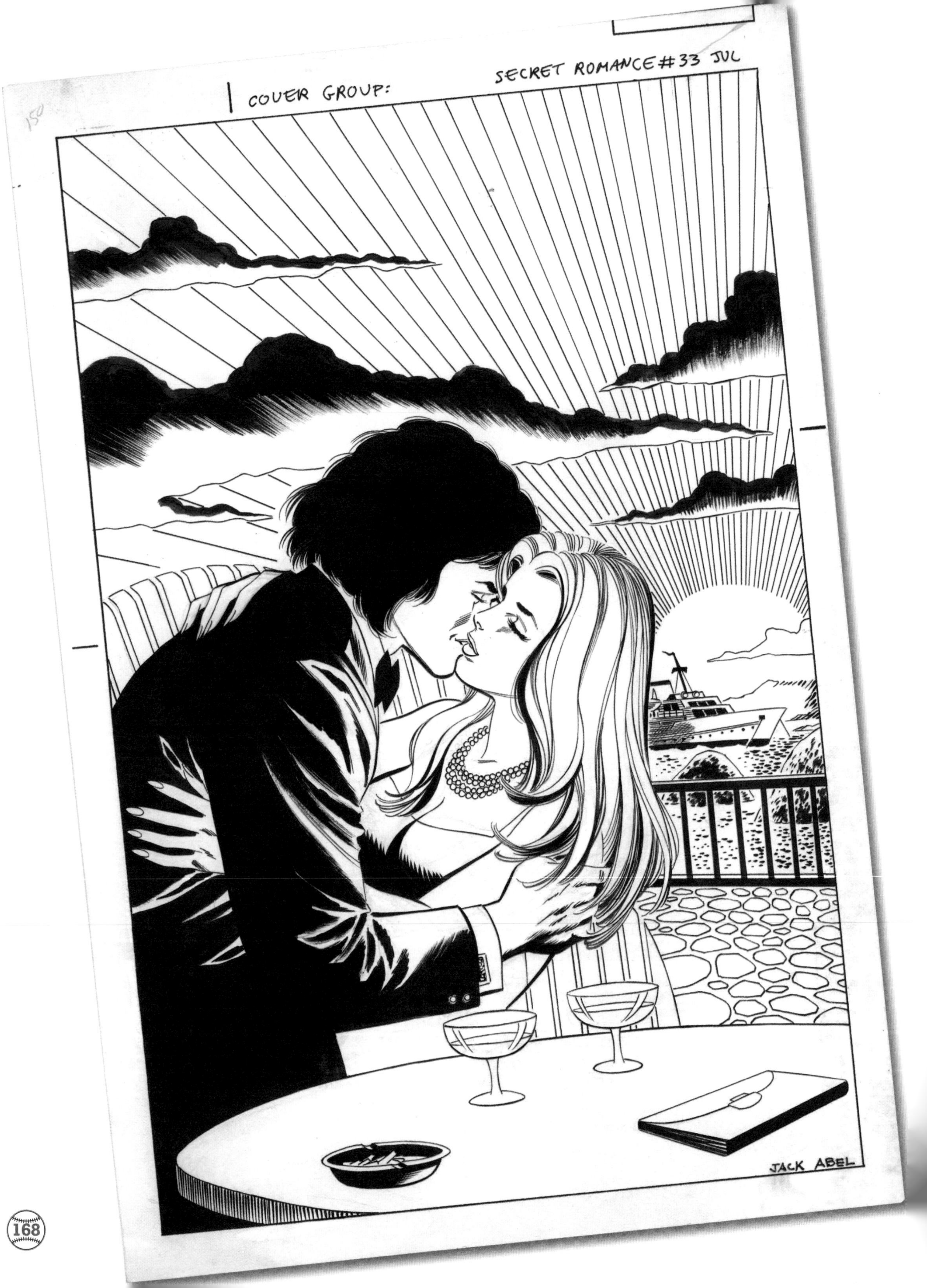

COVER GROUP:
SECRET ROMANCE #33 JUL
150
JACK ABEL

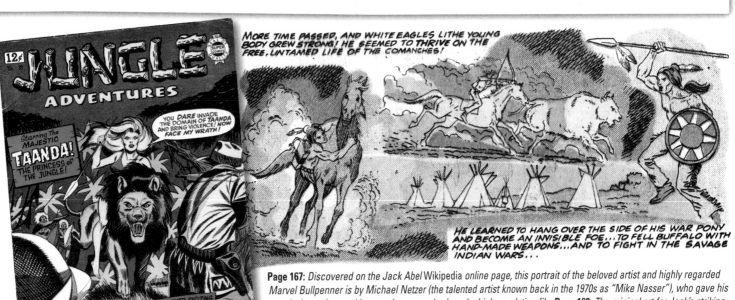

Page 167: *Discovered on the Jack Abel Wikipedia online page, this portrait of the beloved artist and highly regarded Marvel Bullpenner is by Michael Netzer (the talented artist known back in the 1970s as "Mike Nasser"), who gave his permission to be used here and generously shared a high-resolution file.* **Page 168:** *The original art for Jack's striking cover for Charlton Comics' Secret Romance #33 [July 1975].* **This page:** *Maybe if any single feature is best attributed to Jack, it would be the "Hunter's Hellcats" feature (set in the WWII era) in DC's Our Fighting Forces, which evolved from the Robert Kanigher-scripted "Capt. Hunter," a short-lived and, weirdly enough, Vietnam War-based series. The original half-page art at top is from OFF #113 [May–June 1968], which features Jack's pencils and inks. The cheapo publisher Israel Waldman enlisted Jack to draw the Jungle Adventures #18 [1964] cover at left. Above is a panel from the Atlas/Seaboard one-shot, Western Action #1 [Feb. 1975], which included "The Comanche Kid," a story penciled by Jack and, in a rare turn being embellished by another artist, inked by Allen Milgrom.*
Hunter's Hellcats TM & © DC Comics. All others TM & © the respective copyright holders.

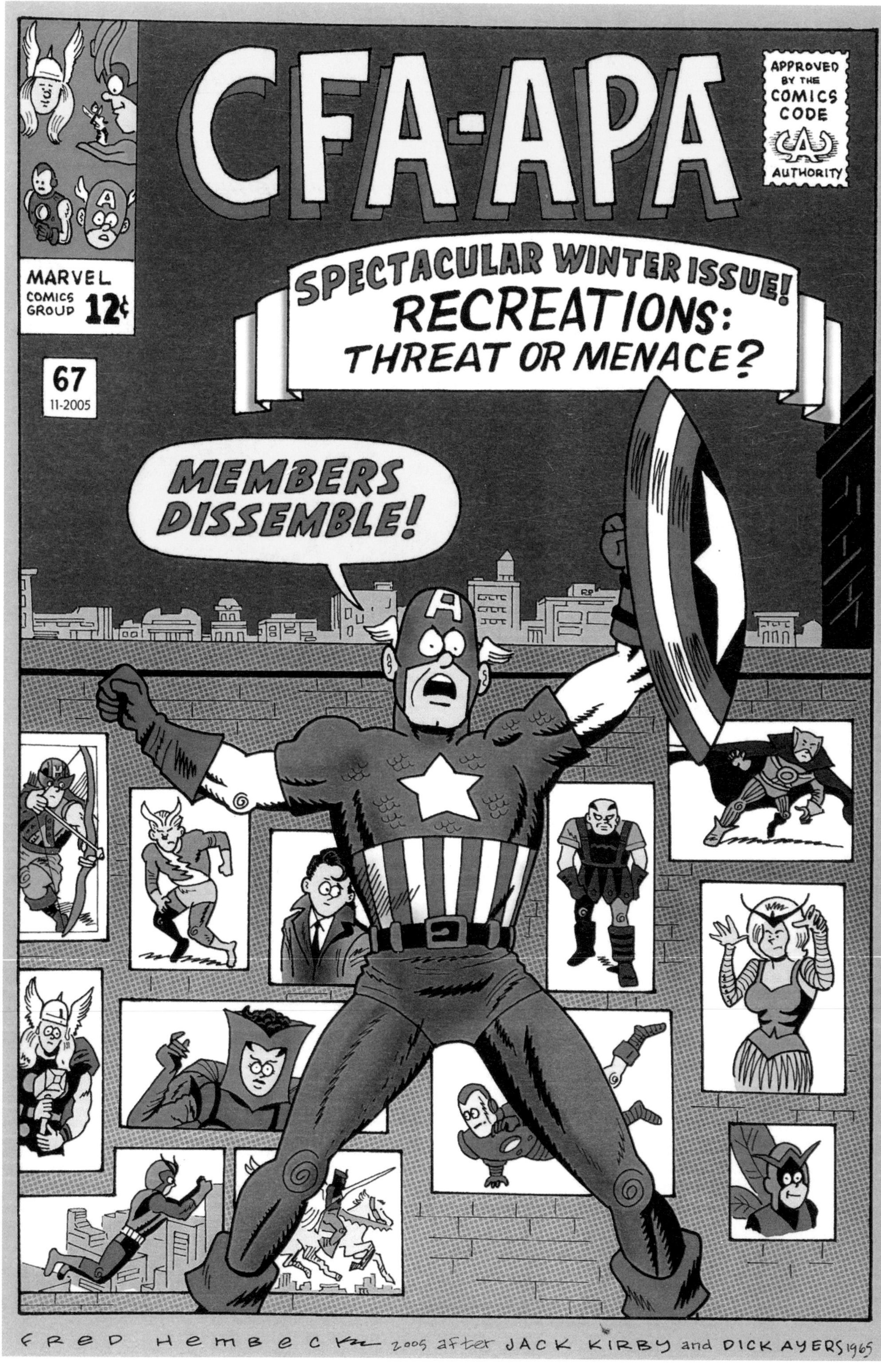
CFA-APA
APPROVED BY THE COMICS CODE AUTHORITY
MARVEL COMICS GROUP 12¢
67
11-2005
SPECTACULAR WINTER ISSUE!
RECREATIONS: THREAT OR MENACE?
MEMBERS DISSEMBLE!
FRED HEMBECK 2005 after JACK KIRBY and DICK AYERS 1965

FRED HEMBECK 2008 After (sorta kinda) DARWYN COOKE 2004

FRED HEMBECK 2013

FRED HEMBECK

Page 170: *Fred Hembeck re-creates the iconic Jack Kirby & Carl Hubbell cover of The Avengers #16 for the Comic & Fantasy Art Amateur Press Association Nov. 2005 edition. All characters TM & © Marvel Characters, Inc. Art © Fred Hembeck.* **Pg. 171:** *A quartet of Fred's pieces (including a pastiche of Darwyn Cooke's cover for your editor's Comic Book Artist Vol. 2, #3 [Mar. 2004]). All characters TM & © the respective copyright holders.* **This page:** *At top is relatively recent recognition by the House of Ideas for Fred's contributions to the publisher over the decades. This 104-page collection featured multiple reprints from Marvel Age, Fantastic Four Roast, Fred Hembeck Destroys the Marvel Universe, and other sources. This wraparound cover for The House of Hem one-shot [June 2015] is, of course, rendered by Fred. At right is Fred's spread from Marvel Age #109 [Feb. 1992], featuring the Sentinel of Liberty regaling kids on the time he (and Hitler) met Santa Claus. All characters TM & © Marvel Characters, Inc.*

Terry Beatty

As COVID-19 has moved through the *REAL* world, so has it affected the lives of our characters in the *FICTIONAL* comic strip town of *GLENWOOD*.

Rex and Michelle have been treating patients at *GLENWOOD HOSPITAL*.

Rex is preparing for his *LAST DAY* working in the hospital's COVID-19 unit. He plans to begin *REMOTE APPOINTMENTS* with his *CLINIC PATIENTS* soon.

Nurse *MICHELLE CARTER* will stay on until the Morgan Clinic opens its doors in a manner other than *VIRTUAL*.

This comic strip *HASN'T* followed Rex or Michelle into their work with coronavirus patients. Frankly, that's just *TOO REAL* a subject matter for the *COMICS PAGE*.

But we will say we admire the *BRAVERY* and *DEDICATION* of the *REAL-LIFE* healthcare workers who have taken on this task -- often at *GREAT RISK* to their own well-being.

Lives are *SAVED*. Lives are *LOST*. Tears of *RELIEF*, and of *SORROW*, are shed.

Life moves on for our *COMIC STRIP* cast of characters, actors made of *INK*, playing out their days on a *PAPER* stage.

173

Pg. 173: *A potpourri of Terry Beatty artwork. Clockwise from top left is Terry's cover painting for Scary Monsters #11 [June 1994]. The publication, which boasts it's "A Real Monster Magazine for Real Monster Fans," has sported Beatty covers for many years; a commission color piece featuring Terry's trademark character, Ms. Tree; Terry designed the cover art (and the model itself!) for this Green Lantern model kit produced in 2011 by Moebius; Terry's Rex Morgan strip for Nov. 8, 2020, dealt directly with the ongoing Covid-19 pandemic. This page: In the background is an ultra-violent Ms. Tree #20 [July '85] page by Terry with Gary Kato. At center is an Adam Strange commission by Terry. Above are the covers for Terry's 1986 two-issue collection of Phony Pages strips originally published in The Buyer's Guide for Comic Fandom. At left is commission piece featuring Crystal and Lockjaw of The Inhumans. All characters TM & © their respective copyright holders.*